24-99

British Tourism:

The remarkable story of growth

Thi

British Tourism:
The remarkable story of growth

Victor T. C. Middleton
with the late L. J. Lickorish

ELSEVIER

AMSTERDAM • BOSTON • HEIDELBERG • LONDON • NEW YORK • OXFORD
PARIS • SAN DIEGO • SAN FRANCISCO • SINGAPORE • SYDNEY • TOKYO

Butterworth-Heinemann is an imprint of Elsevier

Butterworth-Heinemann is an imprint of Elsevier
Linacre House, Jordan Hill, Oxford OX2 8DP, UK
30 Corporate Drive, Suite 400, Burlington, MA 01803, USA

First edition 2005
Re-issued in paperback 2007

British Library Cataloguing in Publication Data
A catalogue record for this book is available from the British Library

Library of Congress Cataloguing in Publication Data
A catalogue record for this book is available from the Library of Congress

ISBN–13: 978-0-7506-8411-8
ISBN–10: 0-7506-8411-9

For information on all Butterworth-Heinemann publications
visit our web site at http://books.elsevier.com

Printed and bound in The Netherlands

07 08 09 10 11   10 9 8 7 6 5 4 3 2 1

Contents

Foreword

It is over 50 years since I first opened my home at Beaulieu to visitors. At the time, although of course we did not look very far ahead in the post-war years, I joined the vanguard of those who foresaw opportunities in the expected growth of interest in tourism and heritage. I have, therefore, taken an active role in the decades covered in this book. I have been privileged to witness many of the events and known many of the people at first hand.

The late Leonard Lickorish first mooted the idea for this book in the mid-1990s and the Board of the British Travel Educational Trust[1] was asked to support it. The Trust gladly endorsed the proposal and Butterworth-Heinemann agreed to publish the book when it was completed. Unfortunately a range of delays and difficulties ensued and through Len's illness and death in 2002 the project stalled. Victor Middleton, a former Chairman of the Tourism Society, whose many publications in tourism are well known, agreed to complete the work. I believe he has done an excellent job of pulling the various drafts and other papers together, adding his own interpretation of key events and developing the chapters for publication.

There cannot be a definitive version of events that are still quite close in time. There are too many pieces in the story and many are not well chronicled. But it is certainly a story of remarkable growth. It gives me pleasure to commend this book to all with an interest in how tourism grew from summer seasonal holidays, using mainly Victorian infrastructure in the 1950s, to a thriving year round modern sector of the UK economy that is relevant

---

[1] The story of the British Travel Educational Trust is covered in Appendix II

to just about every community in the land. Although the full economic impact of the sector is still not known with any certainty, it is now estimated to employ up to 2 million people and generate some 5 per cent of the UK economy – a percentage which rises steeply in many areas of the country with few alternative forms of economic growth and employment.

This book is also a tribute to the outstanding work of Len Lickorish and the countless others who have contributed in this story of remarkable growth. From the most unpropitious origins after the war, tourism has grown from what was derisively dubbed a 'candy floss industry' to what many consider to be the fastest growing sector of the economy. Linked as it now is with leisure, recreation and many forms of business travel, tourism has become one of the largest growth opportunities facing us in the twenty-first century.

Lord Montagu of Beaulieu

Preface

I am a discerning traveller; *you* are visitors; *they* are tourists.

(Anon)

Tourism is a reflection of our society and civilisation.

(Pimlott, 1947)

Introduction to the paperback edition

This book, first published in hardback in 2005 and very favourably reviewed, quickly sold through its first print run. It was decided within a year to produce a paperback version and the opportunity was taken to make a number of minor corrections and improvements to the text. The biggest change is the inclusion of a new chapter (Chapter 8) on the development of tourism in Scotland and Wales, contributed by authors with long experience in each country.

Demand for domestic and international travel has been increasing rapidly among the British population over the last half-century. From the summer season attractions ofseaside resorts in the 1950s to modern gap year trav-ellers, silver surfers and every conceivable business, leisure, recreational and social pursuit, Britons are on the move, around the world, 365 days a year. The story oftourism in Britain is one of remarkable, some would say revolutionary, growth. Chapter 3 offers evidence that there has been at least a tenfold increase in the volume oftourism since the late 1940s.

At the end of World War II in 1945 there was little or no international leisure travel and only limited, highly seasonal domestic holiday taking. Although the desire to take holidays was strong, food and petrol rationing was still in place and very few people had access to cars. In 1950 only half the population could afford to stay away from home, typically once a year in July or August. Day visits and 'excursions' were popular in the summer but they were not measured. By 2005, allowing for day as well as staying visits, the era of frequent personal travel involving the vast majority of the UK population in many visits away from home each year had arrived. Criticized by some as a form of dangerous hyper-mobility, tourism has grown from what was derisively known as a 'candy floss industry' in the 1960s to become what is often claimed to be the 'world's largest industry'.

The remarkable contrast between the economic and social conditions of the population at the middle and end of the twentieth century underlies the growth story of British tourism. Any choice of dates is inevitably arbitrary but there is an attraction in seeking to chronicle and assess the developments that occurred in the half-century after 1945. After that, as set out in Chapter 9, market maturity, global competition, concerns over global climate change, international terrorism, the increasing dominance of Information Communications Technology (ICT) generally and the Internet in particular are shifting tourism into the global patterns emerging today.

The tourism sector, little recognized and certainly not respected by the political, economic and academic establishment in the UK at the end of World War II, has grown to become a leading influence in society and an economic driver in just about every part of the UK. Over the period, most of so-called 'traditional' employment through primary industries such as agriculture, mining and fisheries dwindled and in many areas disappeared forever. In the USA, in mainland Europe as well as in Britain, millions of jobs in manufacturing were lost to global price competition and various forms of automation achieved by information technology. Even newer services, such as call centres, have been 'outsourced' to other parts of the world. Large parts of industrial Britain in the North, West and South West lost their former economic rationale with the virtual collapse in many areas of traditional manufacturing industry. Market towns and rural villages have suffered from deep agricultural recession in all the uplands of Britain, especially in the last decade. As a result, cities, towns and rural areas across the UK have been forced to seek alternative means to secure their survival. Tourism in its many modern forms now plays a leading role in helping to secure an economic future in all these areas.

Other forms of private sector and especially public sector employment have, of course, provided alternative jobs for millions. But, with the benefit of hindsight, it is not so surprising that private sector employment, in wealth-creating services that are essentially locked into the places visited, has gained increasing recognition in recent decades. Such places face strong and growing competition, but by definition tourism is ultimately about specific destinations and, excluding virtual tours, the services cannot be provided elsewhere. London is always and only London; Ludlow is always and only Ludlow; Edinburgh is only Edinburgh, etc., and they cannot be produced at lower cost in China or India. Very few people understood the potential for tourism in 1945 to 1950 and this book is in part a tribute to the visionaries and pioneers who did see the growth trends and helped to push the nascent sector along the paths that are so obvious today.

One might expect that a sector showing such remarkable growth and contribution would be fully understood and recognized for its value to society. But paradoxically, just as it was in the 1950s, 'tourism' is still popularly associated in the media with summertime, holidays and other people. For many in the Establishment it has never shaken off the 'candy floss' jibe. Although travel has become a major aspiration in the individual lives of most people, movement *en masse* continues to attract an ugly terminology; stereotypes abound, such as hordes, lemmings, grockles, bed nights, bums on seats, congestion, spreading the load, lager louts and killing the goose that lays the golden eggs. The notion that *'I am a discerning traveller, you are visitors, they are tourists'* appears to have lost none of its elitist appeal in the last fifty years – even among the second homers facilitated by motorways in the UK and frequenting budget airlines and ferries to access their properties in mainland Europe.

While travel and travelling were and still are respected words in Britain, the word 'tourism' is not. The term 'tourist' has never lost the pejorative meaning that is still enshrined in most dictionaries, as in 'tourist class' travel. The notion of tourism as an 'industry', although it is almost universally used, is also seemingly as misunderstood now as it was in 1945 and its true import still appears to elude our political and media masters. Tourism is not a narrow field. It is the business of 'being elsewhere'. Its internationally agreed definition embraces day and staying visits to places outside the normal environment for business, leisure and social purposes. Almost everything in tourism reflects or influences what is happening in the world at large, i.e. growth in personal incomes and mobility, education, employment prospects, oil and other energy crises, taxation, congestion, the arts, new technology, issues of global warming and heritage conservation, international terrorism, the future for the countryside, the quality of life in city centres and rural areas, and even the UK's creaking transport systems. As Pimlott noted in his classic book *The Englishman's Holiday: A Social History*, 'tourism is a reflection of our society and civilisation' (Pimlott, 1947).

Tourism – invisible 'industry'

Virtually everyone knows in personal terms what it means to travel and to visit places outside their usual home environment. Virtually everyone now does it from the cradle to the grave (literally for many of the mourners). Most of us see it as a vital part of the quality of our lives – as both release from and reward for the multiple pressures of modern living. Misunderstanding starts, however, with the now universal term 'tourism industry' because it is not an industry in any easily understood sense. Travel and tourism are types of consumer demand that are serviced by only very loosely connected sectors of the UK economy such as transport, accommodation, attractions and public sector services ranging from information provision to public lavatories, libraries and policing. Such demand can only be measured as consumption patterns. Len Lickorish knew this well. He was a pioneer of tourism research and always insisted on using the term 'travel trades' rather than 'industry' long after it was deemed to be old-fashioned. Measurement is discussed in more precise terms in Appendix III but simply put, tourism cannot be identified and measured in the way that all the traditional economic sectors are.

We live today in a world in which what cannot be measured, cannot be understood. What cannot be easily understood cannot be reduced and presented in easy sound bites and tends not to warrant government or media recognition. In 2005, as in 1950, although there has been real progress, such measures of tourism consumption as exist are flawed and widely recognized as inaccurate. We do not know with any expectation of accuracy how large the tourism sector in Britain is; we do not know how many people it employs; we do not know the many nuances of its impacts on society. There are broad guesstimates, of course, but they cannot withstand detailed scrutiny at national, regional or local level. The available data cannot stand up to Treasury analysis. By contrast, for example, car production is counted at factory gates and valued at wholesale and retail prices; beef and sheep production can be counted at farm gates; oil can be measured in barrels or metered in pipelines and so on. By its nature tourism consumes the outputs of *parts* of at least two-dozen different sectors of the economy, including retailing, transport, entertainment, food production, sport and every kind of recreational activity, and expenditure and investment in capital goods. (For further technical comment, please see Appendix III.)

Cinderella at the Westminster Ball

Because of its complexities tourism has had limited appeal to politicians seeking simple messages and 'quick wins', especially as the democratic systems in all countries are designed to support and respond to voters' interests as residents in their constituencies not as travellers. Tourists do not have votes in relation to the places they visit. What politicians recognized from the inter-war years onwards, however, was the fact that tourism has economic benefits. Firstly, both before and much more so after World War II, politicians could see the national importance of the balance of payments and the benefits of inbound tourism as an alternative form of export 'industry'. This recognition was positive initially. But it also caused a continuing government fixation on inbound tourism and the large organizations based in London that has continued over the last half-century in ways that many consider unhelpful in the overall UK context. More recently, since the 1970s, the economic and employment value of all forms of tourism has been increasingly recognized nationally, regionally and locally as a primary tool for regional and local regeneration and development: 'Tourism means jobs'. By the end of the 1990s, from the Highlands and Islands, through most of Wales to Lands End in Cornwall, via cities and large swathes of the countryside, tourism was identified as important, even if it was not clearly understood. It is now targeted for growth by local authorities across the UK, by governments in Scotland and Wales and by regional government in England. Since the 1980s, although the flow of funds has dwindled as the EU expanded in the twenty-first century, European financial programmes have been widely available to support regional economic development in many parts of the UK. A substantial part of such aid identified tourism for its employment regeneration value – or sometimes, no doubt, *de faut mieux*.

By the end of the twentieth century the idea of tourism as a seemingly low cost/low risk tool for economic and social engineering had captured the attention of national governments. The more far-sighted local authorities have identified the contribution of tourism to the quality of life for their residents. Increasingly since the election of New Labour in 1997, political interest in tourism has expanded to embrace 'access for all', 'for the many, not the few,' 'devolution to regions,' 'multicultural provision' and 'sustainable development', which gives a nod to environmental values. Presented as 'modern', most of these ideas are not nearly as new as their proponents like to believe. They have their pre-war and post-war origins noted in Chapters 1 and 2.

Although the tourism sectors in Scotland, Wales and Northern Ireland received good government support over the last decades of the twentieth century, this has not been the case in England. Few of the Westminster Governments' actions have translated a continuing stream of good wishes and positive words into adequate financial support for tourism in England, in which some 85 per cent of British tourism takes place. Politicians provide exhortation and seek credit for every success but experience indicates that the Government's attitude to tourism in England over much of the 50-year period under review has been what Lickorish termed 'benign neglect'. The House of Commons Select Committee for Culture, Media and Sport heavily criticized Government policy in 2003 and coined the phrase 'Cinderella of Government'. Given the Government's understanding of tourism and its record in its direct dealings in areas such as public transport, millennium funding, national museums and earlier with its nationalized hotels and transport systems, many would argue that we should be grateful.

In current jargon, tourism is a 'cross-cutting theme' for governments. Directly and indirectly it affects many aspects of the way we live. Reflecting the measurement intricacies set out in Appendix III, tourism is an extraordinarily complex sector of economic activity. Because of its size and relevance in nearly every part of the country, tourism also now has massive social and environmental implications for Britain in the twenty-first century. It is the objective of this book to trace the way that modern tourism developed and grew throughout the twentieth century, especially in the last fifty years.

Who this book is for

This book does not set out to be a textbook and it makes no claim to be a scholarly academic history. It is written for a general audience interested in knowing more about the dramatic changes that have occurred over the last fifty years in the way we live and travel in the UK, and for those who wish to appreciate and interpret current trends in society more generally.

It is also written to be part of the background reading undertaken by undergraduate and postgraduate students of tourism at degree level. It is relevant, too, to the thousands of school pupils now studying tourism and needing to gain a deeper and broader understanding of the subject. With an estimated 1.5 million or more people employed in tourism in recent years, we hope it will also be of interest to some of the thousands of people engaged in the tourism sector both now and over recent decades.

Because tourism is universal in the sense that virtually everyone is a visitor, and ubiquitous in the sense that the business of tourism is now relevant to nearly every community in the UK, the story of tourism is a key part of the story of all of us in modern society.

Errors and omissions

The author accepts responsibility for all errors and omissions. Deciding what to leave out has been the hardest part of the editorial process because the field is so vast; it reflects changes in society and civilization and we are addressing so many aspects of the last half-century as well as commenting on the future. Many will spot important missing detail or even key issues that have been passed over too glibly. Some will doubtless challenge our interpretation of events. Perhaps one day someone will thrash out more of the evidence and improve upon our record. It will not be easy, however, and we hope this record will be of interest to many in the meantime.

For the same reason that it is hard to measure, tourism is not well documented. The hard statistical evidence is at best partial and commonly not comparable over the years, not available or not accessible. At worst it is simply inaccurate and misleading. At least we have had the advantage in writing this book of knowing and speaking with many of those who influenced the 1950s to 1980s when so much of what we recognize today was in its formative stages. Len Lickorish, to whose memory this book is dedicated was, of course, a leading and influential figure in tourism from the 1950s through to the 1990s and witnessed at first hand most of the events covered in this story of tourism. A formal tribute to his career and work is in Appendix I.

Acknowledgements

The principal debt is to the late Len Lickorish CBE (1922–2002) who influenced directly so many of the events in UK tourism over the half-century after the war. This book was Len's idea and with the help of Bill Richards, who took over from Len as Secretary of the European Tourism Action Group, they jointly drafted the initial contents. They were supported in the project by The British Travel Educational Trust (BTET) and the publishers Butterworth-Heinemann. The first draft was subsequently extensively revised and amended and the contents developed for publication by Victor T. C. Middleton. All three of us involved in the writing process met through our work at different times at the British Travel Association, later The British Tourist Authority, and now VisitBritain. The BTET made a much-appreciated financial contribution to the work of getting the book ready for publication as one of its last acts before the Trust was formally wound up in 2004.

The final draft of this book was sent to several people who all made helpful and much-appreciated comments on the chapters. They corrected some, at least, of the principal author's worst omissions and mistakes. They include, in alphabetical order, Colin Clark, Gerry Draper, David Jeffries, Professor Rik Medlik, Lord Montagu, Bill Richards and Ken Robinson. Bill Burnett kindly contributed the appreciation of Len's contribution to European tourism in Appendix 1.

The sections on Scotland and Wales included in this paperback edition are invited contributions written by Brian Hay and Elwyn Owen, respectively. Between them they have over 50 years' experience of tourist boards in Britain. Dr Brian Hay, formerly head of research at The Scottish Tourist Board is a

Visiting Professor at Strathclyde University (Department of Hospitality and Tourism Management); Elwyn Owen, formerly head of research at The Wales Tourist Board is a Visiting Professor at the University of Wales Institute, Cardiff (Welsh School of Hospitality, Tourism and Leisure Management).

Sally North of Butterworth-Heinemann was as helpful as always in supporting and facilitating the production of the book and being patient with the author over delays.

Leonard J. Lickorish, CBE, Director General of the British Tourist Authority

Eras in the story of British tourism

To assist the interpretation of events, the story of modern tourism in Britain has been divided into six defined eras. These eras have no general recognition as such but were chosen by the author because they make broad sense in terms of grouping events and outlining the approach to tourism that characterizes each of them. The chapters are constructed around the eras, which are summarized briefly below in synoptic form as a guide to readers.

The first era deals with the inter-war years; four eras divide the main 50-year span and the final era reviews the period 1995 to 2005 and beyond to bring the story up to date and look ahead. Chapter 1 deals with the inter-war years; Chapters 2 and 3 review overall tourism developments in the four main eras and compare tourism in 1950 and today. Chapters 4, 5, and 7 are constructed around the main developments that took place in each era in accommodation, attractions, transport and government arrangements for tourism. Chapter 6 spans the eras by reviewing the contribution of some of the leading pioneers in tourism development and Chapter 9 looks at the present and ahead to the future.

1. **1919–1939** The inter-war years. Notwithstanding the Great Depression, this was a period of growth in travel within and to Britain. It was a time of transition when the origins of many of the post-war developments of tourism can be traced, such as the powerful links between transport and tourism and the early development of mass tourism. Government granted its first token financial support in 1929 to support the creation of Britain's first national tourist board, at that time a trade association. Acceptance of rights to holidays with pay for manual workers was reflected in an important 1938 Act.
2. **1945–1955** Post-war austerity could not hold back a strong recovery of demand for domestic tourism in an era initially of socialist collectivism and nationalization. A British Tourist and Holidays Board was established by

Government in 1947 but it proved short lived and the British Travel and Holidays Association became the successor in 1950 to the earlier pre-war Association. The first pioneer tour operators began to challenge the then tight regulatory regime for air transport and launched tour operating to take the British abroad to the Mediterranean sea and sun.

3. **1956–1969** A combination of liberalization of the economy and travel, strong economic growth and rises in personal income made possible the emergence of a more mobile society. These factors also fuelled the energy of the 'swinging 60s' and changed so much of the pre-war moral climate and attitudes. This was the take-off period of modern mass tourism abroad as the British preference for foreign holidays grew, ably promoted by dynamic entrepreneurial tour operators. Inbound tourism boomed and Government intervention in tourism was formalized in the 1969 Development of Tourism Act.

4. **1970–1989** Growth years for inbound tourism and UK outbound travel despite two major economic crises provoked by oil price rises in 1973 and 1979, and a major decline in traditional manufacturing sectors of the economy. Overall decline in UK domestic holiday travel to resorts occurred, although structural changes in society supported the emergence of important alternative growth sectors in the domestic market that would take British tourism forward into the twenty-first century. Attractions and day visits achieved record growth. The Conservative Government in this period set out to roll back the State intervention of the 1940s, 1960s and 1970s and, *inter alia*, undermined the organization structure for English tourism in ways that have continued into the twenty-first century.

5. **1990–1995** Deep economic recession in the early 1990s and recovery in the UK took place as a new era of global tourism began to emerge along with tourism market maturity in the developed world economies. 'Hypermobility' characterized the travel of the post-industrial population of the UK. Domestic tourism restructured itself as new sectors and segments gained in significance. The Rio Earth Summit in 1992 put the ideas, at least, of sustainable tourism onto government agendas. Tourism responsibility at government level passed to a newly created Department for National Heritage.

6. **1995–2005** A new UK Government in 1997 set out its aspiration for 'world class tourism' and targeted the sector as a tool for employment generation, and achieving 'inclusiveness'. Devolution in Scotland and Wales, and the creation of Regional Development Authorities in England devolved much of tourism responsibility away from national UK level. The Internet facilitated and promoted individualism in tourism as a majority of the population gained access to personal computers, and budget airlines and budget hotels increasingly challenged the traditional business models of the 1980s. 9/11 (2001) drove international terrorism fears to new heights and highlighted the vulnerability of travellers, especially those travelling by air.

---

[1] The story of the British Travel Educational Trust is covered in Appendix II

CHAPTER 1

The inter-war years 1919 to 1939 and the impact of the Second World War (1939–45)

Evidence suggests that the growth of the services represented by such [sea-side and other holiday] resorts, including the services of transport, has been among the most rapid forms of economic growth since the [1914–18] war, and that its effect upon the movement of the population has been of the first importance.

Royal Commission on the Distribution of the Industrial Population (Pimlott, 1940, p. 240)

In the twenty-first century there are many who appear determined to live in what Eric Hobsbawm termed 'a permanent present'. Some, perhaps, to quote LP Hartley's famous aphorism, because 'the past is a foreign country; they do things differently there'; others, because they fail to see the relevance of past events to modern times. But it is also widely agreed that those who forget their history are condemned to repeat it. At least one can safely argue that most of the seeds of the future can be traced in the past. For tourism this is especially true of the inter-war years. In many ways it was a sad and tragic period lasting only 21 years, characterized by grinding unemployment and poverty for many in the 1930s. Such conditions facilitated the rise of ruthless dictatorships in Germany, Russia, Italy and elsewhere in Europe that would set the scene for the Second World War. But it was also a time of great incipient change, especially in the social conditions of the population, emerging lifestyles, better communications, growing political awareness and action. This period witnessed a transition away from the Victorian Age toward the new world of greater individuality, mobility and innovation in most spheres of daily life, and especially in leisure and travel. Against what one might suppose, as this chapter notes, it was also a period of remarkable growth in travel and tourism and of developing social ideas that are still easily traceable today.

The appalling loss of life and economic ravages of the First World War were closely followed by the century's most vicious outbreak of 'Spanish Flu', which claimed over 21 million lives around the world. Economic recovery was barely under way before the Great Depression (1929–30) spread to Europe from the USA. It quickly brought economic progress to a halt and plunged millions of people into economic misery from which they would only be relieved as industrial expansion was funded by governments in preparation for the Second World War. As economies picked up, the war clouds gathered and wartime conditions and deprivations returned in 1939 for six long years.

A changing society and new mobility

In the 1920s and 1930s some of the main trends of post-war tourism were clearly discernible and some remarkable developments occurred. The First World War had led to major social changes, not least in the position and status of women, half the population, who were finally to get the vote with equal rights to men in 1928. Slaughter in the trenches during the First World War resulted in a much more sceptical attitude to 'authority'. What was known at the time of the 1917 Bolshevik revolution and of Stalin's pre-war communist regime, together with the economic conditions of the 1930s, led to a widespread belief in the ideals of socialism across much of Europe and North America. This belief would change the agenda in the inter-war years and come to fruition in the UK after 1945. The First and Second World Wars took millions of people from their normal home environments, tossed them into a cauldron of feverish activity and change, and moved them frequently within the UK and abroad. Traditional perceptions of home, village and town boundaries were broken; ideas of communication between people altered. Allied to increasing personal mobility such changes laid the social foundations for a growing demand for travel and tourism. In the hothouse of war, technical and technological progress was rapid in aircraft, motor transport, communication systems and the mass production processes needed for weapons of destruction and other military supplies. All of these developments would find applications relevant to post-war tourism.

Rail travel reached its peak of popularity in the 1930s, using leisure excursions as well as holiday travel as a major stream of revenue. The famous steam locomotive, Mallard, reached its record 126 miles an hour in

1938 and the 'Bentley boys' achieved their string of records at Le Mans 24-hour races in the late 1920s and early 1930s. Apart from a few transatlantic services by airships, sea travel was the main form of long distance transport, with the great liners such as *France* and *Queen Mary* built in the 1930s competing for the Blue Riband transatlantic record. Bus and coach travel expanded greatly, helped by the dramatic developments of road vehicles during the First World War, after which thousands of surplus army trucks were turned into the charabancs that were the basis of the bus and coach industry for the next twenty years. Dylan Thomas immortalized the role of such vehicles for leisure travel in his classic 'The Outing', about a day trip to Porthcawl (men only) in the 1920s.

By the 1930s some two thirds of the population already lived in the seven British conurbations of upwards of one million each: 'These imprisoned millions needed little persuasion to escape when they could' (Pimlott, 1947, p. 213). Private cars became an important transport mode, although ownership was still mainly the preserve of the wealthy and the rapidly growing suburban middle class. In 1930 there were an estimated one million cars on the roads of Britain and the first Highway Code was published. By 1939, notwithstanding the depression years, some two million private cars were licensed, including mass-produced Austin Sevens, Ford Eights and Morris Minors that were designed for a budget conscious leisure orientated market. By contrast, the less affluent used bicycles, which were readily accessible and there were estimated to be some 10 million bicycles providing the only affordable personal transport option available to most. Road traffic signs were not standardized in Britain until 1934, which also saw the first pedestrian crossings (Belisha beacons). Motorways were built in the USA and Germany although not in the UK, where dual carriageway roads and the first town bypasses were the height of sophistication. Ferdinand Porsche designed Hitler's 'people's car', the Volkswagen, which was launched in 1936 and London's first Motor Show for the public opened at Earls Court in 1937. The effects of this growth over a decade altered the traditional patterns of tourism in ways that would become much clearer after the war.

Motor drawn caravans, known originally in France as *maison automobiles*, appeared just before the First World War but 'caravan design was revolutionized in the 1930s when Hutchings produced his first Winchester'. This was an art deco inspired streamlined vehicle with egg shaped curves and a clerestory roof that became known as the aero look and set the design norms for at least 25 years (The Times, 2000, p. 93). The first caravan parks were established around Britain's coasts promoting a rash of insensitively located sites that would not be controlled until planning legislation was introduced (Caravan Sites and Control of Development Act, 1960).

Although numbers were still modest, more British people travelled abroad, mainly to Europe, in the inter-war years and volume increased in the late 1930s to about one million visits. Britain was still essentially a class orientated, law-abiding society, relatively insular despite Empire links. It was still steeped in traditional practices and lifestyles that the Great War had powerfully challenged and undermined but not yet greatly altered, at least on the surface. Church going was already in decline but continued to wield a strong influence on national issues. Life was relatively simple, largely home focused, and essentially family orientated. There was no inflation. Indeed there was deflation for a time in the 1930s. Prices had not changed much for over 100 years. Holidays by the working population who were able to afford them were in the main limited to the nearest seaside resort for occasional day trips or a week's holiday at best, in July and August, or to visiting friends and relatives. Travel by train or bus was the norm.

After the First World War most manual workers could not afford to stay away from home on holiday, but the issue became identified as a form of social justice and the pressure for state intervention in support of holidays grew strongly in the 1930s. It led to the formation of the Interdepartmental Amulree Committee in 1937 that produced probably the most far-sighted evaluation of UK tourism in the twentieth century. Perhaps because it focused on demand and not organization, its approach was far more profound and influential than anything produced in the strategic tinkering of the last quarter of the twentieth century – and it led to the Holidays With Pay Act of 1938. Legislators do not work quickly in such areas and the Act was several years in the making. The TUC had first passed a resolution in favour of paid holidays for all workers in 1911 and unsuccessful Bills were put to the House of Commons in 1925 and 1929. However they did not attract enough support at the time and paid holidays was not a political agenda issue in the economic and political circumstances of the next five years. The 1938 Act, arguably the most significant government decision influencing travel and tourism in the twentieth century, meant that a worker's entitlement to holidays with pay would be the norm in the future and it laid a key foundation for developments in tourism after the war. Ironically, it was passed not by a socialist but a Conservative Government. Its provisions were not compulsory although the Act had exactly the intended effect over the following two decades.

New ways of thinking

Influenced by the same movement that had led, before 1914, to the growth of nonconformist churches, trades unions, the National Trust and the ideals of socialism, there was a remarkable inter-war years development of non-profit-making organizations, clubs and societies providing a range of holidays for their members. These included, for example, Youth Hostels, Cyclists Touring Club, Holiday Fellowship, Workers Travel Association, Co-operative Holidays Association and so on. These not-for-profit organizations emphasized in their objectives and practice the educational and social values of leisure and holidays. Interestingly the word 'tourism' was rarely used and even then it had a pejorative meaning. A nineteenth-century dictionary defines tourists as 'people who travel for the pleasure of travelling, out of curiosity and because they have nothing better to do', and even 'for the joy of boasting about it afterwards' (Lundberg, 1985).

The Youth Hostels Association, which began activities in 1929, aimed 'to help all, especially young people of limited means to a greater knowledge love and care of the countryside . . . and thus promote their rest and education.' It had 80 000 members by 1939.

In 1919 the Co-operative Holidays Association claimed to provide holidays that were spiritually and physically bracing. The Workers Travel Association in its Annual Report of 1924 promoted 'travel as the best means of achieving mutual understanding between the workers of all countries. Such understanding is only possible by mutual contact, by interchange of visits, by the study of languages and by an interest in the history, literature, art and social movements of other countries.' The objects of the Holiday Fellowship were 'to provide for the healthy enjoyment of leisure; to encourage love of the open air; to promote social and international friendship; and to organise holidaymaking and other activities with these objects.' The National Clarion Cycling Club (*Fellowship is Life; Socialism, the Hope of the World*), formed in 1895 had its membership peak in 1936 when it had 8306 members in 233 local associations across Britain. Overall there were some 3500 cycling clubs with 60 000 members represented by the Cyclists Touring Club and the National Cyclists Union. It is estimated there were some 10 million bicycles in Britain by the end of the 1930s. The bicycle undoubtedly freed millions from their urban confines and promoted an attitude shift toward the countryside that would develop strongly with the popularization of the motorcar before and especially after the war.

This movement of self-help and self-improvement, often associated with socialist ideals expressed through travel and leisure, was a very powerful force in Britain in the inter-war years, where travel had always been respected as a cultural and educational force. The ideas led also to the rights to ramble conflicts that were focused politically in the mass trespass on Kinder Scout (Derbyshire) in 1932 and influenced the thinking on national parks that would mature during wartime and be expressed in the National Parks legislation of 1949. On the Continent, notions of State or political intervention to provide tourism facilities were much stronger, often associated with social and sometimes socialist motivations, as well as health ones. Both Nazi Germany and Soviet Russia organized subsidized mass holidays for hundreds of thousands of their party members and for youth members in the 1930s, partly as reward and partly as propaganda. In many ways such developments pioneered the forms of mass tourism that would dominate holidays in free Europe after the war, albeit through private sector intermediaries for profit rather than State organizations for political reasons. Religious interests, especially in pilgrimages, were another source of non-profit travel generation.

The role of social organizations in tourism was significant and continued in Britain and more so in mainland Europe in the years of reconstruction after the Second World War, when socialist doctrines were generally popular and often the driver of government policies. Club Méditerranée, for example, was formed initially in line with socialist principles by Gerard Blitz and Gilbert Trigano, both pre-war French communists. Villages de Vacances Françaises and Cheques Vacances provided subsidized holidays for the less well off in France. In Britain, however, paradoxically following the victory of a Labour Government in 1946, the movement declined in significance as entrepreneurs in the holiday industry developed efficient low cost mass-produced package tours. Nationalization and government regulation and control were no match for entrepreneurial thinking and understanding of market forces, and tour operators achieved for a mass or popular market what pre-war idealists had sought in terms of affordability and easy access. Many will regret that the heady ideas of self-development and moral improvement of the inter-war years were rather lost in the process.

The volume and patterns of pre-war tourism

Some pre-war data are provided in Appendix V, but there were no precise measurements of tourism in this period and there was no recognized system of tourism statistics in Britain until the 1950s. Market research was still a relatively unknown art.

Professor Sir Frederick Ogilvie published the first economic study of international travel into and out of Britain (Ogilvie, 1933), devising his own estimates based largely on official migration and transport records. During the period from 1921 to 1931 the best year was 1929 when 692 000 overseas visitors came to Britain, including visitors from the Empire and Commonwealth and expatriates. These numbered 240 000. British residents travelling abroad were estimated as just over one million. Ogilvie was strident in his criticism of the quality of the available data and much of his criticism would still be relevant 60 years later in 1995 and on into the twenty-first century.

Receipts from overseas visitors were estimated at £22 445 000 and spending by British residents on their travels abroad at £32 794 000. Even at that time a substantial debit balance was a concern for the Government of the day. Fare payments from inbound visitors were not measured but it is likely that these would have shown a credit balance of some size. Before the Second World War there was no formal government tourism policy to promote Britain's attractions overseas, only the grant of small funds allocated to the newly formed Travel Association of Great Britain and Ireland since 1929. By contrast, a number of countries, especially in Europe, were making great efforts to attract tourists and Britain was seen as one of the leading markets.

International travel in general steadily increased in Europe in the 1920s reaching a peak in 1928 and 1929, but declining substantially as the deep economic recession took hold. In 1929 there were an estimated one million visitors to Switzerland, 1.25 million to Italy, 1.95 million to Austria and over one million to France. In some cases numbers were reduced by 50 per cent by 1931. However, traffic recovered slowly to reach new record levels by 1938 as the leading countries introduced tourism promotion and development programmes. Tourism was also greatly encouraged by the heavy depreciation of currencies in some important destinations such as Germany and Italy.

American travel to Europe increased rapidly in the 1920s to over 400 000, but was obviously affected drastically by the Great Depression. Indeed this peak figure was not exceeded until post-war expansion in the 1950s.

The volume of overseas visits to Britain recovered slowly from the recession helped by the establishment of the Travel Association with its overseas promotional programme. The peak inter-war year was 1937 when official records reported just under 500 000 foreign and Commonwealth visitors. This did not include visitors from the Irish Free State nor British expatriates returning from short trips on leave or for holiday. It seems likely that the total was a quarter or so higher than the peak arrival figures of the 1920s.

A feature of the overseas visitor movement to Britain was the high proportion of non-European and long distance visitors. Great Britain still rejoiced in its status as a worldwide Empire and in 1937, compared with 100 000 US nationals, there were 200 000 overseas British nationals (Commonwealth etc.) arriving and staying for long periods. Accordingly their tourist expenditure was high, making Britain's tourism traffic a high value, low volume trade. This was quite different from the situation in Europe where countries like Switzerland and France attracted over 90 per cent of their foreign visitors from other European countries. This pattern of travel continued for at least a quarter of a century after World War II until declining length of stay and the withering of former Imperial connections altered the volume–value balance toward more and more people, fewer nights and reduced expenditure per stay. One estimate of Britain's tourism revenue in the 1930s indicated that it exceeded that of France.

With no official or other recognized system for measurement, estimates of domestic travel within Britain were very approximate. The best assessment suggested that by the late 1930s, at the time of the Holidays With Pay Act, one third of the population or 15 million people took one annual holiday staying away from home within the country. It is impossible to quantify growth, therefore, but it does seem realistic to suppose that domestic holiday taking doubled between 1920 and 1938. Such growth fuelled the remarkable investment in resorts such as Blackpool, Eastbourne and indeed most leading seaside resorts during the 1920s and later 1930s. The combination of what is left of the Victorian, Edwardian and Art Deco styles of seaside architecture provide a fascinating visible reminder of the vitality of past growth periods.

Government interest in pre-war tourism

The national tourist organization for the UK had its origins in the 'Come to Britain' movement founded in 1926 by Sir Francis Towle, then Managing Director of Gordon Hotels in London. Its focus was inbound visitors, London and the role of the private sector, especially hotels. This movement created lobbying pressure from the industry and the need for some Government financial aid was immediately clear. The Travel Association of Great Britain and Ireland (TAGBANDI) was formally launched and recognized in 1929 with a modest £5000 grant from the then Chancellor of the Exchequer – Winston S. Churchill. Governments began to take more of an interest in tourism at the national level after the 1930s' Great Depression when the potential for foreign exchange earnings was first recognized.

This new initiative was badly needed as travel declined sharply and suddenly in 1930 as a result of the Wall Street crash and the subsequent depression. More than half of transatlantic business was lost. The Government's knee jerk response was to cut its grant to the Travel Association to £4000 as part of a public finance saving programme, which was exactly contrary to the required economic medicine for recovery. Interestingly the Travel Association was persuaded to change its name in 1932 to The Travel and Industrial Development Association of Great Britain and Ireland in an early recognition of an inward investment role. The Government's £5000 contribution, however, was not restored until 1936 although it increased to £15 000 in 1938 (British Tourist Authority, 1972). Many will see parallels with government responses to tourism in later eras.

Apart from its role in public transport provision and regulation, there were two main reasons for the growing political and government interest in domestic holidays and inbound tourism in much of Europe. Firstly a reforming spirit and socialist pressures led to the widespread introduction of agreements concerning time off and holiday pay. By 1937 workers' holidays were regulated by legislation in 20 countries. By 1939, under arrangements agreed before the 1938 Act in the UK took effect, 5 million workers were already covered by holidays with pay agreements in the UK. In Belgium there was a national office for workers' holidays; in France an Under Secretary for State for Leisure and Sport; in Germany a vacation section of the 'Strength through Joy organisation' (KDF); and in Italy rest houses run by Il Dopolavoro.

The second reason was the economic turmoil brought about by the Great Depression era of the early 1930s. Many governments responded by introducing a tourism programme for promotion and for certain aspects of tourism development. Some countries suffered severe depreciation of their currencies, which boosted tourism businesses. For the fortunate stronger currency countries, such as Britain at that time, outward tourism expanded as it offered obvious bargains to those who could afford it.

As noted above, one motivation for government interest in leisure travel was a political response to a growing interest in social welfare, and the belief that leisure and recreational facilities for the poorer sections of the population were socially and in some cases morally desirable. 'Access for all' 'For the many not the few' were not sound bites of the 1930s (the sound bite age was not invented at the time), but the ideas were the same and they were powerful in their influence. Social tourism, as this policy came to be called in European countries, involved savings schemes, subsidies and cheap transport for families on state railways, state subsidies for spa facilities (the Kurorts), hostels, holiday camps and centres. Many non-profit-making groups were involved, including trade unions, political parties and religious organizations.

In the UK, in the inter-war period, government interest was concentrated more on the perceived balance of payments advantages of tourism and there was no evident recognition of its great economic and social significance and potential. There was from time to time, however, state action and legislation affecting tourism as a result of government policies dealing with major current issues. For example, although not passed until 1943, the Catering Wages Act established a Wages Commission and Wages Councils to protect the large numbers of workers in the hotel and catering industry who were then largely not represented by trade unions. Until that time, in some of the more expensive hotels, waiters and other customer-facing staff were still expected to work solely for remuneration based on tipping. As an interesting addition the Commission was charged with reporting on the provision of holiday facilities, partly a social measure, but specifically to keep under review the requirements of overseas visitors. The Commission actively pursued this task until it was later taken on by the British Travel Association (known as the British Travel & Holidays Association from 1951).

The Hotel Proprietors Act 1932, dealing with the responsibilities of host and guest, notably in relation to stolen property, introduced a more modern definition of an hotel, always a problem area for state regulators.

One of the early pieces of legislation in Britain in support of tourism was the Health Resorts and Watering Places Act of 1921 (Pimlott, p. 244). It permitted local authorities to spend profits from municipal enterprises for tourism up to the equivalent of the revenue of a penny rate, on limited forms of advertising. In 1931 this power was extended in the Local Authorities (Publicity) Act, which granted powers to draw directly on the rates to the equivalent of one half (old) penny for promotional purposes – including overseas promotion for the first time. A further increase to 1.3 old pence was permitted in 1936. These were important steps in recognizing (in principle and practice) local authorities' responsibilities in what would now be known as 'destination management'. Local authorities played a pioneering role in securing government recognition for the importance of tourism outside London and enjoyed a level of recognition, trust and confidence from Central Government in the 1930s that has long since been withdrawn.

The Health Resorts Acts also provided some limited exemptions from the strict Sunday trading laws, which after the First World War closed most shops on Sundays. Resorts were allowed to permit trading on 16 Sundays in the year, then the weeks of the main holiday season, in a restricted list of articles deemed necessary for travellers. The list was odd, permitting for example the sale of herrings and saucy postcards but not the Bible.

In Scotland for many years bars were closed on Sundays, but hotels were permitted to serve drinks to refresh travellers who had journeyed at least three miles from home. There was in consequence a good degree of Scottish mobility on the Sabbath.

Throughout the inter-war years, the evidence suggests that the Government's role in Britain was responsive to industry representation, reacting to the economic and social issues of the day where tourism was seen as a useful aid to their main-line policies. The Holidays With Pay Act was very significant in its implications although tourism was not considered to be an important sector of the economy requiring any significant public support or state intervention.

In many ways one can argue that this proved beneficial and encouraged the development of necessary public/private sector partnerships. It helped to prepare the way for the massive development of the holiday and tourism trades after the war. From its early years The British Travel Association, under its various titles, sought commercial and local authority members. By the 1950s, the Association had several thousand members and could claim to represent a wide range of industry interests making up the travel trades. Although the private sector involvement in the Travel Association was never more than a very small percentage of the total business sector, it did include leading companies and made possible some effective working relationships with the public sector at local and national level. It sowed seeds that would germinate during the war and emerge in post-war conditions.

Role of local authorities

Before 1929 and the limited support for the new Travel Association, public sector involvement in tourism was concentrated solely at local level. A remarkable combination of municipal and private sector enterprise had built Britain's seaside resorts mostly between 1870 and 1914 and local governments competed vigorously for the seasonal visitor market. In the pre-war era local authorities contributed substantially to the national stock of leisure facilities, such as entertainment parks, gardens, piers, swimming pools and promenades, cultural attractions and sports facilities. They also undertook the major task of resort management although this was not a word in use at that time. There were over 200 established holiday towns in the 1930s, mostly seaside resorts, and in addition historic centres prospering from the travel and holiday trades. The British Resorts

Association traces its origins to 1921 when the 'Conference of Health and Pleasure Resorts' was formed. The bulk of the population that could afford leisure travel took their holidays in Britain; the great majority, especially families, chose the seaside. They travelled often to the same resort, in the main by one or other form of public transport, i.e. railways, coach and bus. The growth of day excursions provided another stream of economic wealth for resorts that was promoted vigorously by railways and bus companies, the latter beginning to develop inclusive tours in Britain and abroad in the inter-war period. Active local authorities were represented as members of the national Travel Association, which also lobbied on their behalf.

Many resorts in the 1920s and later 1930s found ways to invest substantially in new amenities, promenades, beach pavilions and swimming pools. Blackpool created seven miles of promenade with sunken gardens and other amenities at a cost of over £1.5 million from 1921 to 1923. Resorts organized entertainment with leading musicians and theatrical stars, and sponsored major events, such as the successful Blackpool Illuminations (which had commenced in the previous century), festivals and competitions. Bournemouth sponsored a leading symphony orchestra, and the Palm Court Trio in the Grand Hotel at Eastbourne became a household name, thanks to the new national radio network.

The large resorts with their piers and promenades had developed their own unique resort architecture, to which great architects of the past had contributed. Pugin, for example, designed beach pavilions and shelters and promenade lamp posts in Margate. In the 1930s these resorts were among the leading mass holiday centres in Europe. A further source of pre-war resort growth was the movement towards retirement out of towns and cities to places well known through regular holiday patronage.

Spas flourished in Europe and still held their own in Britain where their history and Georgian architecture attracted a more affluent clientele. British spas never recovered after the losses of the Second World War and the advent of the National Health Service, which prescribed ordinary tap water in towns for hydrotherapy. It was not until towards the end of the twentieth century that interest in health linked to recreation was commercially viable again in Britain, with large investment by commercial operators in mineral waters, health 'farms' and residential centres usually in the countryside, health clubs, saunas and gymnasia.

In the 1930s, Continental spas attracted a British clientele and promoted a substantial trade in the import of foreign mineral waters when they returned. British spas had forgotten one of the recipes for the early success of Bath and Beau Nash, the first resort director, when it was said 'it was the duty of the doctor to entertain the patient while nature effected the cure'. In contrast to the British Government's policy, in Europe, Germany and France for example, spa treatment 'The Cure' was provided free for employees and their families as a social service. Holidays in Soviet Russia for party members followed the same course.

Transport

Public transport developed rapidly during the inter-war years as the population became more mobile, with holiday taking and other leisure travelling, such as excursion days away from home, increasing substantially.

The railways, which had been government controlled in the First World War, were reorganized in the 1920s with government help into four main-line companies: GWR (West Country); LMS (Euston to Scotland via Preston); LNER (Kings Cross to Scotland via York); and Southern Railways (South of London). These were the glory years of steam trains and companies competed to operate relatively fast and efficient services – with first class luxury for those who could afford it. A number of famous trains were introduced in the 1930s such as the 'Flying Scotsman', the 'Coronation Scot' and the 'Cheltenham Flyer' which reached speeds in excess of 100 miles per hour. Mallard reached the record steam train speed of 126 mph in 1938. International services such as the 'Golden Arrow', the 'Blue Train' and the famous 'Orient Express' to Istanbul were well patronized. It was the peak of railway eminence as the transport of choice and a fifty-year long decline would set in (in the UK) after the war as ever more cars were purchased and freight transferred to roads.

Road transport began its rapid growth in the inter-war years. At first the most significant changes were the creation of a network of long distance coach services as well as the growth of bus services in urban areas and their rural hinterland. By 1938, it is estimated that the number of buses and coaches exceeded 50 000 and that 37 million passengers were carried on long distance routes in 1939. Although private car travel was increasing rapidly, the total number compared with post-war developments was still modest, rising from 132 000 at the beginning of the war in 1914 to two million registered private cars in 1939. The numbers doubled in the 1930s, however, notwithstanding the depression years.

People went on holiday mainly by public transport to destinations in Britain, usually by the seaside. The railway was the dominant transport provider but a substantial proportion made the journey by coach. Both railways and bus companies offered package tours especially to Continental European tourist areas. Tour operators owned their own coach companies just as after the war they developed their own airlines and hotels in a process known as 'vertical integration'. Excursions, particularly by road were popular, not only trips from home but also tours from the seaside resorts during the holiday period. Continental travel by road was increasing rapidly by 1939. Tour operators had formed their own trade body, The Tour Operators Conference, the name providing some indication of their growth and commercial success at that time.

Travel by sea, and in particular on the great ocean-going liners, reached the peak of its development when the *Queen Mary* (80 000 tonnes) went into service in 1936 and completed the voyage to New York in 5 days carrying 2000 passengers. The Blue Riband for the quickest transatlantic crossing stimulated fierce international competition when Dutch, French, Italian,

German, Scandinavian and American State-subsidized liners fought for the traffic that reached its high point in 1929. Volume on routes such as New York to Southampton was substantial, with passengers between Europe and the USA reaching one million in the good years, although modest compared with future growth in the second half of the century.

Liners offered regular and comfortable travel to and from all the continents and Britain played a key role with its Empire connections, its still large merchant fleet and its position as an intercontinental junction. Forced to respond to economic recession and consequent surplus capacity, shipping companies developed cruises in this era, foreshadowing the major development that would take place fifty years later, albeit with the essential contribution of air transport to move the market to the ships.

Air travel developed slowly at first in the inter-war period, with government support primarily through mail contracts, but the competition from highly subsidized European airlines limited Britain's services on the shorter routes. One of the first regular air services, however, was started by the Air Ministry in 1919 to carry passengers from London to Paris to the peace conference. These services had a chequered career as the journey was uncomfortable (no toilets, and took over two hours), the aircraft were unreliable and weather dependent, and a lack of modern navigational aids hindered efficient operation.

The British Government was more interested in the Empire routes where it faced little or no competition and Imperial Airways developed important services with its popular flying boats. The State also sponsored pioneering airships, but these proved faulty and dreadful pictures of the crashes of the R101 and the Hindenburg went around the world. By 1937, the peak prewar year, Imperial Airways carried only 244 000 passengers. A second state supported airline, British Airways started in the mid-1930s on routes to Northern Europe. But even by 1937, the peak year according to the Board of Trade statistics, passengers travelling from the UK to the Continent by air numbered just under 100 000.

Air travel was poised for rapid expansion, however, even before the war started in 1939. The Boeing 307 was the first airliner with a pressurized cabin, for example, in 1938. The war would produce massive technological advance in aviation and the basis for the great leap forward in civil aviation in the decade 1945 to 1955. This would be driven by the development of jet engines that were conceived in the 1920s by Sir Frank Whittle who famously could not acquire government support for development. The first jet engine was not built until 1937 and was first demonstrated in the air in1938.

Hotels and catering

Hotels, catering and many other service trades dependent on tourists and other travellers benefited from post-war recovery after 1918, but were seriously affected by the 1930s depression and the substantial decline in travel and consumer spending which followed. Many hotels, especially in London, had been requisitioned during the First World War. In some respects this was fortunate for the hoteliers as by 1913 the railway boom had encouraged the development of many large hotels in cities and resorts. Overcapacity in rooms was affecting profitability as discounting for trade led to falling prices and revenues. It was a process reflecting the business economics of fixed capacity and very variable demand that would become familiar many more times over the rest of the century. At the end of the First World War, however, compensation was poor and inadequate to meet the costs of restoration. Furthermore, the financial effects of the war had reduced the value of the hotel companies' reserves and led to higher interest charges, making the necessary capital expenditure difficult. The industry was operating on a stock of mainly Victorian buildings lacking more modern amenities, such as bathrooms, increasingly demanded by the clientele, especially in London by Americans, who numbered about 400 000 a year by the end of the 1920s.

As the inter-war years recovery took effect and prosperity improved there was substantial new investment. In London during the late 1920s large new hotels were constructed such as the Cumberland and Strand Palace, the Dorchester, the Mayfair and the Park Lane. Gleneagles was built by the LMS railway company in Scotland. But the Great Depression had a serious effect. Some of the large pre-war hotels were demolished and replaced by offices – The Royal became the Unilever head office, and the Cecil was replaced by Shell Mex House. Few hotels companies were profitable and the industry had a poor reputation with financiers.

Overall the total accommodation capacity throughout the country did not change much between the wars. There was always large capacity in small establishments such as boarding and guest houses, and seasonal accommodation in rented properties, bed and breakfast, farm houses and other temporary provision. Hostels, camping and caravanning were developing. A major innovation was the invention of the 'luxury' all-inclusive holiday camp. In 1939 there were some 200 holiday camps around the country but most were fairly spartan affairs until Butlin built and opened his first holiday camp at Skegness in 1936. At an investment cost of £100 000 it catered for 100 000 during the summer season; the charge was £3.10 shillings inclusive for the week. The clientele was largely white-collar rather than blue-collar workers, as this seemingly modest price was still beyond the means of the average industrial worker with a wage of £250 a year or less. At the Easter opening of the Skegness camp the British weather was traditionally cold and there was snow on the ground. Heating was not provided and dancers took to the floor in heavy overcoats to enjoy the dance hall facilities provided as part of the entertainment. The campers were clearly not daunted and the first season was fully booked. Although the implications would not be clear until after the war, Butlin had broken the mould of the then traditional seaside resort holiday experience (Read, 1986, p. 19).

The catering industry was as yet undeveloped for tourism purposes although a range of small cafes and teashops were found in most places, together with inns and pubs. The latter offered little in the way of food, however, before the war. Significantly there were some significant innovations in popular catering, such as the rise of milk bars and the popularity of Lyons Corner Houses. Charles Forte (later Lord Forte) created his first company to develop catering services in leading-edge cafes known as milk bars in London's West End in the 1930s (see Chapter 6). He did not become involved with hotels, however, until the 1950s. Reflecting the growth in road traffic, inns and hotels along main roads recovered trade that had been lost to railways fifty years earlier and created new customers from motorists. Many resort hotels offered entertainment, and dance halls in all towns and cities as well as in resorts provided mass entertainment for millions in the inter-war years.

The cinema was also a major source of mass entertainment in cities, towns and resorts, and thousands were built in an extravaganza of art deco architectural styles. Many such buildings, often no longer cinemas but bingo halls or restaurants, can still be seen in Britain's towns some seventy years later.

1939 – the impact of war

The immediate effect on travel and tourism in 1939 was inevitably drastic in Britain and mainland Europe. International pleasure travel ceased abruptly for the second time in 25 years. Families were split up when conscription was implemented. Petrol, food and other forms of rationing were soon introduced; attitudes and expectations of leisure time and social life were dramatically altered and put on hold. Private motoring except for business and official purposes virtually ceased. Beaches were fortified and mined in the southern part of the country for fear of invasion. In 1944, all civilians except those who lived there were banned from a coastal strip ten miles wide, which stretched from the Wash to Lands End (*The Times*, 2000, p. 97). In many popular holiday areas, hotels, holiday camps, transport and other tourism facilities, including London Zoo, were requisitioned for military purposes. Many hotels would not reopen. Some were bombed, such as the Langham and the Carlton in London, some converted to offices. The result of the two wars changed the industry substantially. The *Daily Telegraph* reported that by 1955, of the 110 hotels listed in the Baedecker Guide in 1910, only 11 survived.

Main messages of the inter-war years which resonate into the post-war period

1. Although still at a low base compared with the post-war era, the economic and social conditions of the British population, especially personal mobility and lifestyle expectations, changed in ways that

would fan the desire to travel and take holidays as soon as it was afford-able. The era of cinema and radio communications for all and television (for a very few) transformed the role of the media in most people's lives and would extend it dramatically after the war.

2. Depression years notwithstanding, as the quote at the head of this chap-ter illustrates, tourism interpreted as leisure travel and the holiday trades grew strongly in the inter-war years. Such growth would provide a springboard for future development just as soon as post-war condi-tions allowed.

3. The inter-war years witnessed the wide growth of socialist ideals and thinking about the role of holidays and leisure in society that in many ways failed to develop in the UK after the war, notwithstanding or per-haps because of a Labour Government acting according to socialist prin-ciples. Perhaps those ideals have their modern echo today in the notions of 'Access for All', 'For the many not the few' and 'Right to Roam'. The National Parks thinking of the 1930s obviously influenced the 1940s and 1950s and perhaps also finds modern echoes in the sustainable tourism movement of the last decade.

4. The inter-war years also provided opportunities for entrepreneurs that would strongly influence post-war tourism. Charles Forte, Billy Butlin and Wallace Arnold, for example, all pioneered new business models. The art of promotion, since developed as marketing, was important in this period too as 'all the resources of 20th century salesmanship were called into play by the holiday resorts, the transport undertakings, the travel agencies, the hotels and the amusement caterers' (Pimlott, p. 213).

5. With the honourable exception of the Holidays With Pay Act of 1938, the British Government revealed an overall indifference to the potential role of tourism that was in contrast to the interventionist policies of leading Continental governments. The depression years underlined the value of inbound tourism, however, and started a preoccupation with inbound tourism and foreign exchange earnings that would last into the twenty-first century. Driven by holiday resorts of the period, the evi-dence suggests that local authorities with tourism interests were far more dynamic and far-sighted in their actions than they were allowed to be after the war and following local government reorganization in the 1970s. In this sense at least lessons of history appear to have been lost (see also Chapter 9).

6. Professor Ogilvie's pioneering studies and later work by Elizabeth Brunner revealed the inadequacy of tourism statistics. Key aspects of this deficiency would be tackled after the war but even into the twenty-first century the lack of adequate data bedevils decision-making in the tourism sector as it did in the 1930s.

CHAPTER 2

Overview of growth and change – 1945 to 1995

This chapter provides a brief outline and overview of the underlying character and the principal events in the four eras chosen to explain the growth of modern British tourism. It highlights some of the main events influencing the half-century following the end of the Second World War, leaving the detail to later chapters. Readers may find it helpful to read this chapter with the year-by-year chart of main tourism events provided on pages 32 to 49 and the general chronology of dates and events provided in Appendix IV. Chapter 9 takes the story forward into present times and looks ahead.

The eras described were not times of clear-cut or steady progress and expansion. There were the same frenetic periods of daily stop and go and international tension and confusion that we experience today. The half-century witnessed economic and political disasters as well as some triumphs and a process of constant change accompanying the emergence of a global economy. The last fifty years saw the emergence and collapse of regimes in Communist Europe (the former Soviet Union); the Red Guards and cultural revolution created by Mao Zedung in China and overturned by Deng Xiaping; and the seemingly unstoppable growth of the Japanese economy until it hit the buffers in the early 1990s. They also saw wars in the Far East and the Middle East; growing conflict between the processes of capitalism in economically developed countries and fundamentalism in Islamic states; the Asia Pacific Boom; and the creation and growth of the European Union, and the growing involvement in it of the UK. International energy crises plunged countries into recession in the 1970s and 1990s and, for a time at least in the 1960s, the possibility of a nuclear conflict between the USA and Soviet Union over the Cuba crises of 1964 seemed possible. It was a turbulent half-century indeed.

In the UK, many parts of the travel and tourism market and emerging new segments achieved remarkable growth while other parts peaked and declined, and some disappeared. Package tours by air grew from tiny beginnings and created many new resorts along the Mediterranean coastline, for example, that after only four decades of growth would be experiencing many of the problems faced by British and other Northern European resorts since the 1970s. Inbound tourism to the UK increased to around 22 million visits a year and budget airlines, facilitated by EU liberalization of regulations, provided a major shift in customer expectations of scheduled travel by air. The Westminster Government, under both parties, continued to focus its limited tourism interests on a bewildering series of reviews, strategies and rearrangements of the official organizational structure of national tourist boards. The only constant theme – in England at least – has been a steady reduction of government funding over the last twenty-five years.

1945 to 1955 Post-war recovery

The attitudes of the time were initially dominated by recovery from the trauma of war and the continuing impact of wartime conditions of shortages and austerity. During wartime, of course, there was no international leisure travel and no currency allowance was available for the British to spend on travel abroad when it was over. Domestic holiday travel was actively discouraged during the war and large parts of the South and East coast were out of bounds, with beaches in some areas mined or restricted by barbed wire defences against invasion. Many hotels and holiday camps had been requisitioned for wartime use and there was no fuel for private motoring, and very few new vehicles on sale. Unnecessary travel generally had been discouraged with posters at railway stations asking 'Is your journey really necessary?' Immediately after the war, the impact of rationing of food, clothes, petrol, etc., was even more severe than it had been during the war and it felt worse because the war had ended.

The immediate post-war period reflected the great ambitions and expectations of the results of nationalization and national planning brought in by the post-war Labour Government. The 'commanding heights' of the economy were not deemed to include tourism, however, and the generous USA dollar aid offered to support post-war economic recovery in the form of the Marshall Plan was not used to restore tourism infrastructure in the UK but primarily to help support the manufacturing industry. Other European countries took a different view; France for example gave a greater degree of priority to transport and accommodation and other key travel sectors.

Although large parts of seaside resort tourism had been able to survive and, in some cases thrive, by accommodating the massive movements of troops and training, the holiday business waited, as it were, to be reinvented

Figure 2.1 Is your journey really necessary? This figure is reproduced in colour in the colour plate section.

and to start again from ravaged sites and run-down plant. There was clear expectation of pent-up holiday demand, as identified by Brunner, for example in 1945, but for most people the immediate post-war priorities were reuniting families, finding or restoring homes, and buying food and clothing.

Britain in the late 1940s was virtually bankrupt, having exhausted its reserves on the war effort. A political imperative was to earn foreign currency, principally US dollars to pay for essential imports. The Travel Association of Great Britain had prepared a post-war recovery plan (see Chapter 7) and managed to persuade the Government that tourism was potentially a vital dollar earner. This was very much due to the support at the time of Harold Wilson, then a young President of the Board of Trade in the post-war Attlee Government. Limited funds were provided for use on promotion in North America and certain other hard currency countries.

In addition, recognizing that effective promotion had to be linked to product development, a recovery programme was made available for hotels meeting the needs of foreign visitors, including the provision of rations and extra

Figure 2.2 Butlins as a wartime camp. (Courtesy of Butlins Archives)

supplies of goods restricted to essential users. There were even rations of confectionery and petrol for foreign visitors, tax-free shopping, furniture and fittings for hotels, and supplies of liquor for hotels catering for foreign visitors. The links between inbound visitors, foreign exchange earning and spending on promotion were reinforced as key political attitudes toward tourism.

By 1950, reflecting demand that had been frustrated during the long years of war, demand for domestic holidays was recovering quickly, mostly in the form of annual seaside family holidays for those who could afford them. Shortly after the war there may have been some 15 million domestic holidays of four or more nights and by 1955 this had risen to some 25 million domestic holidays, as estimated from surveys first implemented in 1951. The available evidence indicates an approximate doubling of the volume of pre-war holiday travel in Britain by 1955. British travel to destinations abroad also restarted on a small scale although it was restricted initially by the imposition of a very small foreign currency allowance, which varied from time to time (see statistics section in Appendix V). Tour operating based on air charters was then at its very beginnings, impeded by regulations designed to protect the air transport market for scheduled airlines. Vladimir Raitz formed his company, Horizon Holidays, to take his first clients by air to Corsica in the summer of 1950. There were less than 500 clients in the first year (see Chapter 6). By 1953 *The Travel Trade Gazette* was launched, a weekly journal for the travel trade and a sure sign that the number of people involved in the travel business had grown sufficiently to warrant a trade paper.

As soon as peacetime manufacturing was reorganized and the economy began to grow, demand for motoring surged and private car registration almost doubled from 1.8 million in 1946 to 3.5 million in 1955. This was still a small total compared with what was to come. But it was a massive increase in a decade least propitious to such growth and it provided clear indications of the power of the pent-up demand for personal mobility that would be released later as personal incomes rose.

In the general lifestyles of the population, society as a whole remained traditional and home based with little change until the mid-1950s. Just 7500 TV licences were sold in 1946 and TV at that time meant black and white and BBC only. Colour TV, rock and roll and pop music were still in the future and the first national recreation study by the British Travel & Holidays Association, which by then had a mandate for domestic tourism in Britain as well as for inbound tourism, described British people as 'recreationally inert'. The report gained great publicity at the time, with media denouncing the Association for prying into people's private lives. There was at that time little understanding of the role of market research in assessing market behaviour and patterns.

All in all, the decade to 1955 was a world with marked similarities in holiday behaviour to pre-war times and, apart from the indications of pent-up demand, few clear signs of the massive changes to come. The Labour Government of the day believed in a centrally planned economy and society, and proceeded to nationalize the principal means of production according to its socialist principles. Ports and transport were included in nationalization as key industries. Because the pre-war railway companies had acquired a range of interests outside trains, railway nationalization brought into public ownership the country's largest hotel chain, half the coach and bus companies, a major shipping line comprising cross-channel and other passenger ferries, and also principal travel agencies and tour operators, including Thomas Cook and Pickfords.

Thus, although it was more accident than design and certainly nothing to do with any political recognition of the future for tourism, the British Government owned in 1950 what we would now call the largest tourism conglomerate in the country. Although it must be admitted that the task facing them was daunting in its scope, public ownership and management by politicians and civil servants proved to be no more a recipe for efficiency and entrepreneurial innovation in 1946 than it is now. In an age of massive expansion, the public sector hotel group was the only chain to reduce accommodation and close hotels. The bus companies suffered as their railway-dominated owners starved them of capital and forbade competition, and few entered the package tourism business to compete with the entrepreneurial tour operators.

Under public ownership, Thomas Cook was slow to modernize, and did not enter fully into tour operating until after it had been bought back from the Government by a Midland Bank led consortium which in turn sold the company to a German bank. Later, in the 1990s, the firm was sold to a German industrial company that had bought its way into what it saw as the growing travel and tourism industry. Pickfords, more famous then for furniture removals than travel, was also eventually privatized and became a flourishing travel agency chain, later to be part of the Thomson Travel Group. By the twists of fate, both the major British travel companies nationalized after the war, would become German owned some 60 years on.

Growth sectors of tourism developed with the emergence of new entrepreneurs and new investors in the industry sectors (see Chapters 4, 5 and 6), but progress initially was slow. Government and media alike regarded tourism as a sector of no real consequence. Manufacturing was 'good', services, especially non-essential tourism services, 'bad'. Even the Government decision to provide limited financial support to back its British Travel and Holidays Association in the austerity era was greeted with media scorn, with one leader article declaring that 'no foreigner in his senses would willingly come to this damp and dismal island'.

1956 to 1969 Liberalization of travel – and of British Society

Slowly at first and then at an increasingly rapid pace, the structure of British society was changing by the mid-1950s. Personal incomes and leisure time were increasing in real terms as the post-war economy recovered and expanded. Bill Haley's *Rock Around The Clock* hit the number one hit spot via a film *Blackboard Jungle* in 1955. The 'pill' was made available commercially in 1961 offering 'safe sex' for the first time and the previously fairly rigid sexual moral code was relaxed as the 1960s proceeded. Also in 1961 the Beatles released their first LP. The birth rate was soon falling and traditional large families were split up as people moved to find better paid work and there were more small and single households. A seemingly insatiable consumer interest focused on consumer durables, especially cars and television, and it was accompanied by a rapidly growing demand for leisure services and especially holiday tourism.

By 1955, although still travelling mainly by sea routes, overseas visitors coming to Britain exceeded one million in a year for the first time, accom-

Figure 2.3 The Beatles. (Courtesy of ITN stills)

panied by media fears that there would be too many foreigners and no room to walk in central London streets. Total international arrivals by air across the Atlantic first exceeded those by sea in 1957 and international travel to Britain then literally took off. By 1969 overseas visitors reached a figure of nearly six million, with a healthy surplus on the balance of travel payments at that time of £50 million.

Demand for domestic holidays continued to grow, but more slowly and by the mid-1960s some traditional resorts noted their first declines in what was then the all-important main annual holiday visits in the summer. Holidays of four nights or more were estimated in 1955 at 25 million, a figure that would grow to 30 million by the late 1960s. British visits abroad tripled over the same period from two million to nearly six million as the market for package tours to sunshine destinations by air gained massively in popularity and media coverage. Home holiday visitors still spent some £600 million, but those who went abroad spent nearly £400 million, and in a very few years their expenditure would overtake and greatly exceed that on UK domestic holidays.

Associated with rising car ownership, motorway building and rapid extension in air transport capacity, a new growth trend towards more frequent travel for shorter trips and day visits emerged. But while day trips were largely domestic, the longer holiday trips increasingly turned to the attractions and modern facilities – especially the more favourable weather and new accommodation – to be found in foreign destinations, especially on the Spanish Costas and Islands.

For the first time in Britain, a Government took a major interest in the fast growing trade of tourism, mainly because of its implications for earning foreign exchange. A Minister with special responsibilities and a Cabinet Committee reporting to the Prime Minister were set up with a view to creating the right conditions for expansion. A Conservative Government under Harold Macmillan at that time was interested in removing regulation and encouraging commercial enterprise. Customs regulations were eased, passport and visa requirements were revised. Foreign visitors from Europe could make passport-free day trips. Liquor licensing laws were revised to ease traditional restrictions imposed during the First World War and the first casino opened in Brighton in 1962. Sign posting was improved. Road traffic regulation, which at that time tightly controlled the provision of bus and coach services, was liberalized. The Prime Minister, Harold Macmillan, could claim in the early 1960s that Britons 'had never had it so good'. Whatever else that much-disputed claim might mean, there is no doubt that growing prosperity fuelled interest in holidays and travel.

But there were also some setbacks for tourism growth. A new Labour Government in 1966, facing economic difficulties and a run on sterling against other currencies, introduced a severe currency restriction on the British travelling abroad of £50, and gave The British Travel Association a special grant of £300 000 to carry out a national holidays at home campaign. As some indication of its lack of interest or understanding of tourism it also simultaneously imposed a Selective Employment Tax on service industries in 1966. It did not last long (it was removed in 1973 when the UK joined the then Common Market) and it was not intended to damage tourism. But by increasing labour costs it had a major negative impact on the development of labour intensive sectors, such as hotels, at exactly the time they were preparing to modernize and expand. Reflecting slow investment in hotel capacity in the 1960s, the same Government went on to introduce a costly Hotel Development Investment scheme in 1968 as a new initiative to support hoteliers and speed development (see Chapters 4 and 7).

By the end of the 1960s, the key sectors of British tourism, especially the parts concerned with inbound international travel, were finally starting a post-war process of modernization and expansion in earnest. Hotel chains and hotel marketing co-operatives were forming to develop more effective marketing. New hotels were built in London and some of the larger cities, but until the end of this era, the investment in new capacity was modest, estimated at some 2000 new rooms per year in the late 1960s. This was supplemented by substantial improvement in public houses and inns, with better food, comfort and entertainment, which were attracting more women customers as a significant market segment for the first time. New leisure developments, such as bingo and discos, sports centres, and a revived interest in heritage and museums began. Technology and improving productivity, particularly in the international sector, led to remarkable reductions in real prices. For example, measured in real terms after removing the effects of inflation, the New York–London scheduled airfare by 1969 was little more than a quarter of what it had been in 1949. With the growing popularity of holiday travel by air charter and better economies of scale, the cost of overseas holidays for the British fell dramatically. Entrepreneurs were able to challenge and eventually overturn traditional air transport regulation practices that, *inter alia*, had sustained artificially high prices for international airfares by scheduled services.

Equivalent price reductions did not apply to domestic travel, however, dependent as large parts of it still were upon a highly seasonal trade, old facilities in need of refurbishment and a government controlled nationalized transport industry with poor capital investment. A highly taxed accommodation and leisure trade struggled to update products that were not considered as necessities equivalent to manufacturing output. The notion of tourism as a 'candy floss industry' stems from the Labour Government of the 1960s, the hostility of the traditional manufacturing industries and the trades unions. It reeks of the 1930s 'kiss me quick' holiday image that was attached to domestic tourism at that time.

By 1969, the economic importance of tourism as one of the country's major export trades and chief US dollar earner could no longer be overlooked. The Wilson Government produced a White Paper, which highlighted the hotel shortage and proposed a government mechanism for intervention. For example, there were only 900 rooms with an en suite bath at that time in Edinburgh and an even smaller number than that in the whole of Wales. The bulk of accommodation provision had changed little since the massive hotel building development of late Victorian times in most major cities and seaside resorts. Yet 400-seater jumbo jets were about to bring visitors to Britain who had already long been used to staying in hotels where all rooms had private facilities. The first such jet, a Boeing 747, arrived at Heathrow from New York in January 1970.

The White Paper became the Development of Tourism Act 1969 which, although government policy and implementation have very significantly altered over the following decades, has remained unchanged on the Statute Book ever since (see Chapter 7). This legislation replaced the British Travel Association constitution of a public sector/private sector trade partnership with a statutory authority (British Tourist Authority), and it created independent statutory bodies for England, Scotland and Wales. The Act was undoubtedly instrumental in drawing in and engaging many local authorities for the first time (in addition to the leading resorts that had been in membership of the former Association). Through newly created regional tourist boards, the English Tourist Board also engaged many local businesses in issues of tourism policy for the first time and it provided important new channels for communication and advocacy. Unfortunately, or as some saw it, disastrously, the Act made no adequate provision for co-ordination and co-operative action between the new Boards (see Chapter 7). The Act and the accommodation subsidies it authorized succeeded in doubling the total national stock of international standard accommodation within four years, albeit at a far greater cost than the Government ever intended.

On paper this was a massive achievement but, as so often with Government intentions, its success was almost immediately overshadowed by unforeseen events – in this case, the major international oil crisis of the early 1970s that led to a fall in visitor demand and some serious over supply and bankruptcies in the tourism sector.

'Modernization' was the political Zeitgeist of the 1960s, just as it would be again at the end of the 1990s, and in particular the period witnessed major steps to modernize an outdated nationalized transport infrastructure. Dr Beeching launched what many believe to be his infamously radical pruning of the Victorian era rail network (Reshaping of British Railways, 1963). Apart from cutting out uneconomic branch lines, the strategy was to prioritize the main lines, replace steam trains with more economic diesels and introduce High Speed trains. To meet the needs of burgeoning car ownership and improve the essential arteries of road haulage, a motorway and associated road-building programme commenced with the M1 opening in 1956 and the M6 following in the 1960s. Seaports and airports were developed and roll-on/roll-off ferry operations across the Channel greatly expanded to cope with the demand.

There was renewed interest among Local Authorities in economic regeneration and destination development as the first major impacts and implications of industrial decline were becoming clear, especially in Northern industrial towns and cities. Conference trade, sports and leisure centres were built and some seaports and especially airport expansion benefited. Unfortunately also in this period, governments revealed growing distrust of local authority independent spending or trading and this would seriously limit any expansion in public service operations, which had been an important element in destination tourism investment for a century and more. As so often with Whitehall decisions, at the most critical time for resorts, the ability of local government to respond to a downturn in tourism was curtailed by Government action. Of course, tourism was probably the last thing on anyone's mind at the time. The major local government reorganization implemented by the Conservative Government in 1972 would provide mechanisms for further interference from Whitehall and a process that would reduce the status of resorts within wider geographical boundaries often with only a minority (electorate) interest in tourism affairs.

1970 to 1989 Approaching maturity

Following the energy crisis and 3-day week of the early 1970s, the Wilson/Callaghan Governments took control for most of the 1970s, although not until after the Heath Government had engineered the UK's accession to the European Community in 1973. Many will see that accession as one of the defining points of the century for Britain and it has had massive effects on regional regeneration, agriculture and fishing and the communities they supported. In due course, liberalization of air transport and facilitation of intra European travel would have a strong influence on the development of tourism. But its impact at the time was more symbolic than real in most people's lives. The Thatcher Government took over in 1979 as the world was about to slip into its next major international economic recession. The combination of Tory ideology – to disengage the State and reduce subsidies – coincided with massive increases in international competition for manufacturing and new energy sources that would force change and decline on much of the traditional manufacturing economy of large parts of the UK for ever. The Miners' Strike of 1982–83 was faced down by the Government and is seen as a turning point that speeded the inevitable process of British industrial decline. The pace of social and demographic change had never been greater as incomes and leisure time, especially although not only in the more affluent South and South East of the country, continued to increase. Consumer interest grew in most recreation and leisure pursuits, health and fitness, fashion and entertainment, but also in environmental concerns. The British Tourist Authority held its first ever conference on the environment, 'Tourism and the Environment' at the Festival Hall in 1972. That it was addressed by The Rt Hon Peter Walker, then a cabinet minister, gives an indication that the subject was perceived to be important to Government, at least in token terms.

In business, although the installation of mainframe computers had been a key development for large organizations in travel, such as airlines, since the 1960s, it was the communication and technological innovations of the first personal computers (PCs) in the 1980s that revolutionized the flow of information – and the pace at which business could be managed and controlled. The Internet linkages that were possible for the general public in the 1990s are more popularly associated with the information communications technology revolution, but it was the development, for business purposes, of the first generation of office PCs that made it possible and funded the development costs that consumers would later enjoy in their own homes. Although heavy, bulky, costly and not at all user friendly, the first mobile phones were appearing in the late 1980s, albeit initially for business purposes. The first 'I'm on the train . . . and it's running late . . .' shouted conversations began to disrupt the peace of rail travellers.

In Britain and the wealthier European countries, birth rates dropped. In 1971, 5.2 million children were born in the European Community. In 1980 there were only 4.3 million, nearly one million less. By 1980, one in three UK marriages ended in divorce. Households reduced in size, with more single people as the average age for marriage increased. Former polytechnics were awarded university status in 1968 and the first postgraduate tourism degree courses emerged in 1972 followed by the first undergraduate courses in 1986.

The Government elected in 1979, led by Mrs Thatcher, embarked on a radical programme of privatization of as much as possible of what had been government controlled or owned since the 1940s. Telephones and British

Airways were prime examples along with gas, electricity and water supplies. Council housing was sold off creating a demand for home ownership (then supported by mortgage subsidies via tax relief) that would support the boom in house prices in the late 1980s that helped make so many consumers feel more affluent. Tourism was not to be exempt from the reductions in State spending. Tourism subsidies for development purposes under the 1969 Act were withdrawn in England, while the annual grant in aid payments to State-appointed tourist Boards (England and Britain) were put under continuous 'strategic review' and either reduced or pegged below the rate of inflation. In Scotland and Wales a different view was taken and the discrepancy between tourism funding in England and other parts of the UK widened.

Beyond the UK, the inefficiencies of state control of economies were revealed and Communism as a form of totalitarian government began to crumble, as a combination of market forces and political demands for freedom to choose spread throughout Eastern Europe. In 1989 the Berlin Wall, erected in 1962, was demolished and the Communist Soviet Empire collapsed in 1991. The effects of these changes in the liberalization of trading and encouragement of tourism made themselves felt in the 1990s, although the main effects occurred after 1995 and would begin to reach fruition with the enlargement of the European Union in 2004.

The 1980s saw the rapid development and expansion of budget hotel accommodation in the UK and growth in most other tourism services, notably in theme parks and visitor attractions such as museums, heritage properties, health and sports centres. Travel for all purposes boomed; the mobile society had arrived and traffic congestion became a political issue of growing importance. For most of the time it was a period of price inflation, but rising incomes, rising stock markets and affluence linked to house prices fuelled a 'feel good' factor for many and expenditure on travel and tourism was a natural response.

The number of overseas visits to Britain rose from nearly 7 million in 1970 to over 17 million in 1989. British travel abroad increased even faster, from 8.5 million in 1970 to over 30 million in 1989 (see data included in Appendix V). The Queen's Silver Jubilee Year of 1977, which stimulated some 12 million inbound visitors to the UK was in fact the high water mark of the revenue contribution of inbound tourism in the 50 years to 1995. Numbers would continue to increase, indeed they doubled over the next twenty-five years, but with falling length of stay and ever more efficient marketing reducing the cost of travel, the real financial contribution, stripped of the effects of inflation, would seldom match or exceed the contribution of 1977. From the 1980s onward, the UK would have to deal with more and more people spending less per visit as the issues of sustainability began to appear on the political agenda. Many believed that greater effort was required to manage this issue with better research data, improved marketing and visitor management at the destination. But the decisions taken by Government, at least for England, were at best unsupportive and at worst served to undermine such much-needed developments.

The number of main holidays of four nights or more in Britain fell from 34.5 million in 1970 to 31.5 million in 1989. Visits of one night or more away from home for all purposes remained more or less constant at an estimated 132 million in 1972 and 130 million in 1988 (see Appendix V). Although the basis for collecting these data changed in the period, these are the only official data available. The domestic decline may have been less than indicated and the overall figures conceal important growth areas that are hidden within the averages provided. But there was certainly no significant growth in staying visits in the domestic market over these years as British consumers increasingly looked abroad for both short and longer holidays.

1990 to 1995 A mature market and the emergence of a new era of globalization and growing world competition

This period started with military actions in the Gulf to defeat Iraq following the invasion of Kuwait (the first Gulf war). Although the war was brief, the uncertainties surrounding it and the perceived added risk to air travellers generally, especially for Americans, hit international tourism badly. The negative impact of the Gulf war was made worse as many of the developed nations in the West worked their way through the deepest international economic recession to hit them since the 1930s. While China and much of the Pacific Rim entered a decade of remarkable growth, the formally dominant Japanese economy was to fall into recession for more than a decade. Even the seemingly inexorable growth around the Pacific Rim would stumble badly on the 1997 economic and financial crisis originating in Thailand. In the UK, the annual rate of tourism growth had been slowing down anyway, but war and recession at the start of the 1990s exposed the volatility of demand in developed tourism markets. Outward travel from Britain, overseas visits, inbound and domestic trips all declined in 1991. Growth in international world travel worldwide was checked, and then resumed at a much slower rate until the mid-1990s.

In Europe, while Europeans were able to travel more both inside and outside Europe to increasingly far away destinations worldwide, the Continent took pride in being the world's largest international tourism region as measured by the World Tourism Organization. This was always a rather false claim, however, as much of its international tourism reflects frequent travel between adjacent countries (without border controls) that in the USA, for example, would be measured as domestic travel between adjacent states. As the European economy stagnated, its tourism growth rate was well below the world average in the 1990s and its so-called world market share continued to decline. To a large extent this fall in 'share' was inevitable as nascent tourist markets in India and the Far East, especially China, began to exercise their influence on global tourism volume as their economies grew.

Total domestic trips in Britain decreased in 1990 to 96 million from 110 million in 1989, and only slowly increased again to 121 million in 1995. In contrast, British travel abroad recovered its momentum very rapidly as the economy grew strongly from 1994, rising from 31 million visits in 1990 to over 41 million in 1995, with a record travel account deficit (at that time) of over £4 billion. As strong economic growth ensued for a decade, the deficit would grow continuously to £17 billion a year in 2003.

The number of overseas visits to the UK also recovered from the fall in 1991 to reach some 24 million arrivals in 1995, although shorter visits and more efficient management of capacity reduced costs to visitors and the value of spending overall did not rise in real terms.

By the mid-1990s, the British tourism industry faced strong winds of change. Globalization and liberalization in international trade brought new challenges through stronger competition from international destinations. The mid-1990s saw the effective dawn of the commercial use of the Internet as the first travel websites became available on-line to domestic personal computers, which at that time were just about powerful enough to access and download information, although speeds prior to broadband were slow. This was powerful information communications technology and as soon as on-line bookings became available (from 1995) and could be supported later with faster and more powerful PCs with broadband access, it would revolutionize tourism marketing and alter many traditional business models. The dot-com boom did not live up to the revolutionary fervour that greeted all its possibilities, however, and its wilder aspirations fuelled an investment bubble that would collapse spectacularly in the new century. But the Internet would change tourism marketing fundamentally over the next decade, initially for large organizations but quickly for the active smaller businesses that dominate the tourism sector in the UK as in other countries. The implications of that revolution are still emerging ten years on.

Directly allied to the new technology in its effects, one of the most far-reaching changes of the early and mid-1990s affecting travel would be the European deregulation of air transport under its Single Market competition rules, which paved the way for the remarkably fast development of budget airlines. Across Europe these have facilitated massive changes in international *and* domestic travel movements. For the next decade the greatly reduced real cost of travel abroad would radically alter the traditional balance of cost between domestic and international travel destinations – in favour of the latter. It would also promote domestic travel by air as the budget airlines extended their routes across the UK. Although mass marketing by tour operators would remain a dominant force in tourism, its influence would decline as the Internet developments heralded a future of marketing based more on direct communications, with visitors treated as individuals.

The impressive development of air transport liberalization, however, was not matched in the broader tourism sphere and many consider that the institution of the European Single Market following the Maastricht Treaty of 1992 proved disappointing to tourism. With no tourism policy or priority for the industry, taxes, business regulation and constraints increased across the board, eroding Europe's competitive edge in the face of growing competition. Financial scandals surrounded the Directorate responsible for tourism (DGXXIII), which subsequently lost its credibility and separate status in the internal jockeying for power in the Commission. Nevertheless, specific directives covering package tourism and tourism statistics, as well as the air transport controls over emissions and noise, plus a wide range of environmental and health and safety and employment legislation have changed the conditions of business for many in the tourism industry. Many complain of slow strangulation by red tape and failure in Brussels to appreciate the problems faced by small businesses in all sectors of the economy.

The Government at Westminster continued to shed its direct involvement in industry with the dismemberment of British Rail into a collection of private companies variously responsible for the track, the terminals, the operation of trains and the provision of rolling stock under leasing arrangements. The determination to withdraw funding from tourist boards under Westminster control continued, with the English Tourist Board and its successor the English Tourism Council under constant pressure of budget reduction and threat of closure. The final axe was not wielded, however, until 2002 when most of the responsibility for tourism in England was transferred to newly created regional development agencies.

The Brundtland Report of 1987 focused the world's attention on global warming and all the associated issues of sustainability, and in 1992 the major international World Summit at Rio de Janeiro produced an international blue print, *Agenda 21* for sustainable development. International disagreements and unwillingness to act soon undermined much of the good intentions of *Agenda 21*, although the Rio work and its follow-ups through the Kyoto Protocol have arguably changed forever the earlier twentieth-century assumptions about the notion of economic growth without environmental cost. Concerns about the potentially negative impact of tourism on the environment, requirements for impact assessments and environmental audits and issues of consumer protection for health and safety purposes have become major factors in modern destination development.

Tourism, viewed as a massive, mobile, rootless global force played a major part in economic and social life in the UK by 1995. It would continue to be affected by further development of new technology and changing fashions and lifestyles stimulated by the communication revolution in a less ordered and more volatile economic and political scene. The post-1995 developments and implications are addressed in Chapter 9.

Table 2.1 Chronology of events affecting British travel and tourism from 1945 to 1995

Year	External influences	Attractions sites/events	Transport	Other facilities and services	Organization and legislation
1945	Strictly enforced regulations regarding foreign currency allowances both for business and leisure travel outside Sterling area	Seaside resorts reopen after the war and begin to improve their facilities	IATA reconstituted restarting of international air services and facilitation of through ticketing and airline co-operation		Act of Canadian Parliament reconstituted IATA embodying the spirit of the 1944 Chicago Convention
1946			British European and British South American Airways Corporations formed	Opening of first section of Heathrow airport (North Side)	
1947		First Edinburgh Festival	IATA Clearing House opened in London (later transferred to Geneva)	Expansion of holiday camps Holiday travel mainly by rail and motor coach	'Bermuda One' Air Agreement bi-lateral between USA and UK on North Atlantic Services British Travel & Holidays Board set up
1948	Continuing food rationing encouraged the better off to travel overseas (despite currency restrictions)	Olympic Games – London Wembley	Transport Act passed – UK railway companies nationalized Berlin Air Lift – most UK charter aircraft commandeered by Government to ferry supplies into the beleaguered city		Jan 1st – nationalization of the British railway system under the Transport Act of 1947, includes the travel agency chains of Thos Cook & Son, Pickfords and Dean & Dawson

	Growing acceptance of holidays with pay stimulates leisure travel Emergence of 'profitable' independent airlines and entrepreneurs such as Freddie Laker and Harold Bamberg		First Air Car Ferry across the English Channel Railway Air Services taken over by BEA (British European Airways)		500 000 overseas visitors came to Britain Wales Tourist & Holidays Board set up
1949	Sterling de-valued (from $4.03 to $2.80 to the £) People's Republic of China formed	Longleat opens for visitors	BSAA absorbed by BOAC Baltic Exchange air section opened in London to cope with increasing air charter traffic throughout the world		National Parks and Access to the Countryside Act passed Nature Conservancy formed
1950	2.3 million cars registered in the UK		First inter-European air inclusive tour operated from UK to Corsica by Horizon Holidays First flight of British turbo-prop 'Viscount' airliner	Association of British Travel Agents (ABTA) formed	British Travel & Holidays Association formed (replaced 1947 Board)

(Continued)

Table 2.1 Chronology of events affecting British travel and tourism from 1945 to 1995 – (Continued)

Year	External influences	Attractions sites/events	Transport	Other facilities and services	Organization and legislation
1951	Newly elected Conservative Government 'liberalized' air transport regulations to allow private airlines limited competition with BEA and BOAC – the State corporations	Festival of Britain in London			14 million British wage earners now entitled to holidays with pay First market research survey of UK holiday taking – British National Travel Survey (BNTS)
1952		Olympic Games – Helsinki Beaulieu opens for visitors	Tourist class fares introduced on North Atlantic First 'pure jet' passenger service inaugurated by BOAC 'Comet 1' between London and Johannesburg		
1953	One million Britons travel abroad for business and pleasure	Coronation of Queen Elizabeth II London	First scheduled turboprop aircraft introduced by BEA from London to Cyprus	*Travel Trade Gazette* launched – first weekly travel trade newspaper	New Licensing Act consolidated licensing laws in England & Wales

1955	Britain receives one million visitors from overseas	The Westbury, first new large post-war London hotel opened	Inauguration of Independent TV. First travel companies advertise
1956	Suez Canal crisis	Olympic Games – Melbourne First Beaulieu Jazz Festival	Institute of Travel Agents founded (now Institute of Travel and Tourism)
1957	Transatlantic passengers by air exceeded those travelling by sea for the first time	Hertz Rent a Car inaugurated the first 'Fly-Drive' facility at Orly Airport, Paris Boeing 707 jet aircraft entered North Atlantic service on Paris–New York route	Grand Hotels (Mayfair), later Grand Metropolitan Hotels became a quoted company
1958	British Motorway building programme began (M1 opened in 1959) 58 per cent of British people now taking a holiday away from home	Gatwick reopened after refurbishment as London's second main airport First jet service London–New York by BOAC Comet 4 Economy and excursion fares introduced by airlines	Travel Trade Association formed (in competition with ABTA)

(Continued)

Table 2.1 Chronology of events affecting British travel and tourism from 1945 to 1995 – (Continued)

Year	External influences	Attractions sites/events	Transport	Other facilities and services	Organization and legislation
1959	M1, Britain's first motorway opens connecting London and Birmingham			Fortes acquired Fullers and Quality Inns	
1960	Spanish Government commits to the growth of the 'Costas' and Balearic Islands developed by the Spanish Government changing the patterns in British holidays abroad OECD formed	Olympic Games – Rome	To 1965 – large growth of IT European holidays. Emergence of new large tour operators such as Thomson, Horizon, Global, Cosmos, and Clarksons		Act to control the siting and development of caravan sites Definition of the term 'tourist' ratified by the UN through IUOTO
1961	To 1970 – large shift of demand from scheduled to air charter services			Channel Tunnel Study Group formed Skyway hotel, first major hotel at London Airport opened Carlton Tower, first 'skyscraper' hotel in London opened	
1962		First casino in Britain opened in the Metropole Hotel, Brighton		Lunn-Poly created through amalgamation of Sir Henry Lunn with the Polytechnic Touring Association London Hilton opened	

1963	'Reshaping of British Railways' – Dr Beeching's Report which resulted in major cuts in the rail network and end of steam trains. Two million overseas visitors came to Britain, and spent £188 million	Britain's first ski resort opened at Aviemore, Scotland	First computerized reservation systems introduced by airlines. British Eagle Airways collapsed. Scheduled airlines began to create their own charter subsidiaries (British Airtours, Condor, etc.)	Grosvenor House merged with Trust Houses	British Travel & Holidays Association became British Travel Association
1964	'FIESTA' Group of tour operators failed financially, leading to legislation to protect the consumer – first by ABTA in the formation of the Tour	Olympic Games–Tokyo	Large expansion of cross-channel car ferry services with the introduction of 'RoRo' Ferries. Large tour operators acquire and start to	Cut-price holiday schemes introduced by Max Wilson, John Bloom, etc. Grand Metropolitan hotels launch weekend breaks	

(Continued)

Table 2.1 Chronology of events affecting British travel and tourism from 1945 to 1995 – (Continued)

Year	External influences	Attractions sites/events	Transport	Other facilities and services	Organization and legislation
1964 (cont.)	Operator's Study Group and later by the Civil Aviation Act in 1971		develop their own airlines, including Britannia, Monarch and Orion	First university degree course in hotel and catering management began at new University of Surrey Hotel Sales Managers Association formed	
1965	Business entertainment disallowed for tax purposes 8.9 million cars registered in the UK			ABTA introduced 'Operation Stabiliser' and inaugurated bonding for tour operators	Sports Council established
1966	Introduction of first UK Credit Card – Barclaycard £50 foreign currency travel allowance introduced to deter Britons from travelling abroad		BEA introduce Trident jets, which were the first aircraft equipped for automatic landing Laker Airways formed	Travel Trade Association merged with ABTA Prestige Hotels – first major hotel co-operative marketing group formed	Selective Employment Tax introduced UK Gaming laws relaxed
1967	Four million overseas visitors came to Britain and spent £236 million Sterling again devalued (from $2.80 to $2.40 to the £)			Guild of Business Travel Agents formed in London Tour Operators Study Group (TOSG) formed with ABTA – an important move in consumer protection	Countryside (Scotland) Act passed

1968	Olympic Games D Mexico City	British Rail introduces HST125 fast diesel Inter-City trains	Interchange Hotels D second major hotel marketing consortium formed (later absorbed into Best Western)	Countryside Act created Countryside Commission Transport Act gave British Waterways Board recreation and amenity duties and powers
1969	Selective Employment Tax increased by 28 per cent Beginning of a long period of unrest in Northern Ireland	QEII made maiden voyage across Atlantic Maiden Flight by Concorde	Inter-Hotels – third major hotel marketing consortium formed	Development of Tourism Act created: a) British Tourist Authority replacing the British Travel Association b) English, Scottish and Wales Tourist Boards and provided for grants and loans for hotel building (HDI Scheme) and powers for future hotel classification schemes
1970	Holiday destinations for Britons extended to Portugal, Greece, Canaries, and	QEII in service with Cunard Inauguration of Boeing 747 jumbo jet aircraft	Expansion of retail travel agency sector Trust Houses and Forte merged	

(Continued)

Table 2.1 Chronology of events affecting British travel and tourism from 1945 to 1995 – (Continued)

Year	External influences	Attractions sites/events	Transport	Other facilities and services	Organization and legislation
	Yugoslavia Popularization of Miami Beach and other US destinations by Intasun using the Laker Air services Britons took 40 million holidays away from home (5.25 million overseas) Seven million visitors came to Britain		and arrival of first 'Jumbos' at Heathrow BEA introduce Windsor Tours to Britain		
1971		Opening of Beamish Open Air Industrial Museum in NE England	Hovercraft introduced on English Channel routes Increased number of custom-built cruise ships and growth of Fly-Cruising market	Development of 'seat-only' market ex UK by air taking advantage of loophole in the regulations promulgated by the Civil Aviation Act of 1971 – using 'token' accommodation	Civil Aviation Act passed to regulate the development of scheduled and charter airline operations i) merged BOAC and BEA as British Airways ii) Licensing for tour operators iii) Created Civil Aviation Authority

1972	More than 10 million Britons travelled abroad UNESCO convention to recognize World Heritage Sites	Olympic Games – Munich Tutankhamun Exhibition – London BTA holds first national conference on Tourism and the Environment		Thos Cook sold to a consortium of Midland Bank, the Automobile Association and Trust House Forte (by BTC) – later to be wholly owned by Midland Bank First postgraduate courses in tourism offered at Universities of Surrey and Strathclyde	British Home Tourism Survey introduced to measure visits of one or more nights from home for all purposes
1973	First OPEC oil crisis, petrol coupons issued UK joined the 'Common Market' Growth in winter sun holidays	Historic Houses Association formed	Advance Booking Charters virtually killed off the Affinity Charter market and led to the introduction of 'Apex' fares (Advanced Purchase Excursions) British Airways succeeds BEA and BOAC	Launching of ABTA/ITA National Plan for Education and Training for the travel trade London Penta opened, the largest post-war hotel at that time	Selective Employment Tax abolished and Value Added Tax introduced on UK joining the Common Market
1974	Overseas visitors to Britain reach nearly 8 million		British Rail complete electrification of West Coast main line London–Glasgow	Tour operators Clarksons and Horizon collapse in the economic downturn following the energy crisis	Local Government reorganization implemented in England and Wales

(Continued)

Table 2.1 Chronology of events affecting British travel and tourism from 1945 to 1995 – (Continued)

Year	External influences	Attractions sites/events	Transport	Other facilities and services	Organization and legislation
	Economic crisis and severe labour problems in UK – 'three-day week' for part of the year		KLM introduce 'Business Class' on North Atlantic routes	First test of Civil Aviation Act bonding regulation – resulted in the passing of the Air Travel Reserve Fund Act	First policy guidelines issued by Government for British tourism development
1975	Long-haul market to Asia developing Overseas visitors to Britain spent over £1000 million 13.5 million cars registered in the UK	European Architectural Year	British Airways started shuttle service London–Glasgow	First McDonald's restaurant in England	Air Travel Reserve Fund Act passed to protect consumers where the bond held by a tour operator proved to be inadequate (later renamed Travel Trust Fund)
1976	First North Sea oil piped ashore	Olympic Games – Montreal USA Bicentennial	Supersonic air transport began across the Atlantic with BA and Air France 'Concorde' at speed of Mach 2	World Tourism Organization founded as an agency of the United Nations (replacing former IUOTO) Major growth of 'short break' holidays at home and abroad Best Western Hotels co-operative launched in the UK	'Bermuda Two' UK/USA Air Agreement signed – increasing the number of US gateways airports available to UK carriers, and opening the way for Concorde and Skytrain North Atlantic services

1977	Tourism became top British net 'invisible' export	Silver Jubilee of Queen Elizabeth II – marks a peak in inbound tourism revenue to the UK Wembley Conference Centre opened	Introduction of Laker Skytrain service across the North Atlantic	Formation of the UK Tourism Society	Unfair Contract Terms Act – tightened regulations for holiday booking conditions
1978	Overseas visitors to Britain reach 12.5 million and spend £2500 million Britons taking 48 million holiday trips per annum of which 10 million are to overseas destinations		Airline deregulation within the USA under Carter Presidency increased competition resulting in many airline mergers and financial failures. Also strongly influenced international air travel		
1979	Second OPEC oil crisis creates international downturn and major economic recession in UK, speeding the decline and collapse of much of British traditional manufacturing industry				Complete relaxation of all UK Foreign Exchange Control regulations (June)

(Continued)

Table 2.1 Chronology of events affecting British travel and tourism from 1945 to 1995 – (Continued)

Year	External influences	Attractions sites/events	Transport	Other facilities and services	Organization and legislation
1980	Development of long-haul air charter market. Florida becomes popular as a British summer holiday resort Emergence of Time Share market as a response to economic crisis in selling USA apartments/condominiums as single properties	Olympic Games – Moscow Opening of Alton Towers – start of UK theme park evolution	IATA begin to lose influence in fixing air fares and capacity control 1980s see increase in 'seat only' market		
1981	Toxteth and Brixton riots prompt new thinking on urban regeneration	First World Travel Market London	Lord King appointed Chairman of British Airways		
1982	Falklands war	Royal Wedding of Prince and Princess of Wales	Collapse of Laker Airways and associated companies with accusations of 'predatory pricing'. Laker bond found to be insufficient to meet all claims – call on		ABTA's 'Stabiliser' upheld by Unfair Practices Court in London

1983		Air Travel Reserve Fund Satellite terminal opened at Gatwick Airport		National Heritage Act established the Historic Buildings and Monuments Commission of England – 'English Heritage'
1984	Olympic Games – Los Angeles International Garden Festival at Liverpool – first of several such events promoting visitors to areas previously not known as tourist destinations	First transatlantic flight by Virgin Atlantic	First Forte Travelodge marks the start of the budget hotel expansion in Britain	Tourism (Overseas Promotion) Act – Scotland now able to promote directly to overseas markets rather than through the BTA
1985	UK now one of the top six tourist destinations in the world Lord Young, as Secretary of State for Employment, launches 'Leisure, Pleasure and Jobs' report to promote the economic role of tourism	Ryanair launched with one 15-seat aircraft		Responsibility for Tourism in the UK transferred from Dept of Trade to Dept of Employment

(Continued)

Table 2.1 Chronology of events affecting British travel and tourism from 1945 to 1995 – (Continued)

Year	External influences	Attractions sites/events	Transport	Other facilities and services	Organization and legislation
1986		National Garden Festival – Stoke on Trent	Eurotunnel proposals accepted	BTA new travel centre opened in London's Regent Street First undergraduate course in tourism at Bournemouth	Airports Act – Local Authorities to give up major shareholdings in regional airports Single European Act passed by UK
1987	British Stock Market collapse (October) Brundtland Report sets the agenda for new thinking on global issues of sustainable development		Privatization of British Airways completed Opening of London City Airport in Docklands 35 million passengers a year passing through Heathrow Townsend Thoresen Ferries taken over by P&O Ferries	Over 7000 retail agency members of ABTA compared with 4000 in 1977 First Travel Inn opened to compete with Travelodge chain First Center Parc opens in Sherwood Forest	British Airports Authority becomes a 'plc'
1988		Olympic Games – Seoul	Introduction of 'Jumbo' ferries short sea routes to France		Liquor Licensing Act – all day opening of pubs permitted

1989	Berlin Wall demolished – Germany reunified – Tiananmen Square – Beijing crisis 1.8 million UK tourists go to USA 17 million overseas visitors to Britain	UK's Vodaphone network achieved its first half million customers – the start of the popular mobile telephone boom	New North Terminal – Gatwick Excavation work begun on Channel Tunnel	'Tourism Concern', a voluntary organization, was established to find solutions to the environmental and social impacts of tourism Second Center Parcs opens	Channel Tunnel Act passed British Tourism Survey (BTS-M) replaced by UK Tourism Survey (UKTS)
1990	Major economic recession affects developed countries in the Western World UK joins ERM at DM2.95 to £1 Unemployment and the recession cause first fall in package holidays sales for many years 19.7 million cars registered in the UK	'European Year of Tourism' declared by EC and EFTA Glasgow – European City of Culture	Twin engined aircraft now permitted on North Atlantic routes (Boeing 767) Sealink taken over by Stena Line 'Seacat' catamaran service started on English Channel The 200 major airlines lost more than £2.5 billion in 1990 operations	Tour Operators Study Group renamed Federation of Tour Operators	European Community Package Tour Directive issued

(Continued)

Table 2.1 Chronology of events affecting British travel and industry from 1945 to 1995 – (Continued)

Year	External influences	Attractions sites/events	Transport	Other facilities and services	Organization and legislation
1991	Outbreak of Gulf war has devastating effect on tourism movements. 15 000 flights cancelled in first month		Wagon Lits took over Pickfords Business Travel Division London City Airport cleared for operation of jet aircraft Stansted Airport opened United Airlines took over Pan Am Heathrow services and American Airlines replaced TWA at Heathrow	'Bravo' UK's first centralized, computerized reservation system introduced. This was a pioneering effort that would sow seeds that germinated later in the decade	
1992	Outbreak of civil war in Yugoslavia and its component States UK forced out of ERM Earth Summit held at Rio de Janeiro – Agenda 21 adopted	Olympic Games – Barcelona EuroDisney opened in Paris Ebbw Vale Garden Festival in Wales		Thos Cook sold by Midland Bank to German bank and travel holding company	Responsibility for tourism in the UK transferred to Department of National Heritage
1993	97 per cent of British workers now entitled to at least two weeks paid annual holiday. Most now have four		Eurotunnel – first freight services operated Controversial Bill providing for	Demise of ABTA 'Stabiliser' consumer protection scheme	European Single Market inaugurated (January) Lottery Act 1993 establishes Heritage Lottery Fund and

or more weeks

1994	First practical commercial use of the Internet with first travel websites	privatization of British Rail introduced into Parliament		Millennium Commission
	25 million cars registered in the UK	Eurotunnel officially opened with through train services London to Paris and Brussels		Airport Departure Tax levied on passengers departing UK airports
1995		First British Rail service franchises granted under the new Act of 1993	Approaching 10 000 rooms available in budget sector	Sunday Trading Act passed
		Easyjet launched with 2 leased aircraft		

CHAPTER 3

Comparing tourism in 1950 with today

We have stressed in the Preface that tourism is not in any normal sense an 'industry'. It is in essence a powerful and growing market force comprising multiple strands of interest and activity at destinations. In other words, it can only be understood by measuring what people do when they travel away from home (see also Appendix III). There have, of course, been massive changes in the last fifty years, not only in what people do but what sort of people the British are. To highlight the remarkable contrast between demand in 1945 and modern times, especially for younger readers born after the 1980s, this chapter is divided into two parts. The first part illustrates the nature of tourism demand as it was understood and experienced by the British population in the immediate post-war era of 1945 to 1955. The second part reviews the nature of tourism demand 50 years on from the mid-1990s to 2005. Of course, any such review in a few pages requires some sweeping generalizations and it cannot include the finer details. We justify this because we feel the contrasts are truly striking and because it makes it easier to understand the way in which tourism has developed and grown over the last half-century.

There is always an interesting question to resolve as to whether it is changes in demand that bring about changes in supply – or vice versa. Which is cause and which is effect? Major developments in transport technology by air and by road, for example, undoubtedly provided the means to facilitate demand and encouraged its growth. They certainly had a powerful influence on the changing patterns of destinations that visitors chose (and were able) to visit. But they in turn were a response to economic growth and increasing customer affluence and desire for travel. Customer choices were also influenced by the business models and marketing professionalism in the private sector that emerged to nurture – or some would say exploit – the growing demand. Tour operators in particular were a major influence over the nature and volume of demand for tourism by the British and one can argue that they changed both holiday aspirations and expectations of leisure travel. They could not have done so without the technology that brought about reliable large aircraft with usable economics and the ability of customers to pay for their use.

The issues of demand and supply are addressed in more detail in Chapters 4 and 5 and an outline of some of the main changes in business models is provided in Chapter 6. Significant developments in consumer demand, such as the growth and decline in mass tourism, take place relatively slowly over more than one decade and what is in the pipeline in 2005 will have its influence over the next decade and beyond. Such changes are addressed in Chapter 9.

Holidaymakers of the 1940s and 1950s

The holidaymaker of 1950 was very different from the visitors of today. People born in 1900 were still only 45 at the end of the war, but they and their parents were old enough to have survived through two world wars and all the deaths and associated suffering and privations. They had also suffered the impact of economic slumps and hardships of a severity that is simply not recognizable by people born after the 1960s. Those under 45 would for the most part have been called up for war service and survived the dangers and traumas of war. Young single women had also been called up for national service duties. There was no welfare state until the 1940s and infections, illness and early death were the commonplace experience for nearly all but the relatively well-off. Many households in the 1940s still lacked inside toilets and even bathrooms were not available to all; central heating was a rarity. Washing machines, telephones and television were generally not available. Eating out other than in cafes was a rare option for the great majority of the population and drinking wine was little more than an annual event. Although pubs were popular and ubiquitous in the 1940s, and drunkenness commonplace, they were mainly beer houses for men and alcohol consumption for most was limited by income. Nearly all holidaymakers in the 1940s, even little children, had lived for several years under economic privations and wartime conditions in which money was always tight, food was rationed, leisure, entertainment and luxuries were seen as sinful and non-essential travel was actively discouraged. For the few that had cars before the war, driving for pleasure was banned and petrol rationing was brought in in 1942 and not lifted until 1950. 'Is your journey really necessary?' was a classic wartime slogan to make pleasure travellers feel guilty about wasting scarce resources.

For all these reasons the wartime survivors were in the mood to extract holiday enjoyment wherever it was available and affordable. But these were not the discriminating, demanding customers of the twenty-first century and by modern expectations they were easily satisfied. If the accommodation and entertainment facilities were basic, overcrowded and of poor quality by twenty-first century standards, these were very minor inconveniences compared with what most people were familiar with in their daily lives. Seaside resorts were the logical providers of the holiday experience and could sell all available accommodation in the peak summer months. Resorts and annual holidays were seen as the aspirational antidote to the daily grind. They offered fun, excitement, entertainment and a more liberated atmosphere – especially for younger people – that had irresistible appeal at the time. Many would save throughout the year to afford a week's holiday by the sea.

A collectivist, conformist era that was reflected in the holidays on offer

1950 Britain was still primarily the collectivist, conformist, mono-cultural society that it had been in the pre-war era. Immigration was unknown in most places. It was by modern standards a repressed, authoritarian society and far from a golden era measured in health, education and levels of poverty. One can trace criminal activity down the centuries, especially in deprived urban areas, yet communities in both urban and rural areas lived much more closely together and petty crime and vandalism were not significant issues in most communities before and after the war. Drug taking was not recognized as an issue and binge drinking not an option for the vast majority, if only because they could not afford it. Traditional family ties were strong. In Northern England and Scotland working communities even took holidays at the same time (and often to the same resort) through a planned and staggered system of town industry closures. Known in the North as 'wakes weeks' the principal local factories in a town agreed to close for the same week in which their employees were given holidays. It was also a way to reduce loss of production and a convenient time to undertake plant maintenance and replacements. It also suited holiday resorts that could not have coped with the demand if all factories gave holidays at the same time. The wakes weeks system in manufacturing towns lasted until the 1960s and 1970s when the traditional manufacturing base, such as weaving and spinning, was lost to overseas competition.

Although religious observance was in rapid decline, churches were still widely attended on Sundays and their national influence far exceeded the numbers of worshippers. Media meant BBC radio and national daily papers were produced to meet the social class realities and preferences of the day. Most people expected to work with one company for their working lives. If the entrepreneurial culture of small businesses was dominant in retail and home services trades, and especially in the provision of tourism services, it was a far cry from the portfolio careers and enterprise attitudes of the 1990s. Trades unions were strong and collectivism was the political choice of the late 1940s with nationalization as its key agenda. Holiday transport meant public transport for three-quarters of the people – by rail or bus. In parts of Scotland and Wales Sunday drinking was still banned and licensing laws and Sunday shopping laws restricted what could be bought. Single mothers were still stigmatized by the morality of the era and sent away to institutions to have babies that were often then taken away from them shortly after birth and despatched into adoption. Contraception methods were primitive or expensive; this was still several years before the availability of the 'pill', and a combination of religious taboos and a fear of pregnancy tended to govern the sex lives of most young people under the age of 20.

Seaside holidays did not remove all these constraints and taboos, of course, but the fact of being away from home and outside normal community pressures pushed the barriers of accepted conduct in ways that would develop so strongly in the swinging sixties still ahead. It is interesting to speculate that perhaps seaside resorts could claim to have been the real pioneers of changing attitudes in society that are more usually attributed to London and 'Swinging Britain' in the 1960s. Those who recollect walking along the 'Golden Mile' at Blackpool in the 1950s may have disapproved of what they saw but they should not have been surprised at the behavioural shifts of the swinging sixties.

All of these social and behavioural characteristics were naturally reflected in the holiday products and destinations on offer. One might suppose that holidays were relatively dull, drab and conformist affairs. Measured crudely as product specifications this was true. But measured in the attitudes and expectations of the time, in fact the opposite was true for most people. The principal author was brought up in a small hotel in a Northern seaside resort in the 1950s. He recollects clearly that, notwithstanding all the restrictions and limitations of the products available, the sheer release of tension and the fervour of the annual holiday in the 1940s and 1950s made mostly for very contented and satisfied customers. If not quite the summer equivalent of Dickens' Christmas at Dingley Dell, resorts did provide jolly times. Relaxation from the daily grind for a brief period produced palpable expectations of holiday fun that were infectious. Holidays were a good deal rarer and restricted for most to once a year. But because they were rare, they were arguably more appreciated and more enjoyed to the full than often appears to be the case today.

The late 1940s – the annual holiday focus

As outlined in Chapter 1, working class holidays by the seaside were already a well-established tradition that had been growing in popularity throughout the first half of the twentieth century, interrupted by the two major

Figure 3.1   A typical 1950s seaside resort

wars. A massive pent-up desire for holidays was, therefore, given a powerful boost by the ending of the war and return to peacetime conditions. It was part of a yearning for relaxation and pleasure as a relief from the danger and misery of wartime. Demand was facilitated by the advent of holidays with pay covering the bulk of the working population and promoted by the Holidays With Pay Act of 1938. Commentators at the time (Brunner, 1945, and Pimlott, 1947) stressed that the conditions were ripe for a major resurgence of domestic tourism.

One week, or for the better-off, two weeks holiday in the summer by the seaside, was the aspiration for most of the working population who could afford it in the immediate post-war period. The appeal of the countryside was also well established by the late 1930s, however, and the Peak District, Lake District, South West England and rural Wales and Highlands of Scotland were already growing in popularity. But the destination for the great majority would be one of the 200 or so British seaside resorts, mostly in England and Wales. Most were built and developed in Victorian times as a result of the economic development in industrial towns and cities and the railways that provided the essential transport links. Railways enabled the bulk of the population to reach the coast within a typical journey time of up to around two hours.

Even so, in the immediate post-war era, staying away from home for a week or more was a possible choice for only around half the UK population. The choice was strongly influenced by social class, then a far more defining economic and behaviour characteristic of British society than it is today. A large proportion of the middle and professional classes took holidays, but holidays with pay notwithstanding; less than half of all manual or blue-collar workers were able to afford such holidays before the 1950s. Resorts had already established their own images and reputation according to the predominant social class that chose to visit them. Today such images would be defined as 'branding' and 'brand values'. In the 1940s they were just as well understood albeit in less formal ways. For example, Blackpool, Southend and Gt Yarmouth were unmistakably working class resorts. Bournemouth, Torquay, St Annes on Sea and Frinton on Sea received the patronage of the middle classes. Those who could not afford staying holidays could often manage day excursions, however, and many stayed on holiday with relatives.

Although no accurate statistics exist, all resorts with easy access to industrial populations were attractive to day visits, especially in July and August, and these were heavily promoted by the train and bus operators to utilize spare capacity. Just before the war it was estimated that 20 million more rail passengers were carried in August than in May or October (Pimlott, 1947, p. 240) and there is every reason to believe that similar or even increased figures applied in the decade after the war. At that time, ageing fleets of musty smelling trains and buses were retained for such infrequent purposes at a time when the costs of labour and maintenance were low enough to permit such extravagance. Most resorts had extensive railway sidings outside their main stations that were used solely to park the dozens of excursion trains that would arrive on key summer days such as the August Bank Holiday. In an era in which few could afford taxis, the use of rail and bus spawned a 'grey economy'. Youngsters with crudely adapted prams, home-made handcarts and just about anything that could be pushed on wheels, would await the arrival of trains and buses at resorts. For a small tip they would transfer luggage to the boarding houses which were typically located within easy walking distance of the terminals. There were few cars on such roads and the practice was not dangerous as it would be today.

Although there were an estimated 2.3 million cars on the road in 1950, petrol rationing was only just ending and car usage for holidays was not much different to the late 1930s. In any case, many of the cars were pre-war and not reliable and many were not used at all in winter months, being taxed for only six months of the year. AA patrol men mounted on motorcycles with sidecars were still saluting members as they passed them on the road, having time to identify the badges and remove their hand from the handlebars – more or less safely! There were no motorways until the mid-1950s and road journeys were slow. Nevertheless, a quarter of holidays in 1951 and over a third by 1955 were by car and by the mid-1950s there were already notorious (for the day) traffic jams building up on summer weekends in the West Country and the Lake District, for example. 'Bank Holiday mayhem' was as much a media cliché in the late 1950s as it is today.

In the 1950s most holiday journeys where short and of less than two hours duration. Longer distance journeys by all modes of transport, even by road, still held the glamour and excitement of the unusual, and the journey itself was for many a much anticipated and much enjoyed part of the holiday experience. Improbable as it must sound to modern children, brought up to the miseries of overcrowded airports and mass catering of motorway service stations, even a long distance coach journey would be seen as a much-anticipated source of magic and adventure. Scheduled air transport, mostly for the rich and the famous, was for a long time after the war seen as especially glamorous and a flight would be an occasion for wearing suits and ties and best frocks in order to keep up with the expected standards of one's fellow travellers.

The environment

Concern for the quality of the environment was not a tourism issue in the 1940s. People who had just come through world recession and a world war were not in any mood to worry about their impact on the physical, social and environmental qualities of the destinations they visited on holiday. It is highly unlikely that they gave it any consideration at all. Both visitors and the businesses that catered to their needs acted as though they believed that natural and community related attractions were fair game for exploitation. To be fair, most holidays were still located in urban resorts, which were well able to handle the numbers that visited them in the 1940s and 1950s. Visitors to the countryside were still too few at the time to have a major impact and the residents of rural areas were mostly too poor to generate their own observable negative impacts on the environment.

In any case, most industrial workers were still living in heavily polluted atmospheres compounded at that time by the general use of coal fires as the main form of domestic heating. They daily breathed in industrial pollution in their places of work as by-products of processes and with only the minimum of protection, lung diseases were very common. To them the seaside and the countryside were havens of fresh air and resorts still deserved their original title of health and pleasure resorts. If the bathing water was less than salubrious in places, which it was, with direct sewage outfalls on to beaches at low water, very few were aware of it at the time. On the other hand, although it was certainly not identified as a tourism issue, there was national concern for recognizing and protecting the unique qualities of the countryside that had emerged before the war in the Green Belt Act of the 1930s and the Scott Report on the Countryside. That debate matured in the wartime planning process to emerge in 1949 as the National Parks Act. This designated the boundaries of the main national parks in England and Wales as they exist today and provided special planning powers to preserve the natural beauty of special places and provide appropriate access for the public. In different ways these two concerns of conservation powers and promoting public access appear in each of the eras addressed in this book.

The 1945 to 1955 era summarized

Above all else, the recovery of British tourism from wartime was primarily in the collective hands of businesses that serviced the needs of holidaymakers. They were commonly referred to officially at that time as 'the holiday trades' and most were small businesses dealing directly with their customers (see Brunner in Appendix III). The great inflow of visitors from abroad, the exodus of British residents taking holidays abroad and the developments of business tourism were still in the future. In many ways the post-war era was a golden era for the Victorian seaside resorts. Unfortunately most of them continued to offer basic or low standards and overcrowded facilities, partly because of wartime lack of maintenance and post-war shortages but partly because the demand was so strong. It was growing and looked likely to continue for ever. One may speculate that the excess of demand over supply, at least in the short three to four month holiday season, linked with an overall failure to invest, contributed to a fatal complacency and slackness in seaside holiday providers. It would not be forgotten when British tour operators and foreign destinations provided competition that offered customers a better product in better weather at affordable prices. The evidence suggests that this fatal complacency was not recognized until at least 20 years after the spiral of decline started.

Perhaps the primary distinguishing characteristic of the bulk of post-war holiday tourism, as in the 1920s and 1930s, was its extraordinarily narrow focus on a remarkably short 16-week season. This short season caused massive problems of over demand for transport and accommodation, especially in the main four weeks, that led to calls for the 'staggering' of holidays and 'spreading the load'. These themes still have some resonance fifty years later. Residents of popular destinations braced themselves for the annual 'onslaught' and saw little overlap with their own interests. Over the years, the short season would prove to be simply uneconomic, not least because it made employment, refurbishment and improvement difficult or impossible to achieve, and it would force the closure of thousands of accommodation facilities that could not extend their months of operation.

Powerful political and media images of tourism were developed in the post-war decade that mostly owe their origins to the pre-war era; some are still relevant in the twenty-first century. The main images are summarized as:

- Tourism is still popularly assumed to mean mostly holidays and day-trippers, and tourists to London. Business, recreational and social forms of tourism are still not generally considered to be a key part of the tourism economy.
- Tourism is still associated with notions of 'the summer season' and still popularly associated with and linked to school holidays.
- Tourism is an unnecessary extravagance that governments would wish to control if they could, especially when it involves a negative balance of payments. The dismissive political jibes of 'candy floss industry' belong to the 1960s but they owe their origins to the stereotypes noted above.
- The tourism lobby, comprising mainly the bigger players in transport and accommodation, dominated the policies of the British Travel Association through membership in the 1950s and continues to influence VisitBritain today through financial participation/joint funding of promotional campaigns.
- Foreign tourism into Britain is perceived to be 'good' because it involves higher spending, greater use of public transport and hotels and contributes to the Balance of Payments. Domestic tourism is not seen as important because it is thought simply to recycle money within the British economy with little value added.

All of these stereotypes are now false or contain only half-truths but they maintain their hold on much of the media, politicians and, therefore, the perceptions of the general public.

Tourism today – peripatetic society

By 1995, the total market for holiday tourism generated by the British had grown from some 25 million holidays of four or more nights to around 60 million (within Britain and abroad). It has not shifted greatly in the decade to 2005. Unfortunately, given the inadequate state of tourism statistics, that happens to be the only form of tourism for which one can offer any sort of broadly comparable data over the fifty-year period. Main summer holidays, however, the dominant form of 1940s tourism, had become only a minor element of what was identified as tourism in Britain in the final years of the twentieth century; the main growth has been in other forms of tourism.

In broad terms, in the late 1990s (see also Appendix V), tourism in Britain (excluding visits abroad) comprised:

- 40 million long holidays of 4+ nights
- 65 million short holidays of 1–3 nights

- 70 million other trips including visits to friends and relatives and business
- 1200 million tourism day visits (more than 3 hours away from home for non-routine purposes).

It has to be speculation, but judgement suggests these figures indicate that the total volume of tourism is at least ten times the size it was when the ending of the Second World War released its pent-up demand for holidays by the sea. This is the growth that now leads many commentators to claim that tourism is the 'world's largest industry'.

By 1995, most employed people had at least four weeks paid holiday and many had six weeks or more. Many had taken early retirement in their fifties, a phenomenon that may not last long into the twenty-first century as the pressure on pension funds increases. But early retirement and the growing number of well-funded affluent retired people had become key elements in an increasingly active British tourism market in the decade to 2005. Back in the 1950s, average life expectancy for males was still around 70 years and SAGA was just in its very early days, targeting the early retired (see Chapter 6). By the turn of the twenty-first century male life expectancy was over 80 with similar if less dramatic increases for women. The so-called 'seniors market' has become a massive business in its own right and will continue to expand in size over the next 50 years. SAGA had some 8 million prospective customers on its databases in 2004. Twenty-first century pensioners are, of course, far more mobile and travel active than their predecessors in the 1940s. Simple estimates of increases in the number of older people in retirement age groups does not reflect the remarkable shifts in their attitudes and the frequency and intensity of their travel interests. A 20 per cent increase in the number of 'new' pensioners may easily generate 100 per cent increase in tourism activity.

In 1995 compared with 1945 there were so many more reasons to travel for non-routine purposes that fall within the modern definition of tourism. Ten leading reasons, all reflecting the growth in real incomes over the decades, are:

- Massively increased access to personal transport (from 2 million cars to 27 million). Massively increased access to low cost transport for journeys abroad by air, sea ferries, cruise ships, Channel Tunnel and rail.
- Massively increased access and exposure to all forms of media typically extolling travel as a social 'good' in its own right and promoting greater sales through travel related journalism.
- Massive increase in the numbers in further and higher education as the proportion of the relevant age groups approaches 50 per cent. Many of these are travelling to and from home and to stay with friends and relatives as well as pursuing leisure travel as a lifestyle goal.
- Gap year students travelling around the world and second homeowners making frequent visits to their properties.

- Availability of courses and conferences for business, training and leisure purposes.
- Growth of regional airports in the UK that mostly did not exist 50 years earlier, greatly facilitating the growth in budget air travel.
- Explosion of interest in leisure and recreational activities of every kind, much of it involving travel away from home.
- Ownership of sports and leisure equipment from cycles, yachts, golf clubs, fishing rods, caravans and enthusiasm for sporting events of every kind.
- Development of cultural festivals and events in all parts of the country.
- Interest in eating out for both convenience and pleasure and shopping as a leisure activity.

Given the massive growth in the market for travel it is not surprising that imports·have played a big part in absorbing market growth. Just as the British have tended to prefer foreign made cars, electrical goods, clothing, audio equipment and food and wine, so they have tended to prefer holidays abroad to those available in Britain. For both long and short leisure breaks, the market clearly believes that foreign offers better products that are less expensive and better value for money. Given the relative advantages of good weather, newer products and lower labour costs, much of this shift was inevitable. The market, as always, votes with its wallet.

Tourists at the end of the twentieth century

A fairly typical professional family experience of tourism in 1995 would have included:

- Some 45 days travel for business/work related purposes (other than commuting to a regular place of work) split between two partners at work (day visits and some with overnight stay).
- Two weeks main holiday abroad for the family.
- Half a dozen weekends of which some would involve staying with relatives and friends as well as in commercial accommodation.
- If the family were on average or above earnings, access to a boat, a caravan and perhaps a second home would further increase the number of non-routine days away from the home base.
- Children would tend to have their own travel patterns related to their education and recreation pursuits in addition to family activities. These might include regular night clubbing, music festivals and the cinema or active pursuits such as football, tennis or rowing.

On the only available evidence, Britons aged 15+ took an estimated 1.2 billion leisure day visits from home in 1998 'that are defined as tourism leisure day trips' (survey for a consortium of national agencies in 1998). Dividing this figure by some 44 million adults gives an *average* number of tourism day trips from home that is approaching 30 day visits for every adult in the country. With all due allowance for averages, the combined number of days away from home, for both staying and day purposes (allowing for business as well as leisure travel), means that 100 tourism days per person every year, if not the norm, was already a common activity for many Britons toward the end of the last century. These 100 tourism days per person per year compare with around seven nights away on holiday in 1945 and perhaps another five or so day visits. Crude though this calculation is, it provides some powerful support for the view that tourism may have grown tenfold in the last 50 years.

No longer the preserve of the better off, international tourism has become a readily accessible, normal and mostly classless activity for the greater part of the UK population. In any one year, it is still the case that over a third of the population do not take a longer holiday of four or more nights away from home, but those figures do not apply to shorter trips and tourism day visits. Excluding the very old, the seriously ill and those detained at Her Majesty's pleasure, tourism has become a near universal and frequent experience across the whole spectrum of the population. It is so massively different from the late 1940s as to be almost unrecognizable.

Table 3.1 Comparing consumers and travel habits from 1945 to 1950 and from 2000 to 2005

Consumers 1945–1950	Consumers 2000–2005
Few people had telephones and neither mobile phones nor fax were invented; holiday bookings were made by post from pre-ordered brochures	Websites; mobile phones; call centres; direct phones; faxes; high street travel agents. Virtually all customers have instant access to travel choices
Most bookings were made six months or more in advance	Few advance bookings of more than a month. Many same week purchases
Credit/debit cards not invented; payment by cash or cheques for those with bank accounts	Most customers have several credit and debit cards – essential for on-line purchases
No commercial TV available; newspaper ads and resort brochures were the main communication for holiday products	Most have access to dozens of commercial channels and very wide range of advertising as well as the Internet

(Continued)

Table 3.1 Comparing consumers and travel habits from 1945 to 1950 and from 2000 to 2005 – (Continued)

Consumers 1945–1950	Consumers 2000–2005
One or two weeks, Saturday to Saturday, was the norm for bookings. Alternatives were often not accepted	From one night to as long as you wish in any combination you can afford
16-week holiday season; mainly one holiday from home a year in the UK	Year round travel; range of short breaks and longer holiday options in UK or abroad
En suite bathrooms and central heating almost unheard of in resorts. One or two toilets shared by 30 or more visitors with chamber pots for 'night calls'	En suite almost 'obligatory' for most customers. Heating essential
Communal facilities, including shared tables for eating and socializing were common at resort hotels and guesthouses	Privacy and non-contact with others seen as essential by many if not all visitors
Repeat visits to the same hotel in the same resort over many years was normal	Repeat visits far less usual except for owned caravans and second homes
Food was traditional English and bring your own ration books	Whatever you choose with multicultural options to suit all culinary tastes
Travel by train or bus for 75 per cent of people on domestic holidays	Travel by car for over 90 per cent of people on domestic holidays
Formal holiday attire with jacket, trousers and often tie for men; skirts and blouses or dresses for women. Leather shoes for all	Anything goes, the less formal the better; trainers the footwear of choice
Relatively passive holidays with visits to the pier, walks on the prom, tea on the sands, donkey rides and boating pools, and occasional night at a music hall style show or dance hall. Alcohol intake limited by income	Relatively active holidays with every leisure and sport available according to choice. Clubs, discos, theme parks, casinos and infinite entertainment accessible. Drinking normal and frequent; binge drinking common
Branded products in tourism limited mainly to a few hotels (e.g. Trust Houses) and caterers such as ABC and Lyons	Branded products cover almost every aspect of travel consumption except for small businesses at the destination

An age of individualism succeeds the collectivist norms of the post-war era

As noted earlier in this chapter, people born in 1900 had experienced years of dangers and privations that obviously influenced them, while their social conditions and lifestyles in many ways inhibited their behaviour on holiday. After the war, as we have seen, the resorts themselves played a not insignificant part in breaking down established attitudes in the way they facilitated the relaxation of traditional sexual boundaries through the entertainments they offered and the less inhibited atmosphere that prevailed away from home. By 2000, everyone under 50 years old had been brought up within the welfare state provisions for health and education, unemployment, and pensions and care for the elderly and less well-off. They had grown up with colour television and access to one or more cars and lived in homes with phones, central heating and at least one bathroom. They grew up in the swinging sixties with a popular music scene and a media culture that set out to overturn the collectivist, conformist attitudes and standards that influenced the behaviour of their parents. Immigration had shifted the certainties of a former mono-cultural society and the realities of multi-ethnic, multi-faith and multi-cultural lifestyles dominated at the end of the century, albeit with confusion for many. Individualism, egotism and many kinds of 'rage' were challenging authority in every form from schools, doctors, police and nurses, to politicians, lawyers, priests and even bus drivers attempting to manage orderly buses. 'Lager louts' running amok in Mediterranean resorts had overtaken the lesser excesses of the mods and rockers in British resorts in the late 1950s while crime and vandalism, linked often to alcohol and drug abuse, were sadly common at weekends in most urban areas. Even the centres of rural market towns and villages were becoming the exclusive preserve of inebriated youths on Saturday evenings after dark.

Frequent redundancies and whole-scale industry closures had altered and often split the social fabric of many traditional communities, while divorce and re-marriage were altering traditional family attitudes and single parents had become commonplace. Reflected in an intrusive media that revels in the sexual habits and excesses of so-called celebrities (using them to sell their products to a seemingly obsessed population), most of these trends were supportive of increased travel away from home. This was the case despite the fact that many forms of modern tourism were doubtless less harmonious and less satisfying than 50 years earlier.

The environment

Concern for the quality of the environment and human activities that affect it had grown steadily to become a political issue by 2000, at least at international and national political levels. Building on earlier pre-war concerns for protecting national parks and green belts and ameliorating industrial pollution, conservation issues had been debated publicly since the 1960s. In that decade, Rachel Carson wrote the influential *Silent Spring* (1962), and in the UK widespread concern was expressed about the damage of cars and leisure travel on rural environments (Civic Trust 1968). The British Tourist Authority held its first conference on Tourism and the Environment in 1972 and later in the 1970s, Richard Loveluck published *Gaia* (1979). *Limits to Growth* by D.H Meadows et al. was published in 1972 and identified global issues that would be developed in the 1980s as The Brundtland Report of 1987, which in its turn provided the spur to the Rio de Janeiro 'Earth Summit' held in 1992. A voluntary organization in the UK, Tourism Concern, was founded in 1989 to debate tourism-specific problems and begin to seek solutions. The Rio Earth Summit led to the first real international efforts to embrace tourism within overall international, national and local policies to promote more sustainable development. Local *Agenda 21* developments were under active consideration by the mid-1990s in the UK, although progress to date remains limited outside the recycling of waste and compliance with European environmental directives.

In Britain, responding to the international agenda, the English Tourist Board with other leisure and recreation agencies commissioned a series of reports and held a major conference on 'Tourism and the Environment: Maintaining the Balance' in 1992. From that time on, although the tangible results on the ground were rather less impressive, the role of tourism within the environment was taken more seriously and reflected, at least in principle, in all the main tourism strategies within the UK. The World Tourism Organization and the European Commission were proclaiming their overall belief in the concepts of sustainability by the mid-1990s. Not long before the Government wound it up in 2003, the English Tourism Council had published a *Strategy for Sustainable Tourism* based on wide consultation with the tourism sector. Other than general exhortations that sustainable tourism is a 'good thing', that strategy appears to have been lost with the revised structure for tourism imposed by Government in 2003.

Among the population as a whole, environment was not a word in general use in 1945. It was hardly front-of-mind by 2000, although by then environmental issues were in the curriculum for just about every school and college student and some forms of waste recycling were commonly practised in most households. Identified in terms of traffic noise and congestion, litter, poor air and water quality and overcrowding generally, much of the visiting public was actively rejecting polluted environments for leisure purposes. The activities of Green Peace and other environmental lobbies command wide media coverage, and concerns for global warming, climate change, overfishing, destruction of rain forests and over-intensive farming are widely recognized. If the science remains imperfect, concerns about global warming and alternative energy options have become key aspects of the modern political agenda.

Modern tourism summarized

By 2000, the earlier recognition and association of tourism as the 'holiday trades' had moved on to political and media recognition of the 'world's largest industry'. As noted in the Preface, tourism is not an industry and its full economic impact is still unknown, but years of advocacy have succeeded in creating the idea that it does exist as an important sector of economic activity. At least the notion of an industry conveys the idea that tourism is not just about holidays, even if the full ramifications are still not recognized.

The main changes in domestic tourism have been in the overall fall in the market share of traditional seaside resorts, some of which have lost most of their former visitor revenue. Although the seaside clearly retains its appeal and larger resorts are still very active, their growth markets are increasingly associated with non-holiday forms of tourism and second homes. But the fall in one form of domestic tourism has been more than compensated for by strong growth in other aspects of travel. From a low starting base, new forms of tourism have developed; visits to cities, heritage towns and to the countryside have increased massively. For outbound tourism there has been a revolutionary shift of leisure travel by the British to destinations abroad. Over the years to the Queen's Jubilee year in 1977, the growth in volume and value of inbound tourism was highly impressive and it convinced Government of the need to recognize and support that form of tourism at the expense of domestic tourism. Since then, although the numbers have doubled, the revenue in real terms has grown much more slowly.

Perhaps the primary distinguishing characteristic of modern tourism is that of an increasingly year round market that embraces the leisure and recreation activities of residents measured as day visitors, with the additional activities of increasingly year round staying visitors from further afield. Of course, seasonal operations remain but the bulk of successful tourism businesses, from farm houses to hotel chains and many visitor attractions, have found ways to develop year round aspects of their business. Transport operators in particular have managed to achieve the year round flows that are essential to profitability. Looking ahead, the sustainability of the growth in tourism is at least debatable and it represents a powerful challenge for tourist organizations at national, regional and local levels over the coming decade.

The main political and media images of tourism by 2000 were:

- Travel and tourism were popularly understood to be a basic human 'right' and essential elements of the quality of life to which most people aspire. Ownership of second homes, timeshare options, caravans and boats, abroad as well as in the UK, was growing rapidly as personal incomes increased.
- Travel abroad clearly has massive appeal and from the mid-1990s was further facilitated by the budget airline phenomenon. Such preferences

shifted the negative balance of payments on tourism from around £4 billion a year in 1996 to approaching £17 billion a year in less than a decade.

- Nationally, tourism is loosely although imprecisely understood to be an important 'industry' and has become widely recognized as a major employment generator in all communities across the country.
- Tourism has become identified as part of the mainstream of economic options in post-industrial Britain and is frequently associated with urban regeneration and access to EU regional funding options.
- Local and regional governments increasingly understand the importance of tourism and it features in most if not all local development plans. As tourism remains a non-statutory function, however, the funding by local authorities to support tourism promotion and destination management is under severe and constant pressure and, many would argue, is wholly inadequate for needs.
- Scotland, Wales and Northern Ireland invest substantially in their tourism while government decisions for England, which generates and receives some four-fifths of all UK tourism expenditure, are distinguished more by cost-cutting and organizational tinkering than understanding. Government actions suggest it still believes international inbound tourism is the most significant element to be supported.
- The holiday image of tourism still retains much of its hold over general perceptions and in the media, although holidays have for some years been a minor element of total UK tourism.

CHAPTER 4

Developments in accommodation and attractions

1945 to 1955 Domestic holidays by the seaside dominate British tourism

As outlined in Chapter 2, the period began with massive pent-up demand for domestic holidays. It could only be met initially with the pre-war infrastructure of accommodation and attractions, large parts of which had been requisitioned for wartime needs. Much of the capacity was run down after six years of war and little or no possibility of refurbishment. It was not all bad news for accommodation in wartime though as many hotels and guesthouses had found profitable alternative streams of income in providing for war needs. Virtual closure of the South Coast resorts in the last years of the war was a benefit to those in the North. An estimated one million troops passed through Blackpool in the Second World War, for example, with some 50 000 in residence at peak times billeted in over 5000 properties. Billy Butlin was able to use his existing holiday camps and build others with wartime funding that would give him a leading start after the war (see below). Unlike holidays, defence needs provided year round business and Blackpool property prices soared during the war (and fell after it), clearly indicating that there were profits to be made in guesthouses (Walton, 1978).

Fortunately for post-war tourism growth, if the holiday accommodation was often run down, the standards at home for much of the population were also very basic and also run down. So, for several years, the sheer release from pressure made most visitors oblivious to what would now be seen as low standards of food and accommodation. If not exactly Heaven, it was enough in itself to be alive and to be on holiday, mainly beside the sea, especially when the sun shone.

The conditions under which accommodation businesses had to operate were not propitious. Food rationing was still in place until 1954 – anyone staying more than three nights in the late 1940s had to bring a set of emergency ration coupons and there was an overall five-shilling (25 new pence) limit for spending on meals away from home that included luxury hotels. Building materials were needed for war reparation work and closely controlled. Clothing and textiles were rationed, guests were asked to bring their own soap and towels and to economize with water and electricity (heating was mostly not a holiday option). Furniture was in limited supply and much of that had to conform to what was known as a wartime 'utility' standard, which meant it was fairly basic.

Apart from accommodation in towns and cities for travellers on business, tourist accommodation provision in Britain in the early post-war years was primarily for domestic holidays, which at that time was the dominant market sector facilitated by public transport operations of rail or bus. A smaller but important and soon growing market was the stream of inbound tourism attracted as London and other historic parts of Britain recovered from the war effort and depredations. As soon as airports and seaports were available for non-essential travel, British heritage re-exerted its traditional appeal to visitors from abroad and the traffic grew quickly despite difficult circumstances. The domestic and inbound markets were very distinct in that period and mostly did not overlap at all except in 5 and 4 star hotels used by affluent British people for business and leisure purposes. The domestic market was (and still is) divided between serviced accommodations and self-catering, although the latter was relatively much smaller in the immediate post-war era when few people owned a motorcar and were limited to railway and bus destinations and the luggage they could carry on public transport.

The economics of post-war holidaymaking

The economics of holidaymaking in the resorts in the immediate post-war period were essentially as they had been in the pre-war era. At that time, most small businesses could survive and even prosper on a very seasonal summertime basis. But even then they could do so only by providing very basic facilities to undemanding, grateful customers. Other than for a small number of commercial hotels, there was very little business tourism in resorts and the trading year was the holiday season, as it had been in the 1920s and 1930s. The 'season' typically opened at Easter and guesthouses either closed again or operated at minimal occupancy until Whitsun. It then continued with the peak weeks of maximum occupancy being in July and August – the schools holiday period. Most small businesses closed around the end of September to coincide with the ending of seasonal shows on piers and theatres and closure of facilities such as open-air baths, boating lakes, amusement parks, putting greens and other holiday entertainments. Christmas opening was relatively unusual at the time and most small serviced hotels and boarding houses had a season of little more than 16 weeks, and were full up for only about eight of them.

Most holiday businesses in resorts had to operate with seasonal labour. In the North of England such labour was drawn from industrial towns and laid off to return home at the end of the season. Typically, low paid unmarried young women working in textile industries were hired on an annual basis in time for Easter or Whitsun. They were not difficult to attract as many young women sought holiday jobs to get away from their overcrowded home environments and to have what was considered an exciting time in the relative freedom and uninhibited atmosphere of a seaside resort. In many ways these girls were the forerunners of the modern chalet girls now seeking adventure and excitement each winter in European ski resorts. There were, however, far more of them. Even by the mid-1950s the business economics of providing and sustaining a competitive fully catered product (three meals a day) on a part-time basis for little more than 16 weeks a year were difficult to resolve and would become impossible for many over the next 20 years.

The combination of demand for better en suite accommodation and food standards, the rising costs of provision, the drying up of cheap casual/seasonal labour (as traditional industries were driven out of business by new competition from abroad) and a very short operating season would drive tens of thousands of such businesses out of existence over the next quarter of a century. With hindsight it is easy to see that this process was a form of economic attrition as inevitable as the loss of so much of British manufacturing to low wage countries abroad. Another parallel would be with the closure of thousands of small retail shops unable to compete with supermarket chains.

It was also the case that many house owners in popular resorts offered B&B accommodation in the main summer weeks on an unofficial but not illegal basis. They simply put up signs advertising 'vacancies' on an opportunistic 'grey market' basis because the demand was there. But they were not part of the trade associations operating in most resorts. Many were thought to be operating low standards, avoiding business rates and were resented by the more professional tax paying operators of recognized businesses as giving them a bad name. In the absence of statutory accommodation registration and licensing arrangements there was little that could be done about this. Although valiant efforts were made with voluntary classification and grading schemes from the 1970s onwards, the problem of so-called 'cowboy' businesses would continue unresolved in Britain over the whole of the next 50 years.

Blackpool, and to a lesser extent Morecambe, were able to extend their season into October through the illuminations that commenced in Blackpool in the 1890s. But these were the exception, not the rule. Many businesses were only able to survive in the 'low season' by cash flow arising from booking deposits. At that time, because demand exceeded supply, pre-booking with deposits often took place six months or more before visitors arrived. Most proprietors or their spouses also had part-time jobs and as Walton noted, 'women typically operated most small serviced businesses in resorts' (Walton, 1978). These were the famous landladies beloved by generations of comedians.

Holiday accommodation standards

When coastal resorts reopened for business in 1946 and 1947, many still bore visible signs of wartime defence works such as concrete tank traps, barbed wire and gun emplacements. By 1955 'at least half the population took holidays – a total of approximately 25 million people' (British Travel and Holidays Association, 1956) and that meant a main holiday by the British seaside (65 per cent of them in July or August). Only one in ten took an additional holiday and less than one in ten took a holiday abroad. The same study estimated that in 1955, 77 per cent of the population had 'never been outside Britain' – a low figure bearing in mind the travel associated with two world wars, and a powerful indication of just how unusual travel abroad was at that time. Although a few people travelled abroad as soon as they could after the war, there was active discouragement from a Government that could not afford to allow scarce foreign currency to be 'wasted' on leisure travel. Severe restrictions were imposed on the amount of currency that could be spent abroad and the first surge in growth in foreign travel by the British would not occur until the 1960s.

Unlicensed hotels and guesthouses, mainly built in the nineteenth century and offering less than ten letting bedrooms, provided the bulk of all commercial accommodation in the resorts. Serviced accommodation substantially outweighed self-catering options in caravans and apartment houses. Only a handful of rooms in the more expensive hotels provided en suite facilities. Hot and cold running water in bedrooms and spring interior mattresses were strongly featured in advertising by businesses that were able to boast of such facilities; they were promoted as desirable luxuries commanding premium prices. Chamber pots under the bed for overnight calls of nature were still the norm for the great majority. One bathroom for 25 or more guests and one or two toilets were commonplace in guesthouses of the era. Visitors were expected to bathe before they came away and the use of a bath during a stay was generally discouraged through an extra charge levied on those who felt personal hygiene demanded such sacrifices.

Rationing notwithstanding, full catering was the norm and it included breakfast, cooked lunch, cooked dinner or more often 'high-tea', and often snacks for supper. Interestingly, in this still mainly pre-television era, and perhaps because guesthouse dining rooms and sitting rooms were very small by modern standards, visitors whose party did not comprise a full table would be asked to share with others whom they did not know. Close proximity and lack of TV promoted lively social intercourse of a type now generally unknown and unwanted, but surprisingly satisfying to those who recollect the evening discussions and round table banter that flourished in conditions that today would be regarded as an intolerable intrusion on personal space and privacy. The guesthouse market in resorts was very much a family market with some 40 per cent of all holiday parties including children. Many visitors returned to the same resort and the same guesthouses in the same week, year after year. One may only speculate that the socializing process provided for many children, through staying away on holiday in close proximity with adults, was a formative and positive influence on their behavioural development that has long since been lost.

Holiday camps, self-catering and rural areas

Holiday camps flourished after the war. Butlins was the pre-war leader in the 'luxury' sector with two centres built since 1936, targeting what was then the 'top end' of the market, but there were an estimated 200 different camps around the coast in 1950. In a far-sighted deal when the war started, Butlin not only leased his existing two camps to the Navy for wartime purposes, but arranged for other sites to be built for wartime use. These sites were designed to his overall specification, so that they were suitable for conversion to future holiday use and he leased them on the understanding that he could buy them back after the war at 60 per cent of cost price. He quoted a construction cost per person of £75 against the War Office assumption of £125 and secured the business to build four more camps (Read, 1986, p. 42). As a result he was in business very soon after the war with fully built operational holiday centres that could never have been built within the building restrictions operating at the time. Holiday camps were highly successful and popular in the 1950s and Pontins were soon in competition with Butlins – even so, the holiday camp sector catered for only 4 per cent of the holiday market in 1955.

Self-catering, much of it also at the seaside although not all within the Victorian resort boundaries accounted for only 15 per cent of holidays in 1955 (8 per cent for caravans and 7 per cent for apartment houses). The comparable figure for hotels and boarding houses was 42 per cent. Interest in holidays in the countryside, established in the pre-war era, was also important, although at a relatively low level, reflecting car ownership. Even so, Pimlott noted that 'by 1939, thanks largely to the motorcar and the bicycle, there was hardly a village which did not provide some facilities for holidaymakers – teas, bed and breakfast, camping sites – while in hilly districts and in most of the hinterland of the coast, holiday catering had become an important source of income' (Pimlott, 1947, p. 257). Readers of Wainwright's Pennine journey in 1938 will be aware that the author who did most to popularize walking in the Lake District in the 1960s and 1970s, was able to walk for consecutive days, before the war, in the most remote of England's upland rural areas without thinking it necessary to book any accommodation ahead (Wainwright, 1986). Yet he found B&B and meals in every village in which he called.

Caravanning had developed with the growth of motoring in the pre-war years and the development of new designs of caravan in the 1930s. Some caravan parks with vans to let were already established around the coasts, often sited in areas of high scenic quality that would later cause planning problems. However, the major growth in self-catering had not yet started and there were none of the chains of park operators and holiday cottage letting agencies that would come to dominate rural provision by the 1990s.

London and cities

Other than for routine commercial and business purposes, only a handful of heritage cities catered for tourism on any scale. City Breaks and weekend stays in hotels were virtually unheard of in the decade after the war. All industrial cities within flying reach of bombers had suffered damage, with London being the primary target. The impact of the V1 and V2 rockets caused massive damage in London in the last two years of the war and many pre-war hotels were damaged and not restored as hotels after the war.

Nevertheless, the powerful heritage and cultural attractions of London, Edinburgh, York and Bath, for example, were as attractive to inbound visitors as before the war. The energies of entrepreneurs such as Maxwell Joseph, Charles Forte and Henry Edwards were already laying the foundations in the 1950s of what would become major hotel chains in towns and cities over the next twenty years. Inbound visits, minimal immediately after the war, rose from 618 000 to reach just over one million visits in 1955 – the first major post-war milestone of inbound tourism. The great bulk of USA and other long distance visitors still travelled by sea in the years to 1955. Test flights and the first building work did not commence for Heathrow Airport until 1946 and the first purpose-built terminal building did not open for business until 1951. Hard to imagine now but early terminal facilities were provided under canvas structures with duckboard flooring.

The Festival of Britain in 1951, the building of the Festival Hall and other landmark South Bank buildings, and the Coronation of the young Queen Elizabeth in 1953 excited the media of the day. These events appeared to many to mark the rebirth of the post-war era as a new Elizabethan Age. In addition to their national appeal, these three major events carried very positive British images around the world, especially to the USA and the former Empire territories, and promoted the attractions of a visit to this country – especially to London where the events were staged.

Visitor attractions

Visitor attractions at the destination are the primary reasons for travel. In other words, people go somewhere to do something. In the domestic market the early post-war attractions were primarily the natural assets of bathing, beaches, fresh air and scenery. Since Regency times, however, as described by Jane Austen and chronicled by Pimlott and others, these were always supplemented by man-made entertainments, amusements and associated facilities. Victorian resort developers understood that very well and had specialized in entertainments from their inception. For the inbound market, heritage and cultural traditions and the opportunity to visit with friends and relatives, especially having regard to Britain's former Empire connections, provided the principal appeal. Visits to cathedrals, churches and leading historic houses were made in relatively small numbers before the war – continuing a tradition that went back at least a hundred years before that, but these were not activities for a mass market at that time.

Visitor attractions aimed at holiday visitors were naturally associated mainly with resorts. Blackpool's Pleasure Beach was the leader then but it had its smaller equivalents in most seaside resorts. Piers generally offered the same range of what were always called 'amusements' as they had since Victorian times. These ranged from coin operated slot machines with simple games of chance, to 'what the butler saw'. If such machines had survived to the 1990s except in museums, they might have had a field day with the Princess Diana revelations. Most resorts had piers with auditoriums that also housed glazed conservatories replete with potted palm trees and rubber plants that were used daily for tea dances and orchestral performances. Seaside theatres and pavilions offered a range of mainly raucous humour and forms of vaudeville, music hall or variety shows that operated on a limited seasonal basis. Butlin's camps provided their own amusements, entertainment and variety style shows and, together with the resort shows, launched the careers of many artistes who would later become the national stars of television.

Within resort boundaries, open-air swimming pools, typically with no heating were popular, at least in July and August. Parks, boating lakes and mini golf were found almost everywhere. 'Beauty Queen' and 'Mother and Baby' contests had no difficulty in recruiting volunteers and were a traditional part of the entertainment for at least 20 years after the war into the 1970s. Strolling along promenades and sitting or lying on beaches were attractive activities for most unless it was actually raining, supplemented by brass bands and other musical provision in the season. Rides on donkeys and horses, deckchair rental, Punch and Judy shows, pots of tea for the beach and ice cream kiosks were also part of the provision to be found everywhere. If the resort had a harbour, it would certainly offer a range of boat trips. Some that did not have harbours provided tractors to take people out to boat depth off beaches. For many years after the war, redundant wartime amphibious vehicles known as DUKWS, widely used in the Normandy landings in 1944, performed more peaceful activities along resort beaches. Painted in garish holiday mode and colours, they could carry about a dozen people a time for brief trips in the sea. If a resort had an airfield (mostly very small), 10–15 minutes trips by air, typically in propeller-driven biplanes of the 1930s with either open cockpits or cabins for up to half a dozen people, would be promoted to those who could afford it.

Historic houses, under considerable threat after the war with a disinterested Labour Government ideologically opposed to hereditary wealth, were becoming active in this period. The pioneers in opening to the public were Longleat in 1949, Wilton in 1951 and Beaulieu in 1952. Although the story of the growth of historic houses and their influence on tourism belongs to a later era (see below), there is no doubt that the widespread media publicity attained by these pioneers acted as a spur to others and helped to change the public and political attitudes toward heritage matters. The post-war arrangements for visitors were generally very rudimentary; as Lord Montagu, owner of Beaulieu put it, 'often with the butler selling the tickets and the cook making sandwiches' (Montagu, 1998). At Beaulieu, the first historic cars that would form the basis of the collection for the purpose-built National Motor Museum some 20 years later were located in the entrance hall to Palace House, with drip trays underneath them to keep the oil off the carpet.

While cafes and ubiquitous fish and chip shops provided for the hungry and serviced a large morning coffee and afternoon tea trade, pubs were still

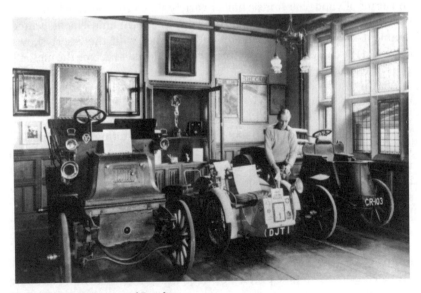

Figure 4.1 Lord Montagu of Beaulieu

typically beer houses catering mainly for men. Food in pubs was limited to snacks and was a very incidental part of the trade as visitors expected to eat in their hotels and guesthouses.

1955 to 1969 Changing times – the origins of modern tourism

As the 1950s ended and the 1960s began, a number of significant changes occurred that would influence the shape of modern tourism. British tourism at that time was still essentially domestic, dominated by seaside holidays in traditional resorts. Holiday travel was still primarily by trains and buses but private car ownership extended very rapidly in this period of rising incomes and facilitated the rapid growth in self-catering holidays at home and later abroad. The first reports were published in this period expressing concerns about car-borne holidaymakers swamping the English countryside and destroying its environmental charms (for example, 'Challenge of Leisure', a Civic Trust Survey on planning for increased leisure in 1965).

Clearly identifying the business opportunities of attracting British holidaymakers abroad using chartered airplanes, from the start of the 1950s the first entrepreneurs were already challenging the rigid rules then affecting licences to operate air transport (see Chapter 6). At that time state regulation stemming from the international 1944 Chicago Convention (see Chapter 5) dictated which airlines could fly what routes at what prices. The challenges by a new breed of tour operators succeeded in making some inroads into the rules initially and they offered the first air inclusive packages abroad. 1950 is commonly identified as the dawn of mass tourism abroad that would very quickly come to dominate British holidaymaking for the rest of the century (see Chapter 6). The new business model involved economies of scale achievable by chartering airplanes, contracting bed spaces in large volume at 'wholesale prices' and offering combined low package prices that were achievable and profitable – provided the operators could sell over 90 per cent of their capacity. In good years they could, but when economic crisis struck many operators were financially exposed and collapsed, with consequences for travellers that would have to be addressed.

Travel agencies thrived and grew rapidly to provide the national distribution patterns needed to service this business. Scheduled airlines responded relatively slowly and reluctantly and BEA did not create its own charter subsidiary until 1970. But they could not drive away the competition from what they doubtless considered to be fast moving reckless tour operator entrepreneurs with minimal investment in airlines, hotels or destinations and no interest in expensive scheduled airline networks. Modern jet aircraft for the charter airlines very soon replaced the piston engined and turbo prop post-war fleets, which were consigned to the scrap heap being no longer acceptable for holiday charters. Standards and expectations were rising.

For inbound tourism other than from Europe, the soon to be ubiquitous Boeing 707 performed its first commercial transatlantic flights in 1958 and in various guises would become the long haul airliner for the world. Although supplanted in the 1970s by the larger 747 it was still being produced right up until the mid-1990s. Inbound tourism, supported by air transport developments thrived and the pressures were already being felt in this era for a third London airport to supplement Heathrow and Gatwick.

In Europe, The Treaty of Rome was signed in 1957, establishing the European Economic Community (EEC) and the first six European countries began their long journey toward the European Union that the founding fathers envisioned. General de Gaulle, then President of France, delivered his first famous 'non' to the UK's application to join the EEC in 1963 (and *encore non* in 1967), declaring that Britain was too transatlantic in its attitudes to be a good European partner. Over 30 years later, some of the same attitudes have clearly not been extinguished.

Accommodating domestic tourism

The British seaside retained its majority hold on the domestic tourism market throughout most of this period. Many regard the 1950s and 1960s as the golden age of the resorts. In volume terms it was, but ominously for the future, the leading contenders were still offering what to the more travel experienced customers was now recognizably the same tired product formula as they had 50 years earlier. Most resorts were then approaching 100 years old and it showed. There were clear signs of decline and decay, compounded by rising car traffic congestion by the end of the 1960s, although such signs were evidently not enough to stimulate effective response by the local councils responsible for their areas. The unsustainable economic realities of the 16-week holiday season were becoming clearer every year and post-war 1940s accommodation standards were increasingly perceived as just not good enough. There was by now a clear international yardstick to measure such standards.

As car ownership increased to around 9 million cars in the mid-1960s, with the first full length British motorway (M1 from London to Birmingham) opening in 1959, increasing numbers of visitors expected car parking. This was provided in some resorts to some extent by concreting over the front garden areas of guesthouses (where they existed), but only at the expense of a resort's appearance, ambience and appeal. En suite rooms were still the exception not the rule but the demand was growing and the chamber pot era was ended as guesthouses had to install more toilet facilities. Often this was achieved by dividing rooms with cheap partition walls that simultaneously damaged the original ambience and created unfortunate sound effects that were not conducive to a good night's sleep. The domestic market was ripe for the plucking by the entrepreneurial tour operators with the promise of good weather and good value in newly built hotels along the Mediterranean coasts.

Associated with rising car ownership, self-catering provision both at coasts and in rural areas grew massively in this period because it provided value for money and also freedom from the relative regimentation and constraints of serviced accommodation. Serried ranks of visually obtrusive, overcrowded caravan sites were located in areas of scenic value to exploit the 1950s growth in car ownership. The largely uncontrolled trade, with no concessions to environmental considerations, led to the 1960 Caravan Sites and Control of Development Act to regulate the future location, planning and use of such sites. The Act did not concern itself with the quality of the facilities on offer and that would have to be tackled in later periods.

Butlins and Pontins were the vigorous and highly successful leaders in the holiday camp market, now seeking to change their 'Hi de hi' image to that of more sophisticated holiday centres and introducing self-catering into a business model that originated with fully serviced provision. Dining rooms with several hundred seats at every sitting began to give way to provision of alternative smaller fast food style outlets but the overall regimentation of the mass catering and entertainment process was still in evidence in this period.

Overseas inward

If domestic holidays dominated the trends in the first decade after the war, inbound tourism dominated the second decade. The number of visitors to the UK rose from just over one million in 1955 to nearly 6 million in 1969 and triggered a major hotel investment boom with government support. London was the primary target of most inbound holiday visitors, often linked with a circular tour route that would take in heritage towns and cities such as Oxford, Bath, Stratford-upon-Avon, Edinburgh, York and Cambridge. Accommodating the growing inflow became a major issue and the business model of hotel chains that were to dominate the rest of the century developed strongly. Trust Houses, Grand Metropolitan, Forte, Lyons, Centre Hotels and Rank grew strongly in this period and the issue of new hotel capacity, especially in London, became urgent by the late 1960s. The first hotel to be built after the war in London was the American owned Westbury in 1955, followed by the first hotel at Heathrow in 1960 and the Park Lane Hilton in 1963. More American chains would follow but the emerging British chains dominated supply in the 1960s.

Air transport (see Chapter 5) was revolutionized in this period when passenger jet aircraft performed their first commercial transatlantic flights to London in 1958. The Boeing 707 also undertook its first transatlantic flights in 1958 and revolutionized the reliability and unit costs of longer haul travel. It would be joined and rapidly replaced by the bigger 747 that first arrived in London in 1970. Even so, the volume of passenger travel by air only exceeded travel by sea for the first time in 1957. From that time on the fleet of liners that had dominated the inter-war years and nearly a century of transatlantic travel would quickly become irrelevant as a means of transport and most were scrapped. The development of air transport undoubtedly drove the inbound demand for accommodation and stimulated the introduction of the government funded Hotel Development Scheme noted later. Sea cruises were popular at this time, but only for a small affluent minority market, and this kept some of the liners in commission. But it was the combination of fly-drive cruise products out of Florida in the USA that restored significant commercial interest in leisure travel by sea later in the century and a much more popular, some would say downmarket style of cruising crossed the Atlantic to Europe. By the 1990s, cruise ships had become self-propelled floating resorts, not forms of passenger transport.

UK to abroad

After the war, the traditional cross-channel ferry routes resumed as soon as the government eased its foreign travel controls in 1948 and by the 1960s volume was expanding rapidly to France, Belgium and Holland with the development of roll-on/roll-off ferries. But the most significant developments influencing the mid-1950s onwards were taking place using air travel. Vladimir Raitz, still in his twenties and trading as Horizon Holidays, had operated his first pioneering air package holiday from Gatwick to Calvi in Corsica in 1950 (see also Chapter 6). He used charter flights but was restricted to a market of students and teachers under the air traffic regulations of the day. The inclusive price for a week under canvas in a type of beach resort that would later be known as a Club Med style village was £32.50 including meals and wine. It compared with the BEA return airfare to Nice of £70 without any accommodation, food or transfers. In 1950 Horizon booked some 300 clients over 16 weeks (the classic British holiday season at that time). The first year's holidays, using 32-seat DC3 Dakotas, did not break even but with just over 400 holidays in 1951 a profit was turned. In 1952, when the teacher/student restriction was dropped under easier regulation, Majorca was added to Calvi and, with a new airline, Raitz began his expansion into the then nascent Costa Brava in 1954. He was closely followed by Universal Skytours which offered its first air packages in 1953 and Eagle Airways that bought Sir Henry Lunn Ltd in 1954 (Bray and Raitz, 2001).

By the mid-1960s the newly formed Thomson Holidays Group and Clarksons were engaging in fierce competition with Horizon, Global, Cosmos and others that increased the number of UK residents taking holidays abroad to around 6 million in 1969 compared with around one million in 1955. The mass-market model of chartered airline seats, matched to what were in effect chartered hotels, was firmly established. Most of these hotels were newly built at this time, in formulaic clusters of ugly, concrete, identical high-rise buildings that would be outmoded in little over 30 years. Built for mass production holiday operations, these hotels were, perhaps, the model T Fords or Volkswagen Beetles of the tourism industry – and many would prove to be hardly more durable.

Visitor attractions

The 1950s and 1960s were important growth years for historic houses as the number of cars rose rapidly with the growing affluence of the population. Up into the 1970s this was perhaps the golden era of driving for pleasure, especially at weekends in the summer, and a mobile public was hungry for day out experiences as well as holiday activities. Weekend congestion was certainly perceived as a problem on some routes even then, but not at the level of disincentive that would occur after the 1990s as car ownership and usage continued to expand.

With Len Lickorish as its General Manager, the British Travel Association was very well aware in the 1960s that the growing appeal of heritage attractions was significant for inbound tourism. As Lickorish put it 'very early on, the British Travel Association realized that the heritage and historic properties in general were a major attraction; in effect our answer to Spanish sunshine competition'. Lickorish worked closely with historic house owners to create a committee in 1966 (Historic Houses Committee) to promote the interests of historic houses and to lobby for their survival at a time when the Labour Government of the day was strongly opposed to all forms of hereditary wealth. This committee was the forerunner of the Historic Houses Association that was formed in 1973. The National Trust also expanded its interests and public access considerably in this period as owners unable to cope with mounting debts and death duties donated properties to the Trust to secure their survival.

Although it was doubtless the last thing on the good doctor's mind, the Beeching report of 1963, which closed down so many branch lines and ended the steam train era, created a powerful heritage railway movement. Saving the trains and rolling stock and preserving some of the lines released the passion and engagement of volunteers in the 1960s that would so stimulate and distinguish the independent museum movement of the next two decades. Although Beamish Open Air Museum would not be ready to open until 1972, its formative years date back to the late 1950s and early 1960s and the then curator of the Bowes Museum, Frank Atkinson, who would later become the first Director at Beamish. Plans to develop the Ironbridge Gorge Museum also date back to the 1960s with its formal opening in 1973.

1969 to 1989 Major changes in UK tourism – modern tourism emerges

In the twenty-year period to 1989, the key patterns and characteristics of tourism emerged as we still see them today in Britain. Domestic tourism shifted slowly at first and then rapidly from its former primary focus on seaside resorts. The resorts were destined to begin more than a quarter century of continuous decline from which many would not recover. Domestic tourism growth shifted to self-catering in the countryside and to heritage towns and villages. Although there was no means of counting them in this period, day visits undoubtedly grew rapidly in line with disposable income and the freedom conferred by rising car ownership. The former concentration on a relatively passive form of holiday tourism gave way to ever-growing interest in the pursuit of every kind of active and passive recreation.

Outbound holiday tourism would escalate from around 6 million in 1969 to some 21 million in 1989, while inbound tourism reached a significant peak in value in 1977 associated with the Queen's Silver Jubilee year. Ominously, perhaps, as an indication for the future, two major oil crises (in the early 1970s and again in 1979) provoked international economic recession as the first implications of a global economy made themselves felt. The collapse of Clarksons, a casualty of the early 1970s recession, sounded alarm bells for outbound tourism. Its demise paved the way for the creation of another major tour operator, Intasun, that would, in turn, collapse for almost the same reasons in 1991 in the major economic recession of the early 1990s.

The fact that tourism could not escape the effects of the wider world became more obvious. Britain engaged in the Falklands War in 1982 and the Chernobyl nuclear disaster in the Soviet Union (1986) produced fallout effects that were still not fully worked through in parts of Cumbria in 2004. The UK joined the Common Market formally in 1973 although the immediate effects on tourism were slight.

Under Labour Governments of the 1960s and 1970s a philosophy of collectivism, regulation and overall planning guidelines influenced the tourism scene for the 1970s and 1980s. National statutory boards and councils were created to oversee just about every aspect of tourism and visitor movement in terms of countryside recreation, waterways, arts and sports. Most created regional bodies as part of their operation, doubtless influenced by the national decision (1968) to create a short-lived Department of Economic Affairs. Countryside planning was also restructured in 1968 when the national parks established in England in the 1940s gained new powers through the designation of national park authorities. Known as Quasi Autonomous Non Government Organizations (QUANGOs), the new range of national and regional bodies produced an explosion of strategies, policies and guidelines (the term 'visions' was not then in general use). These would be echoed and reinforced after 1997 when Labour returned to power after the Thatcher era that began in 1979. The term QUANGO was by then out of favour although the bodies established in the1960s were retained and their successors in the 1990s would become designated Non Departmental Public Bodies (NDPBs), which is just another word for the same thing. In the early 1970s and again in the 1980s, the spirit of deregulation was in the air as the 1971 Civil Aviation Act dismantled much of the then restrictive clauses on charter airlines, enabling them to achieve major growth in taking the British abroad on holiday.

Accommodation in the 1970s and 1980s

In the accommodation sector, the British seaside probably reached its high point in volume in 1973 when holiday camps in particular were judged to have had a record season (Norris et al., 1974). But the biggest event in this period in Britain was the government decision to implement a Hotel Development Investment Scheme (HDI) in 1968 to force the pace of hotel development that by common consent was holding back inbound tourism development at that time. The access issues were solved by the new aircraft technology and regulation changes but the provision of accommodation had not kept pace. Under the HDI scheme, new hotels to be built before 1973 could claim a grant of £1250 per bedroom in London and £1000 elsewhere. Subsidies were available also for extensions. The result was a massive building programme, which in the end cost the taxpayer more than £60 million (over £1 billion in 2000 prices). It was estimated that until the scheme some 2000 new rooms a year were being built. By 1973 some 70 000 beds had been added, almost doubling the capacity of international quality stock in a very short time. Between 1968 and 1976, in London alone, a total of 129 new hotels were built with some 12 352 rooms.

As appears to be almost inevitable with such schemes, the massive new capacity, which also reflected the potential of airline capacity with the arrival of the Boeing 747s, ran swiftly into the buffers of the unforeseen 1973 international oil crisis. An already fragile UK economy was badly hit, airlines were plunged into crisis and inbound tourism fell, creating its own crisis conditions in the hotel sector. Heavily borrowed hotel organizations, even allowing for the government subsidy, found themselves faced with falling revenues and rising interest rates as inflation forced up the cost of loan finance. London Airport Hotels were reported at the time to be 'a disaster area as a result of chronic overbuilding' (Norris et al., 1974). The major collapse was the Lyons Group, but most others faced similar pressures on profits and a series of forced mergers and acquisitions took place. By the late 1970s there were more than 20 hotel groups in Britain with more than 1000 rooms each.

The government subsidies also facilitated the first hotel chains in Britain to be built to a standard formula, with the first UK Holiday Inns opening in this period and providing a new form of competition with the size of their bedrooms, swimming pools and gymnasia. In 1970 Forte merged with Trust Houses to become THF, then the largest chain in the UK with nearly

Figure 4.2 Holiday Inn, Portsmouth

20 000 rooms in some 200 hotels (Medlik, 1978). THF opened the first of its Post Houses. In London, just off Russell Square, Centre Hotels provided the first formula built hotels in the 3 star range. None of these were budget hotels although they provided a business model that underpinned the later development.

Conditions of excess supply over demand unleashed marketing initiatives such as the development of short break products in hotels at weekends. Taken for granted by the 1990s, short weekend breaks as they are understood today had been launched in the mid-1960s by Grand Metropolitan Hotels and by Forte about four years later, but the concept took off in this period in response to the economic conditions facing operators. An attractive business formula emerged across the UK whereby most business hotels between Monday and Thursday could cater for a weekend leisure market between Friday and Sunday. Another initiative, with the active support of British Airways and other scheduled airlines, saw the development of low cost packages for the inbound market brokered between airlines and hotels. The British Inbound Tour Operators Association (BITOA) emerged to focus on developing packages for inbound tourism.

Mostly outside London, the evident business success of the hotel chains created a response among independents that formed consortia to survive and prosper. As Groups they could access for themselves at least some of the benefits of marketing and branding, and the savings achievable through the economies of scale that the chains had developed. Consort Hotels, Interchange Hotels, Prestige Hotels, Minotels and Inter-Hotels were established and operating effectively in the 1960s and 1970s. Strongly supported by marketing campaigns developed by the English Tourist Board in the 1970s, they too were able to capitalize on the short break marketing phenomenon and help to change the attitudes of the population to weekending in hotels.

Although still seen in the 1970s largely as a business of sales management, hotel marketing as it is practised today effectively dates from the capacity explosion of the early 1970s and the need to market excess capacity more effectively. The Hotel Sales Managers Association (HSMA) was formed in 1964 and became the Hotel Industry Marketing Group (HIMG) within the Institute of Marketing in 1972.

As so often when looking at the history of tourism, a new business model occurs that changes industry perceptions (see Chapter 6). In accommodation provision for the domestic market in the 1970s and 1980s it was arguably the Dutch concept of Center Parcs that did most to change the prevailing attitudes toward resorts and holiday centres (see also Chapter 6). Center Parcs opened its first park in Sherwood Forest in 1987, followed by a second in Norfolk in 1989. These parks were not, as some believed, just a new form of holiday camp. Working on a formula of combinations of three and four night products or stays of one week, they broke traditional British holiday attitudes to seasons by demonstrating that year round operation was achievable in domestic tourism. With some 90 per cent occupancy and direct marketing to reduce distribution costs, it was also highly profitable. The profits sustained the cost of putting the key central areas under cover and heated as necessary around the year. Equally impressive, Center Parcs designed its villages around environmental concepts, turning relatively unproductive and scenically average areas with little or no farming value into centres for biodiversity and wildlife. They even managed to prise visitors from their cars on site and onto bicycles – a remarkable achievement in 1980s Britain.

Visitor attractions

The period 1969 to 1989 witnessed a major expansion in the provision of visitor attractions, with the heritage focus very much to the fore. Section 4 of The Development of Tourism Act in 1969 gave tourist boards in England, Scotland and Wales powers to provide loans and grants to visitor attractions in ways that were in some ways equivalent to the HDI scheme for hotels, although not with anything like the same sums of money.

The combination of growing inbound tourism, the post-war shift of domestic visitors into rural areas away from resorts, plus the unleashing of day visit demand by ever-growing access to motorcars created a large market for visitor attractions of all kinds. It was a market that would grow for at least the next quarter of a century up to the mid-1990s and the capacity measured in the number of attractions open to visitors would grow even faster and for longer. The British Travel Association had collected claimed numbers of visitors to attractions since the 1960s. But the first formal measures of visitor attractions date to 1978 when the English

Tourist Board introduced its series of *Sightseeing in the UK* Surveys that would later embrace the whole of the UK. Although these figures are based on un-audited claims for visitor numbers, they represent the only available annual assessment of changes in the number and types of attractions in the UK. Dominated by various types of heritage provision, the ETB survey categorized attractions according to types agreed with operators at the time and its record reveals the remarkable growth that took place in a short space of time in sectors such as historic buildings, museums and galleries, and gardens.

For example, looking backwards from the survey of 1998, it can be seen that nearly half of all the museums open in England first opened between 1970 and 1989, as did one third of all historic properties and 46 per cent of wildlife sites. These data do not include theme parks or retail attractions but do give some indication of the sheer growth in the capacity of attractions over the twenty years to 1989.

Theme parks in Britain also date from this period. Drawing on USA precedents, the largest with approaching or over one million visitors a year each were Alton Towers, Thorpe Park, World of Adventures (Chessington), Pleasurewood Hills and Drayton Manor. With one exception (Drayton Manor originally opened in 1950), all of these were opened between 1979 and 1983. Collectively, as major players in the attractions sector, they altered the attitudes of customers to expectations of quality, value for money and the nature of the visitor experience.

In the heritage field, the Historic Houses Association was formed in 1973 with Lord Montagu as its first chairman. The Association received strong encouragement at the time from the British Tourist Authority under Len Lickorish who provided office space and a seconded manager to support and undertake the work. He also organized publicity support in the Authority's international promotional work. The Association was plunged into fighting a proposed Capital Transfer Tax and an annual Wealth Tax planned in 1975 by a new Labour Government and a Chancellor, Dennis Healey, who promised to 'squeeze the rich until the pips squeak'. In fact Dennis Healy was responsive to the lobby – accepting the case that heritage assets were a key element in earning foreign exchange – and historic houses, grounds and works of art were exempted from the planned Capital Transfer Tax in 1976 – with conditions set for public access. In 1976 Lord Montagu led an influential delegation of peers and other representatives of heritage organizations to salute America on the occasion of its Bicentennial and promote Britain's attractions.

By the mid-1980s the consumer interest in all things historic had generated the idea of a 'Heritage Industry' that would be embraced a decade later in 1994 when the Government created a Department of National Heritage to be responsible (inter alia) for tourism. In the 1980s the Conservative Government decided to end the State's traditional ownership and civil service operation of heritage resources and pass the assets and management to

Table 4.1 The decades in which UK visitor attractions opened to the public

Year of first opening	Historic Properties %	Gardens %	Museums and galleries %	Wildlife Sites %	Total – all attractions %
Pre 1959	51	24	28	18	26
1960 to 1969	8	13	10	11	8
1970 to 1979	15	18	20	18	19
1980 to 1989	17	26	28	28	27
Total 1970 to 1989	32	44	48	46	46
1990 to 1998	9	19	14	25	20
Total	**100**	**100**	**100**	**100**	**100**
Actual no. of attractions known in 1998	1418	347	1724	300	5890

Source: Sightseeing in the UK Survey, 1998.

a new agency called 'The Historic Buildings and Monuments Commission for England'. The Commission quickly adopted the more appetising title of 'English Heritage', of which Lord Montagu was appointed the first chairman. Hewitt's interesting polemic on the heritage industry was published in 1987. It identified what Hewitt termed 'a new cultural force . . . the heritage industry [which] is more and more expected to replace the real industry upon which this country's economy depends. Instead of manufacturing goods, we are manufacturing heritage . . .' (Hewitt, 1987).

Garden Festivals were another significant development of this period that had a powerful lasting influence nationally on local government understanding of the role of tourism and the economic regenerating of cities. Festivals, each drawing millions of visits over a year were held at Liverpool, Glasgow, Stoke-on-Trent and in the South Wales Valleys in the 1980s. They changed both public and private sector understanding of what could be achieved by tourism events.

1989 to 1995 Global tourism emerges

Key events in the decade to 1995 reflected the extent to which tourism was becoming dominated by international affairs. There were, for example, the tourism repercussions of the first Gulf war in 1990–91 and the effects in Britain of the major international economic recession of the early 1990s following the 1988–89 boom. The effects of the recession on consumer spending was exacerbated in the UK by the negative equity problems caused when house prices collapsed in the early 1990s and some 1.5 million homeowners were affected, of which an estimated 150 000 were effectively dispossessed. Recession appears to have reached its depth in September 1992 when Britain was forced by speculative traders out of the European Exchange Rate Mechanism (ERM) it had joined in 1990 as an expected precursor to joining the Economic Monetary Union. The strong economic recovery of the UK throughout the 1990s and into the twenty-first century dates from that time, as successive governments ceased to defend the pound and practised more effective demand management and control over inflation.

Although its volumes and structures had changed massively, there was a resurgence in domestic tourism in the 1990s. This was fuelled by day visits, business and other work related tourism, visitors to friends and relatives, growing ownership of second homes (including caravans), the organization of year round events and festivals, and the growth in recreational activities of all kinds. In particular, shopping for pleasure, often dubbed 'retail therapy' was enormously facilitated by the formal abandoning of Sunday closure for shops in 1994 (Sunday Trading Act) as part of the drive for deregulation by the Conservative Government of the day (see below).

Although the number of inbound visitors to Britain continued to increase over the decade, despite the effects of international events, the real expenditure per capita did not shift in parallel. 1977 remained the high water mark of inbound tourism expenditure in real terms until the late 1990s.

Deregulation of air transport, introduced in the US domestic market in 1978 had a growing effect on European decisions in this period. The Common Market was always designed to provide a basis for increased competition on level terms between member nations. But this was transparently not the case across Europe in transport in the late 1980s where several nations still heavily subsidized their state airlines and railways and prevented the competition of low cost carriers on their national territory. As explained in Chapter 5, this situation was changing rapidly under EU rules, releasing the energy of low cost, budget carriers in the 1990s and stimulating increased international tourism within Europe.

Visitor accommodation

The development of branded chains of budget hotels in Britain was one of the most impressive accommodation developments in this era. They reflect another example of a business model change or 'paradigm shift' that changed both consumer and business expectations, in much the same way that budget airlines did for air transport. Using mass production methods for buildings and standardized bathrooms, and furniture manufactured to a formula off site and installed on locations, the concept originated in the USA in the 1960s and 1970s (where development land was relatively cheap). Forte Hotels introduced budget hotels in Britain in 1984 with their Travelodge brand developed on sites adjacent to Little Chef fast food restaurants generally close to petrol stations on main roads and later on motorways. The success of this business model quickly attracted competitors with Travel Inn commencing in 1987 and others following very quickly. Initially designed for a family leisure market, the budget hotels immediately found favour with business travellers and those travelling for the many other reasons common to late twentieth-century populations. Very high occupancy levels year round, low staffing costs and direct marketing (rapidly facilitated by Internet bookings from the mid-1990s) proved to be profitable for operators and attractive to customers, especially through offering highly competitive prices.

The budget hotel expansion accompanied recovery from what many in the UK believed to be the worst economic recession since the 1930s. As business recovered and business travel grew after 1992–93, the attractive prices available in the budget sector were assisted by the heightened cost consciousness and cut back on expenses that developed in the recession years. When Travel Inn, for example, a Whitbread product, was launched in 1987 there were already some 3000 or so branded budget hotel rooms. By 1997, with the market then growing at some 30 per cent a year, there were at least ten budget chains developing the UK market. Travel Inn, by then the market leader, had some 200 hotels accommodating some 5 million guest nights a year and the total number of branded budget rooms had increased to over 10 000.

In self-catering there was a remarkable resurgence and process of rein-vention in the caravan park industry. For decades considered to be a down-market operation, the sector modernized itself by agreeing to operate to stricter codes of quality assurance and by using a business model based more on the sale and site rental of units as second homes than on tradi-tional seasonal holiday lettings. The Bellamy Award for good environmen-tal practice was introduced in the mid-1990s and helped to change the traditional image of caravan parks. Nationally branded chains for letting holiday cottages also thrived in the 1990s and their marketing was enormously facilitated by the advent of the Internet.

Visitor attractions

The attractions sector, especially the heritage sector, was hit by the early 1990s recession and the associated downturn in tourism as Britons were forced to tighten their belts. Capacity in the sector had massively increased in the 1970s and 1980s as noted earlier and an unexpected lifeline was made available in 1994 by the government decision to run a National Lottery for which heritage would be one of the sectors to benefit. Section 4 funding for England had been withdrawn in the late 1980s, but Heritage Lottery Funding and Millennium Commission Funding created a remark-able windfall of new finance. The money was available only to new devel-opments and extensions rather than refurbishment of existing attractions and it would repeat in the late 1990s some of the same issues as those that faced hotels in the 1970s after the government's intervention in subsidising hotel capacity in the HDI scheme.

Although its impact comes strictly outside the period under review in this chapter, Lottery funding was an initiative that precipitated a wave of appli-cations for new heritage attractions that would lead to the disbursement of some £1 billion by 1998 for some 1650 new capital projects committed since 1994 (Middleton, 1998, p. 9). A further £4 billion was allocated in 1998 but not spent at that time.

Public interest in heritage continued to grow as the National Trust approached a membership total of just under 3 million in time for its cente-nary year and English Heritage passed the half million mark for its mem-bership operation. Museums of all kinds attracted friends and volunteers and drew in thousands of local residents to participate in their survival and continued vitality.

As so often, competition comes from unexpected quarters. It was the decision to permit Sunday trading in an Act of 1994 that opened the flood-gates for the development of retail malls, discount villages and speciality shopping centres that determined so much of the shape of British retail developments in the 1990s. Supported as part of the economic regeneration of former industrial cities such as Glasgow, Leeds, Manchester, Newcastle upon Tyne and South East London, 'Bluewater', 'Trafford Centre' and other large sites created, in effect, massive new visitor attractions for day visitors, thus becoming new resorts of the twenty-first century. Within a decade, some two thirds of the population were engaging in shopping on Sundays and many stores could do a fifth or more of the week's trading on the Sabbath. With a throughput of some 30 million visits each across a full year (including many repeat visits), the largest of the new centres offered entertainment, cinemas, events, bars, cafes and restaurants, and facilities for children to support the retailing core. Some have hotels located on adjacent sites or close by. By their choice of flamboyant architecture, theming and planned ambience, these are not just out-of-town shopping centres; they are new purpose-built resorts that are an integral aspect of modern tourism (Middleton, 1999). In total contrast to the 1940s and 1950s holiday resorts' 'season' of 16 weeks, these day visitor resorts are open 7 days a week, over 360 days a year and some are open 24 hours a day.

In the 1960s, 1970s and 1980s, Sunday had been the traditional popular visiting day for many heritage and other leisure attractions. The competition to them from the combination of new attractions and the new major retail centres would tip many older attractions into difficulties and some would be forced to close. Many would argue that, notwithstanding the fact that government provided a lifeline to many attractions through Lottery funding, the process effectively subsidized growth in the capacity of new attractions at exactly the wrong time for the sector. It also created unfair competition for commercial visitor attractions that were not eligible for such funding. In this period the die was also cast for the Millennium Dome costing some £750 million of public sector funding that would underperform its volume and revenue targets in 2001 and create massive negative publicity for the public sector use of such funding.

Summary

Perhaps the most powerful message emerging from the developments reviewed in this chapter is the way in which the sectors of accommodation and attractions have changed and developed in response to, as well as leading changes in market demand. Significantly, business models have changed and adapted and whole sectors of provision have reinvented themselves and their product offers to appeal to modern markets. Some parts of both sectors have disappeared, unable to compete, but new sectors have emerged. The processes of successful private sector reinvention and adaptation offer positive messages for the future, in which change is certain to be a constant preoccupation.

CHAPTER 5

Developments in transport

Transport is the tail that wags the tourism dog. (Seekings, 2001, p. 223 in Lockwood and Medlik)

Transport is one of the three primary elements in modern tourism, along with accommodation at the destination, destination attractions and other facilities. Transport is, however, arguably the most influential of the three since, without convenient access at affordable prices, there could be no tourism as it is understood today.

Convenience and affordability have changed radically over the last fifty years as new technology improved the size (carrying capacity) and speed of the vehicles, routes possible and costs per mile charged. Transport developments have profoundly altered consumer options in terms of destinations that can be visited and the relative costs of visiting them. Before the 1950s, passenger travel by air was minimal and ocean liners undertook the long distance routes. Aircraft technology has obviously revolutionized international travel and the growing use of cars totally altered the characteristics of British domestic tourism. The search for convenient access and affordable prices also provides opportunities for new models for the conduct of business operations, while innovative marketing can influence customer preferences and destinations visited just as dramatically as technology shifts. Tour operators demonstrated this convincingly in the 1950s and 1960s; Britain's scheduled airlines' marketing was the main force in generating inbound visitors to the UK and budget airlines have demonstrated in the last decade just how powerful an influence innovative business models can have over tourism developments.

In the early post-war period of the story of British tourism, railways, coach travel and ferries were still the dominant forms of access to holiday destinations. After the war they were mostly taken over and owned or controlled directly by the State. But, apart from roll-on/roll-off ferries, each of these transport modes dwindled in relative importance to tourism in the decades after 1955. For staying visitors, both train and coach continue to play a role in taking visitors to their destinations, not least for example via the coach operators that effectively drive the large present-day pensioners holiday market in the UK. But this role is now at the margins of development, not at the forefront. For day visitors, group arrangements and for moving people at the destination, coaches continue to play a vital and growing facilitation role, but it is travel by car and air travel that have dominated the key developments in British tourism over the last half-century.

A regulatory morass?

To the interested observer not directly involved, the story of transport must seem confusingly bound up by bewildering regulatory issues. Unfortunately it is. Market demand dominates much of tourism developments and operators compete for business. But transport is different, especially where it involves large operators capable of achieving monopoly positions that could be used against consumer interests or where it involves government controls over national air and sea spaces. The story of transport developments is both the result of regulatory decisions and, as technology changes, the new transport options are the primary cause of regulatory change. One cannot tell the story without a brief introduction to this process.

Regulation is the business of governments and their agencies and, because tourism is an international business, it has to involve agreements between governments. Lawyers are employed to advise governments and their processes are not noted for their speed of decision-making. Nor, because the law aims at precision in definitions, are regulations intended to be flexible. The process is compounded because lawyers have to use statistics as evidence and travel statistics are often unreliable, only partial in coverage and may be two or more years out of date, while markets change rapidly in the fast moving business of tourism. Regulatory decisions mostly have implications for the cost of travel, which influences the prices paid by customers whether or not taxes, also controlled by government, are involved. It is widely agreed that relative prices are a primary motivator in most travel decisions and even small changes influenced by regulation can stimulate or depress the volume of bookings.

Because of the speed of change in tourism, usually led by private sector entrepreneurs, there is constant and unavoidable friction between government regulation and market realities. Market circumstances change and regulations often become out of date. Political objectives also change, with different governments swinging, for example, between preferences for more or less regulation. As a result, impatient business entrepreneurs, such as Freddie Laker in the 1970s, typically see the law governing transport as 'an ass' and set about challenging it in order to provoke the changes in which they have a commercial interest. Other vested interests may seek to retain the existing regulation, and the arguments and counter arguments are a goldmine for the legal profession.

Visitor accommodation and attractions are also subject to regulations, of course, and to the planning and development controls and influences of local and regional authorities. At least in the UK, however, neither accommodation nor attractions are officially licensed and the bulk of the regulations they are required to comply with were not designed for the tourism sector but for businesses generally. That is not the case with transport regulation for which the statutes and agreements are specific to the sector. Because governments are involved and the costs and benefits to society of transport decisions are important, regulation is also subject to political objectives, such as coping with the environmental and social impacts of transport decisions.

Reasons for transport regulation – why it is important

For reasons of safety in particular and for rather more spurious reasons, such as national interest and control of national air and sea space, transport has always been heavily regulated and often controlled directly by national governments. In the second half of the twentieth century, the driving force has been economic regulation – to influence the prices, capacity and route structure of airlines in particular to ensure fair competition, protection for consumer interests and to hold the ring against mutually destructive competition. Since the 1940s, regulation of air transport has had to be operated on a multinational basis because tourists have increasingly crossed traditional national boundaries. In Europe, since the 1980s, the regulation of key parts of travel has been increasingly transferred to the European Union with whose decisions national governments such as the British have to comply. Most recently the Union has taken responsibility for the international treaties that govern global air traffic movements into and out of Europe.

Regulation can be defined as 'the attempt by Government or their agents to ensure certain objectives are met, which might not be met under the operation of free market forces' (Shaw, 1982, p. 90). It is not a new process. Railway safety regulation to protect passengers was introduced 150 years ago in the Victorian age as a response to accidents, not long after the development of the first railway companies. Bus travel in Britain was first regulated in the 1930 Road Transport Act that established traffic commissioners, requiring operating companies to apply to operate specific agreed routes and covering the standards to be achieved by the drivers they employed. Licensing provided operators with a stable base from which to

develop and form collaborative pooling arrangements with other companies. London Coastal Coaches was one such pool based at the new Victoria
Coach Station in London that opened in 1932.

Regulation and intervention in transport continues in multiple guises for
reasons including:

- Licensing public transport operators to ensure they meet minimum stan-
  dards before being allowed to market their services to customers.
  Traditionally such licences have been for particular routes and with spe-
  cific controls over capacity and prices that effectively controlled who
  could enter the market and engage in competition.
- Agreeing the location of airports and seaports and the road systems generally.
- Controlling airspace and managing the movement of aircraft.
- Health and safety procedures and inspections in the consumer interest.
- Promoting competition or preventing consumer exploitation by
  unfair/anti-consumer monopolies.
- Holding the balance between competing interests on major routes such
  as that across the Atlantic in ways that aim to promote maximum efficiency and achieve the lowest prices that are economically viable for
  operators.
- Determining and overseeing vehicle specifications (e.g. noise and emissions controls, aspects of recyclable materials and passenger protection).
- Licensing vehicles (including cars) in part for tax purposes but also for
  controlling standards.
- Controlling driver training and licensing drivers to ensure passenger
  safety.
- Operating a tax regime in the public interest or in the interests of the
  environment – including setting airport landing charges and airport
  taxes.
- Endeavouring to ensure that the costs to society of transport systems, for
  example to residents affected by roads and airport developments, and the
  environmental costs of operations, are reflected in decisions taken.
- Regulation to promote better co-ordination between different modes or
  forms of transport, for example between air transport, local public transport (such as trains and buses) and the use of cars.

In addition to these reasons, the public sector is often directly responsible for
funding, building and maintaining large parts of the transport system
infrastructure, from motorways and other roads, to airports and ferry ports.
Traditionally, the State has also been a major investor in aircraft and shipping manufacture, with an interest in seeing a return on investment. It reg-
ulates and taxes transport systems, in part at least to fund this direct
expenditure, and in all countries it controls a planning and development
system that determines where the infrastructure should be located. Debates
about a fourth London airport, for example, have continued for years as the
multiple issues and interests are evaluated, not least residents' interests for

which governments are also responsible. More recently regulation has had to tackle the issues of passenger security under threat from terrorist organizations around the world who identify transport systems and terminals as easy targets. Environmental issues of noise pollution, global warming and CO_2 emissions, unknown or insignificant in the post-war era, are also likely to dominate the political agenda for transport in the twenty-first century.

1945 to 1955

Railways and coaches

Taken over by Government in 1939 for the duration of the war (as they had been from 1914 to 1918), the railway companies were nationalized after the war under the Transport Act of 1947. At that time the railway companies also owned sea ferries and at least half the bus companies in Britain as well as British Waterways (still a freight transport business at that time) and former railway hotels. All were brought together into a conglomerate known as The British Transport Commission in 1948. Railways and buses were the primary means of access to seaside resorts at the time and in 1951 railways carried some 47 per cent and coaches 27 per cent of people travelling on holiday. By 1948, coaches were carrying some 59 million passengers, nearly 79 per cent more than in 1939 and by 1955, some 100 million journeys were undertaken by coach. Not all of these were for holidays, of course, but the figures give some indication of the popularity of this form of transport after the war. The economics of transporting millions of holiday visitors, mainly in July and August, were as fundamentally unviable for transport as they were for resort hotels and guesthouses (see Chapter 4). Standards were low in the holiday transport sector because of the lack of money for refurbishment of old and infrequently used rolling stock/vehicles. Older readers will doubtless recollect the characteristic unmistakable smell of musty dampness that pervaded such aged rolling stock. (In this period, Britain's railways still operated 3rd class railway carriages.)

Cars

Just under 2 million cars from the 1920s and 1930s survived the war years and rolled out onto post-war roads, although petrol was still rationed until 1950. As soon as production could be geared up they were joined by another 1.5 million by 1955 and the first foreign imports – Volkswagens from Germany and Renaults and Peugeots from France – began to influence the British domestic market. At that time, many cars were used only for leisure and laid up from September to March and there were no MOTs to ensure good maintenance. AA and RAC patrolmen, still on motorcycles and sidecars at that time, continued to salute members as

Figure 5.1 Exmoor traffic

they passed. This practice was continued until the early 1950s – an anachronistic but charming reminder of pre-war motoring. By the mid-1950s, with increasing freedom to choose when and where to go, there was a massive shift from seaside resorts toward self-catering in other (rural) coastal areas and inland.

There were no motorways in Britain then, and relatively few bypasses had been built in the 1930s for towns. Areas such as the West Country and the Lake District, growing in popularity for those with access to cars, were already recognizing tourism car congestion at summer weekends by the late 1950s.

Sea transport

For long-haul travel (North America and the former British Empire and Commonwealth nations) liners still ruled the oceans and the volume of passengers by air travel did not overtake sea travel across the Atlantic until 1957. The first *Queen Mary* had been launched in 1936 and the *Queen Elizabeth* in 1940, and both were used in war service as troop ships for US forces. Refurbished after the war, they entered a golden decade until the arrival of jet airplanes. Then, increasingly unprofitable in the face of price competition from airlines, both were withdrawn in 1967. The *Queen Mary* survives in a tourism role at Long Beach California but the *Queen Elizabeth* was destroyed by fire in Hong Kong Harbour in 1972.

Taken over by the nationalized British Transport Commission in 1948 the classic Dover and Harwich routes to Calais and the Hook of Holland returned to operations. Cars could be taken, but in the early years before the introduction of purpose-built roll-on/roll-off ferries, they had to be lifted on deck one at a time and disembarked in slings.

Limited competition across the channel by Bristol Freighter air transport was provided by Silver City Airways on the Lydd to Le Touquet route starting in 1948, which could carry a small number of cars in their holds. Before more effective ferry competition and hovercraft developed in the 1950s, this route carried some 45 000 cars and 170 000 passengers.

In the air

With wartime developments forcing the pace and revolutionizing the size, speed and load capacity of aircraft, the first post-war airliners were based on the airframes and engines of planes developed as wartime bombers. The ability to fly long distances and carry large loads (of bombs) had developed enormously since the 1930s and the payload of bombs was readily converted into seat loads for passengers in the 1940s.

Just as a surplus of military trucks provided the base for the development of bus and coach services in the 1920s, so a surplus of military airplanes provided the basis for the development of air charters in the late 1940s and 1950s. The Berlin airlift, instituted to lift the Russian blockade of road and rail routes into Berlin in 1948, produced an urgent demand for air freight charters and many mothballed aircraft were brought back into service for several months until the blockade was lifted in 1949. Their operators, often ex wartime pilots using their wartime service payments, found this a profitable if short-lived business and with the money they earned some would become the natural operators of the first air holiday charters in the 1950s. Harold Bamberg, Ted Langston and Freddie Laker were among the leading entrepreneurs of this period.

The key event in international air transport after the war was the Chicago Convention drawn up in 1944. In the arguments over regulation for post-war flying between countries there was widespread fear in Europe that the Americans would dominate international air transport because of the sheer size and development of their own air transport market, the vigour of their economy and their aircraft production capacity, which had been massively stimulated and not damaged in the war. American airlines were the dominant world competitors and war-torn European nations needed market protection to re-establish their own airlines.

Since the Paris Agreement of 1919 after the First World War, the principle had been accepted that states have sovereign rights over the airspace above their national boundaries. The Chicago Convention of 1944 confirmed that principle and defined so-called 'freedoms of the air' that were intended to guarantee the ways in which each country would continue to control its own airspace and control routes and capacity. Any airline wishing to fly between countries would have to negotiate with each individual country for rights to enter the national airspace of the intended destination and to obtain rights to fly over any other airspaces en route. To fly across the Atlantic to Germany, for example, generally meant flying over France – subject to agreement.

'The philosophy of the Chicago Convention was that the scheduled traffic between two countries is to be reserved [and shared] between their own airlines' (Burkart and Medlik, 1974, p.130). Negotiations to achieve this goal became, in effect, bilateral treaties between countries of which the Bermuda Agreement between the USA and UK became the model when it was agreed following the Convention. For several decades the Chicago Convention would be the basis from which international air service arrangements were made and amended. The 1944 Convention also led to the creation of the International Air Transport Association (IATA), a conference or trade association of airlines that would agree fares and debate the issues of economic regulation, subject to government ratification. It is important to note that these agreements only covered scheduled airlines on international routes and did not cover the regulation of domestic airlines or charter airlines. Those sectors were left to be regulated directly by each Government or its appointed agency. The close identity of national scheduled carriers and their Governments was inevitable and it would be the cause for constant friction and bargaining as competitors to national carriers sought to establish their own rights to fly routes. Similarly, some countries, notably France, Italy and Spain were thought to provide unfair subsidies and therefore establish unfair competition to support their national airlines.

An uncontroversial agreement within the Chicago Convention, which still stands, was that the purchase of planes would not be subject to normal sales or purchase taxes and that the provision of aviation fuel would be tax exempt. At the time such benefits were justified by the need to encourage the growth of aviation, but the repercussions have become very significant 50 years on as concerns over global warming have increased and the role of aircraft in polluting the skies has become more focused.

Heathrow airport opened its first terminal in 1951 and in the post-war era until 1960 BOAC (long haul) and BEA (European and domestic flights) were the principal British operators of scheduled international passenger and cargo services. They also represented the British Government's interests at the time in civil air transport. Both were government owned and, of course, closely regulated. Both were mainly used by business and government employees and a wealthy clientele, and were not widely accessible to the general holiday market at the time. BOAC introduced services to New York in 1946 and in 1952 introduced tourist fares across the Atlantic in an early bid to promote traffic; London–New York return fares were reduced from £254 to £173. Further reductions were made in 1958 when economy fares were first made available.

Also in 1952 BOAC flew the first jet propelled passenger service to South Africa, halving the time taken by propeller driven planes, using the ill-fated Comet 1. After major crashes in 1953 and 1954 that grounded the first Comets, the final version, the Comet 4, was developed and operated the first jet flights from the UK to the USA in 1958. But the reputation of the plane suffered disastrously from the media exposure generated by the series of crashes caused by metal fatigue with its early version. The Boeing 707 was flying the Atlantic later in the same year and quickly became the plane of choice of long-haul airlines. A later version of the Comet (4B) was developed and operated very successfully in Europe by BEA.

1955 to 1969

Rail and bus

Travel by coach and bus as a means of reaching holiday destinations continued to thrive in most of this period, reaping the benefit of its more competitive pricing compared with rail and being able to exploit the developments to the road network. The National Bus Company was formed at the end of this period (see below). The railways, however, were struggling as passenger and freight traffic declined. By the time of the Beeching Report in 1963, it was widely recognized that a major overhaul was needed and the infamous Beeching 'Axe' was applied as noted later in this chapter. By 1969, rail was ceasing to be a major player for holiday transport and was increasingly marginalized as other forms of transport took the initiative and developed marketing muscle. Many would argue that the combination of government ownership, Treasury control and constant union disputes created a form of management sclerosis on the railways that would continue for the rest of the century, even after denationalization in the mid-1990s.

In 1968, Barbara Castle in the Wilson Government of the time passed the Transport Act with its ambitious plans to provide for integrated transport in Britain. Nearly 40 years later the prospects of integration of transport modes appears as far away as ever although it remains a Government objective. *Interalia*, the 1968 Act brought the private and public sector bus operators (nationalized since the 1940s) together as the National Bus Company (NBC), controlling 93 bus companies grouped into 44 operating units employing 81 000 staff and having a fleet of 21 000 vehicles. The 1960s collectivization process was clearly still well in evidence there.

Cars

As the number of cars on the road almost quadrupled to over 11 million in this period, and motorway building proceeded, this was perhaps the golden age of popular motoring. Car parking was relatively unrestricted, fuel prices were low, speed restrictions were not heavily policed and congestion was minimal by 1990s standards. Nevertheless, media pictures of so-called 'Bank Holiday Mayhem' on the roads were common in the 1960s – a foretaste of what was to come by the end of the century. The first major international energy crisis of the early 1970s that threatened to bring back petrol rationing in 1973 and restrict the use of cars, was still in the future. Caravan parks and holiday centres were major recipients of shifts in holiday demand and cars flooded to the countryside, leading to the first serious alarm bells ringing about the environmental impact of cars by the late 1960s.

Sea transport

Roll-on/roll-off ferries with bow opening doors for easy and rapid access were first introduced on channel routes in 1952. Acting as a form of 'moving road bridge' such ferries developed rapidly and soon came to dominate the provision of capacity to accommodate the growing number of cars travelling to and from Britain. Hovercraft were introduced at the end of this period and, although they never gained more than a minor share of the total ferry market, they provided competition for many years until the Channel Tunnel finally rendered them no longer viable.

Air transport

As noted earlier, the Boeing 707 commenced its long-haul flights in 1958 and was followed just over a decade later when the first generation of 747s arrived in Heathrow in 1970. The M4 motorway significantly improved the road access from Heathrow into and out of London in 1965, but a direct service by underground would not open until nearly twenty years later in1986.

In the UK, the Civil Aviation (Licensing) Act of 1960 established a formal system of licensing for the civil aviation industry based, in its thinking at least, on the 1930s system of licensing for bus operators. 'Among other measures, the Act created an Air Transport Licensing Board (ATLB) . . . to which all UK airlines were bound to apply for licences to operate air services. Non-scheduled operations in the 1960s grew at an annual rate some three times faster than scheduled operations and the bulk of this growth was in flights for tour operators taking British holidaymakers to the new Mediterranean resorts' (Burkart, 1974, p. 51). The ATLB, as a semi-judicial tribunal thus presided over the first significant inroads into what had been previously a virtual state monopoly. Effectively, the automatic discrimination in favour of state airlines was ended and privately owned airlines were free to bid for scheduled services, which they did; state-owned airlines could apply to operate non-scheduled services, which they did, but not to any significant scale initially. ATLB was not, however, responsible for licensing tour operators as businesses and had no jurisdiction over them. Its remit was restricted to granting permission to operate charter flights and there were some damaging failures of smaller tour operators in the mid-1960s that a decade later would bring the licensing of tour operators into scope.

This regulatory shift in the rules governing air transport licences opened the way for British air tour operators and their private airline partners. Recognizing the growth potential in demand for holidays abroad, they successfully challenged the scheduled airlines. In the summer of 1961 charter inclusive tour traffic from the UK amounted to 295 000 passengers; ten years later it reached 2 698 000 – a ten-fold increase.

Internationally, across the Atlantic, charter airlines were also challenging the power of the scheduled airlines and finding ways around the regulations to offer lower fares. 'During the ten years 1960 to 1970, the major development in civil aviation was the shift in demand from scheduled services to charter operations. On long-haul routes, charter airlines provided carriage for groups of passengers with some common interests [affinity charters], while in Europe development took the shape of the inclusive tour whereby a tour operator combined air transport with accommodation and sold the resultant package to the public' (Burkart and Medlik, 1974, p. 111).

The use of charters operated only on routes with high demand where keen pricing would fill the available seats and generate profit – much to the discomfort of traditional airlines with their network operations and staffing commitments that included many marginal or unprofitable routes. At that time, state airlines operated many routes under a public service ethos that involved using 'excess' profits earned on popular routes to subsidize the unprofitable ones. The 'common interest' clause for 'affinity charters' across the Atlantic was soon treated with contempt for the law – with made up names such as the Irish Ploughboys Association – and the affinity requirements eventually lapsed.

By the mid-1950s it was being recommended that Gatwick should become the official second London airport and in 1958 the airport opened, greatly facilitating the growth of air packages from London and the South East of England where the major market was located.

1969 to 1989

Rail and bus

By 1970, only 13 per cent of domestic holidays taken by the British used rail as the means of transport. Coaches at that time provided transport for around 15 per cent of holidays. The dominance of holidays by car was already well established.

Throughout the 1970s and 1980s rail transport was digesting and disputing the Beeching remedies, which resulted in the closure of around one in three stations and some 5000 miles of line. Diesel trains followed by electrification facilitated main line travel but the volume of passengers and freight continued to fall throughout this period in which holiday-taking by rail dwindled to insignificance. In 1974, the National Bus Company became National Express and a further Transport Act of 1980, enacted by the new Thatcher Government, deregulated bus transport to allow for competition on long-haul routes and more competition on local bus routes. It released competition that had been controlled by Government and its agencies since the 1930 Act, and on the longer distance buses the number of passengers grew almost immediately from 8.5 million in 1979 to 15 million in 1980.

A further Transport Act in 1985 brought deregulation to short local bus services for the first time since the 1920s and required that National Express should be sold into the private sector; the company was privatized in a management buyout in1988.

Sea transport

By the 1970s, scheduled services by sea had all but disappeared apart from the few sailings of the *QEII* and *France* across the Atlantic in the summer only. As inbound and outbound leisure traffic to and from Britain grew, the shipping focus remained firmly on the ferry fleets. Linking ports in England with those on the Continent, ferry services developed to provide transport for about half the market to and from mainland Europe, especially for those travelling with their own cars.

By 1973, there were some 40 short sea routes, mostly serviced by pur-pose-built vessels. At that time the principal operators were British Rail in a consortium with Belgian and French railway companies and a private oper-ator, Townsend Ferries that later became Townsend Thoresen through a merger in 1968. Led by Captain Townsend (see Chapter 6), Townsend Thoresen was a pioneer in cross-channel ferry developments with the design and quality of its roll-on/roll-off vessels and its associated market-ing. Its success was, perhaps, partly influential in the decision to sell off Sealink (British Rail Ferries) to the private sector in 1984. The firm and its brand name was to become forever tarnished, however, with the disaster that overtook the *Herald of Free Enterprise* when 193 people died as the ship capsized outside Zeebrugge Harbour in 1987. Townsend Thoresen was later taken over by P&O and the brand name disappeared.

Cross-channel traffic, supported by the building of the M2 motorway, led to Dover becoming Britain's largest passenger port, handling nearly three-quarters of all inbound and outbound passengers by sea.

Air transport

Apart from the continuing growth of car ownership, the principal tourism stories were in air transport. Britain's national airlines (then BOAC and BEA) played a leading role in developing inbound tourism, which grew rapidly in this period from less than 6 million visits in 1969 to over 17 million visits in 1989. Working closely with the British Tourist Authority, each airline invested millions in marketing campaigns and especially in advertising overseas. The main theme was 'Visit Britain' and the US campaign for some years featured the actor Robert Morley, well known for his role as the perfect English butler. Morley made such an impact that many Americans at the time thought he was the British Ambassador! In 1970 BEA introduced Windsor Tours to Britain, a tour programme later developed by British Airways, which became the largest inbound package tour programme covering all the major overseas markets for Britain.

Also in 1970, to develop its share of the UK to abroad holiday market, BEA created its own charter airline. Under the brand name BEA Airtours the airline was able to compete effectively with the fast growing tour operators who had already developed themselves into major players in the air charter holiday market. At the same time as setting up BEA Airtours, the airline also established a very successful group of package tour companies including Sovereign, Enterprise and Martin Rook Holidays that came to rank second at the time to Thomson Holidays.

The 1971 Civil Aviation Act was passed in recognition of the need to regulate competition rather more effectively than under the former ATLB. It created a holding board for BOAC and BEA and established a second force airline brought about by unifying various independents. As a result, British Caledonian was established, taking over what was then British United Airways. In 1972, BOAC and BEA were combined under the newly formed British Airways Board with the separate airlines coming together as British Airways in 1973.

The airlines owned by the tour operators were the third element in air transport competition. The 1971 Act replaced the former Air Transport Licensing Board with a new body entitled The Civil Aviation Authority that was given authority to license the number of tours to be sold each year by tour operators, thus regulating tour operators on a systematic annual basis for the first time. This Act set the scene for the further rapid growth of the non-scheduled airlines and the long running challenge to liberalize the rules governing the provision of air services that would continue into the 1990s.

By 1971, continued air traffic growth brought urgency to the issue of a third London airport and a decision was announced by the then Conservative Government to develop Maplin Sands off the Essex coast, just north of the Thames estuary. The decision was overturned in 1974 by an incoming Labour Government on the grounds of cost and Stansted became in effect the third airport designate while a new terminal (Terminal 4) opened at Heathrow in 1986. Since 1984 there were investigations into the possibility of a fifth terminal at Heathrow and the argument would drag on for nearly 20 years as the various parties argued the merits and demerits in the context of growing resident opposition on environmental grounds.

In 1976, the first Concorde commercial flights were inaugurated across the Atlantic between USA and France and the UK. The plane immediately became an icon of design and excellence and an aspirational form of travel for those who could afford it that would continue for nearly 30 years. It was an ideal branding and marketing tool for British Airways. But a combination of powerful environmental interests concerning noise pollution combined with the major hike in fuel prices in the 1973 OPEC crisis – just as the new plane was seeking buyers – meant the plane would never begin to repay its initial investment. With 100 seats, compared with over 350 in jumbo jets, price competition could never be an issue. Less than 20 Concordes were finally built and were only operated by British Airways and Air France, the scheduled airlines of the original investor countries.

Of far more significance for the future of air travel, in 1977 President Jimmy Carter appointed the noted free-market economist Alfred Kahn to be Chairman of the American Civil Aeronautics Bureau (CAB). His concern was to tackle the regulatory restrictions then affecting the growth of air travel, especially the effective control of fares by existing scheduled carriers and the prevention of new entrants to the domestic market from flying beyond individual state boundaries. Because of the size of the country and its lead in development, the US domestic airline market was the largest in the world and influential internationally. In 1978 a revolutionary Airline Deregulation Act was passed and almost immediately followed by the second OPEC oil price crisis that plunged airlines into crisis and led to price battles as capacity exceeded demand both domestically and internationally. Deregulation also had its downside. Long-established airlines with globally recognized brands such as Pan Am, TWA and Eastern collapsed as more carriers were enabled to compete with them by cherry-picking the profitable routes and operating with lower costs.

Domestically the Act made possible the remarkable growth of Southwest Airlines. Originally formed in 1971 within the State of Texas, Southwest produced a winning low cost, friendly staff and 'fun' formula, and carried its millionth passenger in 1974. The 5 million passenger total was reached in 1977 and by 1979 the airline was using self-ticketing machines and could now expand outside Texas. In 1990 it had achieved the 'magic' billion-dollar revenue turnover with a string of awards for its customer service and by 2003 the airline was flying over 60 million passengers to 58 US cities. The airline became an international model for other low cost airlines to follow and Ryanair and Easyjet would follow the same basic pioneering business model in the 1990s as soon as European deregulation made it possible (see Chapter 6).

In 1977, after trying to obtain a licence for five years and with a successful court case behind him, Freddie Laker scented the likely direction of deregulation in the USA and achieved permission to launch his London–New York Skytrain across the Atlantic. Laker already had an established record of success in tour operating and charter flying out of the UK. He had been managing director of British United Airways and formed Laker Airways in 1966. He was a strong, determined entrepreneur and set out deliberately to take on 'the system'. He was also something of a maverick with a flair for publicity. Permission for Skytrain was achieved because the fares were intended to be quite different and, therefore, create a new market, not competing directly with scheduled airline fares to dilute their established revenue. Skytrain tickets were initially 'walk-on' fares available on the day of sale only, with no prior booking. It also meant there were no costly reservation systems and associated agency commissions and Laker provided only limited back-up of planes in the event of problems. The immediate popularity of the low fare offer was never in doubt and it led to queues of some 2000 people at Victoria station with travellers waiting for up to five days to get a flight. The original concept did not last long, however, and having secured the licence, Laker clashed with the scheduled airlines by introducing bookable seats at higher fares. Laker's operation was extended to Miami and Los Angeles but it was hit by over-borrowing, high interest rates and the effects of the 1979–1980 recession – and he would argue 'dirty tricks' by other airways to whom he represented a serious threat on the routes. As a result Laker went bankrupt in 1982 although by then he was already the fifth largest carrier across the Atlantic. BA and other USA carriers retaliated against Laker by introducing standby and Advanced Purchase fares that effectively eliminated most of the fare differentials on which the Laker service was based (see Chapter 6). The fare wars and the media publicity they received further stimulated demand across the North Atlantic.

The US Act of 1978, although it did not extend internationally, nevertheless had a powerful influence and served to open the way to greater competition across the Atlantic, especially the legitimization of new lower fare options. It also influenced revisions to the original Bermuda Agreement. Some would argue that by forcing the pace of regulatory change, Laker pioneered the route for subsequent airlines such as Virgin Atlantic and helped to usher in a more liberal approach to fares and greater competition across the Atlantic. IATA had become a much-maligned organization during the 1960s and 1970s and it was accused of operating as an anti-consumerist cartel, keeping fares higher than they needed to be in the interests of the profit to scheduled carriers. IATA airlines were forced to set up a task force in 1977–1978 to debate the issues and there seems to be little doubt that Laker's Skytrain initiative at this key time was influential.

In 1979 the decision to privatize British Airways was made and a new Civil Aviation Act of 1980 was passed to make it possible. Privatization took place in 1987. Over one million applications for shares were made, making the flotation eleven times oversubscribed.

Among the package tour operators the major event was the 'seismic' collapse of Clarksons in August 1974. Clarksons had purchased a fleet of wide-bodied Lockheed Tristars, too big for viable winter operations at the prices being charged, and became overstretched financially after the OPEC induced energy crisis and demand fall-off following the Yom Kippur war of October 1973. Arab/Israeli conflict was a major international political influence on tourism more than a quarter of a century ago when tanks, armoured vehicles and infantry were deployed around Heathrow Airport in

January 1974. Paradoxically, the collapse of Clarksons created an opportunity for another entrepreneur, Harry Goodman, whose Intasun brand was built on the ashes of Clarksons' failure. In due course, however, Goodman would follow the same trajectory as Clarksons and his company found itself overstretched financially and collapsed in 1991 when demand fell following the major international economic crisis and events following the first Gulf war against Iraq. History, as so often in tourism, repeating itself once again.

1989 to 1995

Bus and rail

In 1989 the first Channel Tunnel breakthrough was made to link Britain and France and the official opening took place in 1994 when the first trains began running commercially, carrying Le Shuttle and Eurostar trains. It had taken 10 years since the British and French Governments had agreed in 1984 to invite private developers (on the understanding there was to be no government funding) to provide proposals for the crossing. The tunnel type and route was chosen and work had begun in 1986. In common with so many other major transport undertakings the tunnel was soon in severe and recurrent financial difficulties as capital costs rose and projected revenues failed to meet rising operating costs. Although the route has become well established for freight and provides an attractive alternative in the South East to air travel for the near Continental routes, the future financial viability of Eurotunnel remained uncertain at the time of writing in 2004.

In 1991, reflecting the Thatcher Government era of deregulation of state controlled enterprises, National Express Holdings was bought by a consortium of city investment companies and became the National Express Group Ltd. This new company was floated on the stock exchange in 1992 and a refurbished Victoria Coach Station was opened in London. By 1995 all coach and bus companies in Britain had been privatized, completing the reversal of the transport nationalization era of the 1940s.

The 1993 Railways Act was passed to provide for denationalization of the railways, which was achieved in 1997 amid huge controversy, just before the Conservative Government of John Major fell to New Labour. In a nice comparison with the 1948 nationalization of buses along with railways, Stagecoach, which had prospered in bus services since the deregulation of 1980, became the first operator of a major railway company – South West Railways.

Cars

Car ownership reached just over 20 million in 1992 and by now the trend of multiple car ownership per household was well established. Combined with the growth in average personal disposable income that would accelerate in the 1990s after the recession of 1990–1993 was over, the rise in car ownership and usage underlies the rise in day visits, short breaks, self-catering, recreational and leisure activities of all kinds, and the frequent practice of visiting friends and relatives. The growth in car ownership has inevitably brought about what many condemn as a form of 'hyper-mobility' and massive, routine congestion was now occurring in and around cities, and on much of the motorway system for most of the year. Many rural areas also experienced routine congestion, especially at summer weekends, bank holidays and school half-terms. By 2000, living with traffic congestion had become a normal part of life for most people in Britain and future projections offer grim reading. Although congestion charges would not be introduced in London for several more years, the future implications of such charging and for motorway tolls were already clear. The effects of congestion in depressing the demand for domestic holiday and leisure travel is not measurable at the present time but it seems certain to be an important factor for the future.

Between 1960 and 1992, car ferries increased their vehicle traffic volume from 5.7 million cars to 20.1 million in the latter year. Some of this was the growing trade in short shopping visits to purchase low duty cigarettes and alcohol (booze cruises), but much of it reflected holiday movement by the British abroad.

Figure 5.2 London congestion. (Courtesy of ITN stills). This figure is reproduced in colour in the colour plate section.

Campaigners espousing environmental causes exercised their muscles in two key battles against road bypasses for Winchester and Newbury. They lost, but only after gaining immense media publicity and not a little sympathy from those who stood not to lose by the traffic congestion arising in the affected town centres. Britain created an unlikely media hero called *Swampy* whose exploits encouraged housewives and pensioners to protest and some to chain themselves to trees and to contractors' lorries. The political awareness and fallout of such protests was considerable and has certainly influenced subsequent road development proposals.

In the air

The deregulation arguments and processes launched in the USA in the late 1970s were echoed in Europe in the 1980s as the European Union developed a ten-year, three-phase programme in 1987 to dismantle the traditional bilateral agreements approach that had existed since the 1940s. The programme was designed to favour a multilateral approach to the liberalization of air transport regulation within the Single Market that had been formally adopted in 1993. By the late 1990s, any airline with an Air Operating Certificate in the European Union could not be prevented from operating on any route within the EU, including flights wholly within another country. This was a revolutionary change to the conditions that applied in the early 1980s. It provided massive opportunities for new budget entrants to the industry as noted below and in Chapter 6.

In tourism terms, the 1990s were perhaps best characterized in the air by the seemingly unstoppable success of no frills budget airlines. They were modelled in many ways on America's Southwest Airlines and not a little influenced by the successes as well as the failures of Freddie Laker and his premature Skytrain in the 1970s, and the greater success of Richard Branson and Virgin Atlantic. In the UK and in other European countries too, Ryanair and Easyjet were the leading contenders in the budget field, stimulating parallel developments across Europe as the deregulation era gathered pace after 1997.

Ryanair started flights in 1985 with a 15-seater turbo prop airplane on the route from Waterford in Ireland to Gatwick, and within a year had overturned the established Aer Lingus/British Airways control over fare prices. By 1995, Ryanair was the biggest carrier on the London–Dublin route, with some 2.25 million passengers in the year. Once the European Union deregulation of airlines took full effect in 1997, Ryanair Holdings was listed on the Dublin and New York stock exchanges and was poised to develop services across Europe. In 1998 the airline placed an order for 45 new Boeing 737-800 planes and was set for major expansion. In mid-2004 Ryanair was proclaiming its intention to be 'Europe's largest airline in the next 8 years' (Ryanair website, June 2004).

Stelios Haji-Ioannou, who at the time was just 28 years old, founded Easyjet in 1995 to take advantage of the EU's liberalization of airline regulation. First flights were from Luton to Scotland with leased aircraft but expansion into international routes started in 1996, to Amsterdam. An award winning website was launched in 1997 and accepted its first bookings over the Internet in 1998. By 2000, Internet bookings exceeded 2 million and by June 2000 Easyjet carried its ten millionth passenger and was listed on the London Stock Exchange. Stelios entered the Guinness Book of Records as the youngest chairman of an international scheduled airline. Both airlines have cut traditional costs by targeting only profitable routes, using direct marketing and booking procedures available via the Internet, stripping out in flight services and using relatively lower cost secondary airports where capacity is readily available.

Between them, the budget airlines have broken through British customers' perception of airfare pricing. For many people, the train fare to the airport and certainly the car parking charges often cost more than the flight. They have powerfully influenced the growth patterns of tourism and greatly facilitated the use of second homes, frequent business and leisure travel and a massive growth in short break travel around the year. Smaller airports have been vying for their favour and been willing to offer subsidies to attract them.

As a counter balance to growth, however, since the late 1980s airports and airlines have increasingly become logical, relatively easy targets for international terrorists of all persuasions. There are dangers from guerrilla activists hijacking aircraft, bombs placed in airports or aircraft for political reasons or the more recent ever-present menace of suicide bombers. Such

Figure 5.3 Easyjet plane taking off. (©Easyjet Airline Company Limited). This figure is reproduced in colour in the colour plate section.

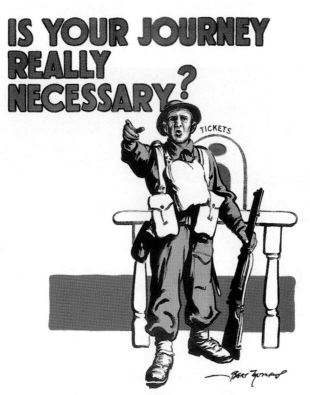

RAILWAY EXECUTIVE COMMITTEE

Plate 1 Is your journey really necessary?

Plate 2 London congestion. (Courtesy of ITN stills).

Plate 3 Easyjet plane taking off. (©Easyjet Airline Company Limited).

Plate 4 Air congestion. (Courtesy of Digital Vision CDs).

dangers, heightened obviously by the traumatic events of Lockerbie in 1994 (Pan Am flight from Heathrow to USA) and of September 11th 2001, have altered, perhaps for our lifetimes, the traditional easy passage of people and luggage through airports around the world. There is a new climate of security at airports and the range of measures including extra policing, luggage screening, personal searches and sky marshals are increasing the costs of airport charges.

Paradoxically, while the real cost of travel by air was coming down as the budget airlines launched their competition, the era of relatively easy going international travel was effectively coming to an end. The majority of short-haul passengers are likely to spend longer in the airport than they will in the air – and many will spend more money on car parking than they will on fares. It remains to be seen how great a disincentive the sheer hassles of air travel will turn out to be in controlling the growth of tourism.

Summary

The post-war story of transport developments in Britain reveals:

- Step changes in affordable and convenient access, often driven through against opposition by new, entrepreneurial business models that broke the traditional mould of travel patterns. Collectively these changes have

Figure 5.4 Air congestion. (Courtesy of Digital Vision CDs). This figure is reproduced in colour in the colour plate section.

driven down the real costs of travel and done most to make tourism a year round option.

- Whatever successes British Governments claim for their transport policies, their record when in direct ownership and control of transport operations appears almost uniformly weak. The business of transport does not appear to sit easily within Whitehall corridors.
- For international travel, political commitment to market deregulation has freed the development of effective competition, firstly by charter operations and since the 1990s (in Europe) by budget airlines.
- Low cost airfares have changed the patterns of international travel and challenged the UK domestic market on its prime territory of short breaks.
- Growing car congestion and the effects of future traffic congestion charges are ominous for the future growth of UK domestic tourism, for the bulk of which the use of public transport is no longer a serious option.
- Although government regulation of routes, capacity and fares has been largely dismantled since the late 1970s, other forms of regulation, especially for environmental and passenger security reasons are likely to become more important in the near future. In the list in the first part of this chapter, economic/market regulation was only part of the 12 main reasons for intervention. Most of the others will assume greater significance in the next decade and provide convincing grounds for political intervention. Transport regulation is not dead. Although the rationale has changed over the last fifty years, the process is clearly alive and kicking.

CHAPTER 6

Marketing developments and trends – entrepreneurs and changing business models in British tourism

Industries don't 'evolve'. Instead, firms eager to overturn the present industry order challenge 'accepted practice', redraw segment boundaries, set new price-performance expectations and re-invent the product or service concept.

(Hamel and Prahalad, 1994, p. 303)

Reflecting the scale of the opportunities created by massive growth in demand, travel and tourism have been fortunate in the number of individuals, and some companies, that have challenged accepted practice, reinvented product concepts and in many ways helped to create and revitalize demand over the last half-century. This chapter provides brief notes on ten individuals and companies whose initiative, energy and clear vision has driven the tourism industry forward – in each case by overturning whatever was 'accepted practice'. All have created a new (or new to the UK) business model that stimulated a significant market/product shift, altered the industry norms and has stood the test of time over at least a decade. The list is offered in alphabetical order to avoid any inference that one or other of these individuals is more important than the others.

This list is, inevitably, illustrative only but it is indicative of the energy, vitality, opportunism and risk-taking flair that has characterized the private sector in the half-century following World War II. In different ways, each of the ten broke the 'rules' surrounding the existing provision of products in their chosen sectors and created new ways of doing business as well as building profitable enterprises in the process. In most cases, others have followed in the wake of evident success. All of these individuals have dealt over the years with millions of customers.

Although it was not a criterion for selection, it is of interest that nearly all of these entrepreneurs developed their business, at least initially, by direct communication with customers, not via travel intermediaries. Direct marketing initially provided major advantages in customer knowledge and response and lower costs, especially if there was a loyal customer base to draw on. Such advantages were further facilitated by the Internet marketing revolution since the mid-1990s that made possible distribution cost reductions beyond even the entrepreneurs' visions.

Where sources are specific, they are quoted. Other sources are trade and general press cuttings kept over a number of years by Victor Middleton, as part of teaching materials used on tourism courses, and original draft material for this book prepared by W.S. Richards.

Piet Dirksen – Center Parcs

Not invented in Britain, Center Parcs was the brainchild of a Dutch Entrepreneur Piet Dirksen who founded a chain of retail outlets for sportswear and equipment under the name Sporthuis Centrum in 1953. The company became the largest retailer of its kind in the Netherlands and, for example, it expanded into production of equipment including a tent factory estimated to sell some 40 per cent of its production through the Sporthuis Centrum chain. It also owned a travel agent and a tour operator business in its own name. The story has it that, in true entrepreneurial style, Dirksen opened the first clay courts for tennis in Holland, raising money for the project by issuing shares to friends and relatives. The company is of interest in this chapter because it radically changed the year round business possibilities in the British domestic market with its innovative concept of self-catering short break products based within enclosed and managed resorts. These were at the opposite end of the product (and profit) spectrum from the offer by traditional British seaside resorts and holiday centres in the 1980s.

Dirksen expanded his retail business into vacation villages in Holland in 1968, creating a concept of 'villas in the forest' with close access to nature. In 1978, the 17 Sporthuis retail outlets were sold to focus on the village developments and shares in the company were massively oversubscribed when it floated under the new name Center Parcs on the Dutch Stock Exchange in 1985. The company was sold to Scottish and Newcastle Breweries in 1989 when Dirksen retired at the age of 75. Interestingly, Dirksen became as concerned with philanthropy as he was with profitable business and from 1983 he gifted the profits from Center Parcs while he controlled it to a Trust called the Living Waters Foundation. The Foundation was to support deprived people in the developing countries. By 1990 there were 15 Center Parcs with a total capacity of around 10 million nights in the Netherlands, Belgium, France and Germany as well as the UK.

Center Parcs were built to a formula that had been honed in the Netherlands for over 15 years. The concept needed sites of around 400 acres, selected for their rural location within a two-hour drive time of at least 8 million people. The first such site to open in England in 1987 was in Sherwood Forest in a conifer plantation bought from the Forestry Commission. It was not scrubland but nor was it located in an area of obvious scenic value or environmental interest. The environmental benefits, which have become central to the marketing of Center Parcs, were designed by an initial Environmental Impact Assessment followed by careful and dedicated landscaping and ecological management. The improvements in Sherwood Forest included an artificial 12-acre lake and construction of some 3 miles of streams and small waterfalls running through the site to add natural diversity, interesting outlooks and to attract wildlife. Further Center Parcs were opened in Elvedon Forest, Norfolk and at Longleat in Somerset. Oasis Whinfell Forest in Cumbria was added to the group in 2001.

The formula within the forest location required the construction of a large central dome, which contained what is marketed as 'a subtropical swimming paradise' with a maintained 28–29°C temperature, regardless of the outside weather. The dome complex was extended to embrace a fully covered village plaza incorporating shops, restaurants, cafes and a wide range of retail outlets, all within a controlled temperature. The subtropical area was no mere swimming pool, however, it included 'wild water rapids' and water slides as well as solariums, jacuzzis, saunas, Turkish baths and a wide range of massage and other health and beauty treatments. The dome incorporated natural materials, plants and trees and provided a focal basis for the whole village. This was a quantum leap in conceptualization from the modern swimming pool areas found at the time in UK holiday centres. Sports halls were located close by and a very wide range of indoor and outdoor sports activities were available including tennis, squash, ten pin bowling, snooker, horse riding, cycling, archery and wind surfing.

Marketed as the 'ultimate short break' and claiming to be the world leader in short break holidays, Center Parcs targeted the family market selling three and four night holidays (Monday to Friday and Friday to Monday) over 365 days a year – 'all year round, whatever the weather'. The business formula was based on some 600–800 villas, accommodating around 300 000 visitors per annum at over 95 per cent occupancy around the year. The financial economics are based on the expenditure generated by some one million bed-nights a year on each site. As direct marketing based on call centres was the chosen marketing formula in the 1980s and 1990s, the business was ideally placed to take advantage of the Internet as soon as it became commercially available from the mid-1990s onwards.

Reflecting the interests of its founder, Center Parcs was a leader among UK tourism companies in exercising care for its environment. The special quality of the environment, reflected in product design and site and operational management, has become a major selling point of the brand. As long ago as 1992, the company in Britain produced its first Environmental Policy Statement, formalizing existing good practice and stating unequivocally that 'caring for nature and the landscape is a key objective of our business'. One hesitates to use the word 'unique' but at that time, and still in 2004, that level of clear and far-sighted commitment was unusual.

In summary, Center Parcs:

- Broke the UK mould of product expectations and quality standards of holiday centres in the domestic short break holiday market in the UK.
- Effectively overturned the seasonality and economic viability expectations that still operated in the domestic leisure market in the 1980s by achieving year round business at 90 per cent occupancy levels from its first year of operation.
- Created and maintained high environmental standards within a wholly managed enclosed site providing security for adults as well as children.
- Prized the British from the umbilical cord of their cars by restricting the use of vehicles on site to arrival and departure and providing bicycles for hire.
- Used direct marketing to best effect with repeat customers and an extensive database that were ideally suited to the Internet developments of the 1990s.

Source: Clive Gordon (various reports in 1990 and 1991); Lavery, P. (1990); company website; and information and promotional material and press cuttings held by the author.

Charles Forte (Lord Forte)

Charles Forte's family came from the village of Montforte between Rome and Naples, where he was born in 1908. He was moved to Scotland in 1913 where his father, who had previously worked in the USA had settled with other members of the family. By that time the enterprising Forte family were already running retail businesses and cafes, including a Savoy Café in Alloa. His father was importing soda fountains from the USA and coffee machines from Italy – bringing revolution to the product standards of snack bar and café catering in Scotland before the First World War.

Although still an Italian national, Forte was brought up and educated initially in Scotland but later in Italy in what was now a 'well to do' family that had already expanded its business into England. He was determined to make a success in business and joined his father's business at the age of 17. Significantly, perhaps, he first undertook a crash course in bookkeeping and accountancy and learned the principles of drawing up a balance sheet and keeping financial records. His first job was in a 'spacious and elegant' café in Weston-super-Mare called the 'Ice Cream Parlour' owned by his uncle, where he worked up to 18 hours a day.

Within two years Forte had joined his father in the café businesses, first in Bournemouth and then in Brighton. He was ambitious to make his own way and formed his first catering services company as Forte and Company in 1935 at the age of 27. He opened his first Meadow Milk Bar, a large and impressive operation designed to his specifications in Upper Regent Street in London and quickly added four others in the West End, including the Leicester Square business, before the war. When Italy declared war in 1940 he was arrested and interned for a while in the Isle of Man but he was soon released and returned to London to operate his milk bar/cafe businesses in wartime conditions. After the war Forte expanded rapidly again, purchasing the Rainbow Corner and Criterion at Piccadilly Circus and in 1954 the famous Café Royal. In 1951, such was his reputation that Forte was appointed as one of two official caterers to the Festival of Britain, his first venture into mass catering. Later in the 1950s, when the motorway era was just beginning in the UK, Forte won the contract to operate the first motorway service station. Later he developed the Little Chef chain across Britain's main roads in the 1980s whose sites would in due course provide an ideal location for many of the Travelodge units that were another Forte initiative.

Maxwell Joseph, a rival in the post-war years to the 1970s, had bought his first hotel in 1947 and added others in the 1950s that would become the Grand Metropolitan chain. Forte did not enter the hotel business until 1958 with the purchase of the Waldorf and his company went public in 1962. By 1970 Forte was operating 43 hotels in addition to the catering operations and took the decision to merge with the Trust Houses group of hotels and its partnership with Travelodge, a US motel chain with international links. Trust Houses had had a total of 222 hotels in 1938 but many were requisitioned in the war and were never to open again. The group had, however, modernized itself in the 1950s and 1960s and the merger would make the new company the largest hotel and catering company in Britain. But the merger, which included a joint Board of which Forte would initially be Deputy Chairman, immediately exposed strong cultural differences between the management styles of the two very different companies. In Forte's view the differences amounted to an 'unbridgeable gulf'. The merger was, therefore, immediately followed by an acrimonious board battle for control of the new company that at one stage involved a take-over bid from Allied Breweries in 1971. The bid was defeated and the battle for company control finally won by Forte in 1972. Trust Houses Forte added the distressed Lyons Hotels, a victim of the 1973 economic downturn, to its empire in 1975.

Inter alia, encouraged by Len Lickorish of the British Travel Association, Charles Forte was one of the leading founders of the London Tourist Board in 1963 with the support of the then London County Council. He was Chairman of that Board until 1965.

In 1996, four years after Lord Forte's retirement as Chairman in 1992 and with his son Rocco Forte as the new Chairman, Granada won control of the company then named Forte in a contested take-over bid of £3.9 billion.

Lord Forte's career clearly illustrates what can be achieved by:

- Powerful determination to succeed and introduce innovative ideas, taking risks with capital as his judgement indicated.
- Clear insight into emerging customer needs.
- Entrepreneurial approach and clear flair for growing the business via acquisitions and new developments.
- Total commitment to the business and careful choice of trusted senior colleagues.
- Aggressive cost and quality control of the businesses.

Source: Forte, C. (1996) and W.S. Richards' original draft and press clippings.

Sydney de Haan – SAGA Group

Born 1919, died in 2002, Sydney de Haan was the man who was said to have 'turned silver hair into gold' – unleashing the grey pound. Sydney was an Eastender, one of 11 children born to a working class family who left school at 14 and went to work as a trainee chef at the Waldorf Hotel. He joined the army in 1939 but was captured at Dunkirk and held as a prisoner of war. After the war he bought a 12-bedroomed hotel, *The Rhodesia* in Folkestone.

As the close of the then 'normal' short summer season in 1949 approached, the De Haans were sitting on a park bench when his wife noted they were surrounded by pensioners. Sensing an opportunity, De Haan decided to put together inclusive low priced out of season holidays targeted at the retired population and based on coach travel and three meals a day. Travel agents he contacted were not interested so De Haan targeted Yorkshire and County Durham and travelled around the area contacting clubs and knocking on doors. He set up his own tour operation using chartered coaches. It was an immediate marketing success; a second hotel was bought and others soon followed on a contracted basis. Saga, as the company was named, initially targeted the over-60s but soon became identified with the over-50s.

All the core basics of charter operations for accommodation and transport were in the Saga business model from the start. More importantly this was a direct marketing operation under the company's sole control. With hindsight one can see that De Haan had precisely targeted the growing market of better-off older people with the time and inclination to engage in leisure travel that others would not follow successfully for decades to come. As the business grew, De Haan could not continue to contact customers directly so the *Saga Magazine* was launched in 1966 using the database he had built up – many years before most competitors followed the same example. Trains were soon being chartered from the North to the South Coast and Saga developed into selling student accommodation during the vacation periods and then into abroad holidays, commencing with Romania and Yugoslavia as good targets. Saga later acquired Golden Rail Holidays from British Rail when it disposed of its hotel and rail transport package tour operations.

Saga was floated on the stock market in 1978 in one of the most oversubscribed issues of the year but later bought back by the family. Valued at over £1.2 billion in November 2003, the process for selling the company was in progress as this book went to press. In 2000, the company employed some 2500 people. By that time, the business had diversified and expanded within its well-established target market to include publishing, radio, financial and insurance services, and share dealing, as well as holidays and cruises. Some 80 per cent of the turnover then came from non-holiday sales. By 2002, the *Saga Magazine* was the second largest subscription magazine after *Reader's Digest*, with a circulation of more than 1.2 million, many of them repeat customers, and a monthly readership of 2.5 million. By this time, the total database was said to be some 8 million.

Sydney de Haan's career, apart from his obvious market foresight into the potential spending of the affluent over-50s, illustrates:

- Entrepreneurial initiative and drive in identifying cost effective ways to reach customers directly that were well ahead of his time.
- The potential of direct marketing of holidays rather than distribution through travel agents, providing effective communication with customers as well as significant savings on distribution costs.
- The subsequent development of additional forms of complementary services for the same target base of customers using the commercially highly valuable opportunity provided by the database.
- Effective use of chartering transport and accommodation to achieve lowest possible prices through purchasing in bulk (economies of scale).
- A major marketing contribution to seasonality for operators, increasing the financial viability of operations and securing lower prices for customers.

Source: Facts based on *The Times* 27.11.03; obituary of 2002; and author's press cuttings.

Hoseasons Holidays

Wally Hoseason, born 1888, died 1950, and James Hoseason

Wally Hoseason, originally a Shetland Islander, had been Harbour Master at Oulton Broad in Norfolk before he retired after the war in 1945. He witnessed at first-hand the growing interest in boating in the 1920s and 1930s and the interest in the Broads as a location for safe leisure boating in a pristine environment. As harbour master he would have encountered many such visitors at first-hand over the years and was, of course, on familiar terms with all the yards that supplied the hire boats.

He created Hoseasons Holidays in 1946, which in its first year booked about 200 people for holidays on the Broads based on hired boats. The business clearly attracted customers and prospered from these small beginnings. When Wally died in 1950 his son James (Jim) gave up his career as a civil engineer to run the business.

Jim developed the business from its Lowestoft base by adding holiday bungalows and cottages to the boat business, initially in East Anglia. By the 1950s, although the company did not provide transport to the destination within its product offers, Hoseasons was nevertheless acting as an entrepreneurial commercially managed tour operator in the domestic market. The company took on and developed the approaches to holiday taking in the UK that had been pioneered in the 1920s and 1930s by the dedicated not-for-profit specialist providers such as Holiday Fellowship, Workers Travel Association and the Co-operative Holidays Association.

In the late 1960s, the purpose and style of the business was reviewed, broadened and repositioned to shift beyond its East Anglia base. The company developed into booking boating holidays on all the waterways in Britain, added caravans to its established holiday home sector and extended the business to include Wales, Northumberland, Lincolnshire and eventually the whole of Britain. Ten years on and the business had expanded to offering boat hire and holiday homes in France and Ireland. Hoseasons' primary focus at that time and now was as a holiday organizer and the company did not expand into ownership of boats or holiday homes.

By 2000 the company was one of the largest domestic holiday operators in the UK, offering some 12 000 places to stay, arranging holidays for over one million people a year and bringing over 100 000 overseas visitors into Britain. Over the years the company has won over 50 awards and distinctions for the quality of its product offer and the manner in which it runs its services and trains its staff. For example, Hoseasons won the Best Holidays Afloat Company Award (12 times), Best Operator UK holidays, and Best domestic holiday company as well as awards for staff care and training.

Still based in Lowestoft, the company claims to be 'the UK's leading self-catering holiday specialist' and it is the largest private sector employer in the town. Under Jim's lead as Chairman, the company was an early adopter of information technology. The company bought its first computers in the 1960s and its database included around 4 million names and addresses by the turn of the century. Although Hoseasons worked with travel agencies in the 1970s and 1980s and sought their support, retailers were never a major source of distribution and Hoseasons, like Saga, was and is primarily a direct marketing operation with a large customer database.

Hoseasons pioneered telesales for holidays, dial-a-brochure services to facilitate customer service, colour advertising in national newspapers, and TV commercials for UK holidays. Because of its structure and operating ethos, the company was one of the pioneers in the UK holiday market to perceive and exploit the distribution power and holiday booking opportunities available through the Internet in 1995 and 1996.

When he retired as Chairman in 2000, finally severing the original family link, ownership of the company was transferred to fellow directors in a management buyout. Jim was awarded the OBE for his services to tourism in 1990.

James Hoseason's career, picking up the baton from his father's initiative after the war, demonstrates:

- Entrepreneurial flair to sense and develop a market with great growth potential.
- Willingness to diversify the product base in order to expand the business nationally and later internationally.
- Skilful marketing targeted mostly directly at clearly identified customers.
- Careful management of product quality.
- Commitment to introducing and using new technology in pursuit of business objectives.

Source: Press cuttings and information kindly supplied to the author by James Hoseason OBE.

Sir Freddie Laker

Laker (1922–2006) was a buccaneering entrepreneur in the classic mould. He was a member of the Air Transport Auxiliary Team during World War II from 1941 to 1946, giving him early knowledge of the aviation industry. It is reputed that Freddie originally went into business with a loan of £600 from his mother, foreseeing the vital role that civil aviation would play at the end of the war. Purchasing war surplus aircraft and spare parts he was well placed to take advantage of the sudden surge of demand for charter aircraft when the Russians closed all the land routes to Berlin in 1948. The governments of the USA, Britain and France pledged to maintain a 24-hour freight service to supply the West Berlin garrison and civilian population with all their requirements.

The profits from the Berlin airlift enabled Laker, along with others, to capitalize the purchase of more suitable aircraft for passenger services and, when the tight regulation of air transport was slightly relaxed in 1951, Laker was at the forefront in cross-channel route operations. Interestingly, his service was known as the Channel Air Bridge. It carried cars and passengers and it preceded the subsequent major development of roll-on/roll-off sea ferry routes.

In the early 1960s, Laker was Managing Director of British United Airways, one of the earliest and most important of the independent airlines operating in the mid-1960s as government transport regulation was eased to favour independents. Impatient to operate his own business again, he went on to form his own airline – Laker Airways, in 1966.

A pioneer of the idea of budget air transport for scheduled services, Laker made his first application for permission to operate his no frills 'Skytrain' service between London and New York in 1973. His proposed fare at the time was about a third of the price of the established competitors on the route and he clearly had support within Government for his concept. After four years of wrangling and opposition from US carriers as well as British Airways, and certainly influenced by the US debate on deregulation and its likely outcome, Skytrain was eventually licensed and operated from Gatwick in 1977 using DC 10 aircraft that Laker had acquired at bargain prices.

Skytrain finally achieved its licence because it could claim to offer a different type of service rather than act as a direct competitor. Skytrain was planned as a form of walk on shuttle service. There was to be no prior booking and no guarantee of passage on a particular flight. The queues that formed in Victoria quickly achieved massive media publicity that made Laker and his brand a household name. Skytrain was soon allowed to accept bookings and operate a more obvious rival to existing scheduled services – including the introduction of a Regency Class with premium fares – to the obvious consternation of his rivals. His media popularity no doubt helped secure his knighthood in 1978.

Laker rapidly expanded his operations, with two inclusive tour operator companies, Arrowsmith and Laker Air Holidays. He had become the second largest carrier across the Atlantic before he was caught out in a classic travel company failure, overexposed in borrowing as the effects of the 1979–80 oil and international economic crisis hit airlines badly. In 1982 Laker Airways collapsed and acrimonious legal battles followed with the scheduled carriers whom he felt had undermined his operations with their price war tactics and what he called 'dirty tricks'. The established carriers saw it rather differently, of course, and were never likely to allow a major new competitor to take significant market share without some form of commercial retaliation, including standby fares to compete with Laker's prices. Laker returned to airline operations in the 1990s from the Bahamas but never again made the impact of his Skytrain operation. The Wikipedia website describes him as 'a big man who took on big business, burned brightly for a time, and failed gloriously as all heroes inevitably must'.

Freddie Laker's career, apart from his own robust initiatives and restless energy, illustrates:

- What can be achieved by a willingness based on a 'larger than life' determination to take on and overturn the establishment – and not take 'no' for an answer.
- Entrepreneurial flair and foresight – the gambling instinct.
- A no frills, low cost business model approach to air transport, cherry picking routes and adopting operational practices unhampered by traditional overhead costs. It was a model that others would soon develop and exploit and Sir Richard Branson cites Laker as one of his supporters and role models for Virgin Atlantic, which was launched in 1984. Branson named one of his own aircraft 'The Spirit of Sir Freddie'.
- Publicity flair to get the public on his side.

Source: Material based on author's press cuttings over the years and Bray and Raitz (2001).

Sir Fred Pontin

Born 1906, died in 2000, Fred Pontin left school at 15 and worked after leaving school on the London Stock Exchange, which gave him a valuable experience of business and financial operations that was to stand him in good stead in his own businesses. He was already running successful businesses in the 1930s. Medically unfit to enlist in the Second World War, he was still eligible for national service and was sent to run hostels for construction workers which gave him first-hand experience of operating mass catering and accommodation services. At the end of the war he was sent to Bristol in 1945 to run hostels, one of which was for workers rebuilding the Bristol docks.

Identifying the opportunities in post-war holidays, and no doubt influenced by the success achieved by Billy Butlin with his pre-war holiday camp innovations, he bought his first holiday camp in 1946 at Brean Sands, Burnham-on-Sea. The site was a farm that had been used as a holiday camping site before the war. In 1946 it was being used as a transit camp for US forces awaiting repatriation at the end of the war. With an eye for containing costs he paid his Bristol dock workers as labour at weekends to construct the new holiday camp to his plans. Using his financial knowledge and contacts he bought Brean Sands for £23 000, financed by an £11 000 loan and £12 000 from former city associates. He purchased army surplus furniture, crockery and cutlery, etc. for equipping the camp for visitors. Clearly such standards would not be acceptable today but were well judged for the needs and expectations of the post-war market he was aiming to tap into.

Profits were £16 000 in year one, £3.6 million by 1975. Pontins went on to grow to 24 sites in UK and 15 abroad by 1979, catering for around one million people a year when Coral bought Pontins for £56 million. Abroad the sites were a combination of holiday centres and hotels, established in the 1960s and located in Majorca, Greece, Morocco, Sardinia and Tenerife.

Knighted in 1976, Pontin was the first major operator to develop the holiday camp product from full catering (three meals a day) into modern self-catering offers, along with the shift of name from holiday camps to holiday centres.

Fred Pontin's career, apart from his own initiative and energy, illustrates:

- An entrepreneurial ability to identify at an early stage a product concept that would tap effectively into a growing demand and match or beat most of the existing competition.
- The use of effective purchasing controls to achieve the lowest possible prices through purchasing in bulk (economies of scale).
- Efficiencies in operation and financial control of the sites under his control.
- Provision (as with Butlin) of a standard of accommodation, catering and associated facilities at 'all-in' prices that were new to the British market and marked a quantum shift in the quality of the product offer and holiday experience then available from small hotels and guesthouses in seaside resorts.

Source: *Times* Obituary in 2000 and author's press cuttings.

Vladimir Raitz

Vladimir Raitz was 27 in 1949 and working for Reuters when he found his way (by steamer) to Calvi in Corsica for a holiday with friends. He had no background in the travel business. He stayed in a tented (US Army war surplus) village called Club Olympique on the Calvi beach. Although the facilities were primitive, Raitz noted 'everyone seemed to have a wonderful, carefree holiday'. This club would arguably be the midwife for air inclusive charter tours and tour operators that would change the face of British holiday taking for the next fifty years.

In 1949 Club Olympique was more popular with the French and Belgians than the British and its agent for Belgium was one Gerard Blitz. He was equally impressed with the potential of the operation – and the holiday village concept for vacations – and he set up his own company in 1950 with Gilbert Trigano. That company was Club Méditerranée, which went on to become one of the most successful and largest holiday businesses in the world, with some 116 villages in 36 countries. Although suffering downturns in business by the mid-1990s, Club Med was one of the early pioneers of all-inclusive holidays and resort management practice.

Raitz talked with friends during the 1949 holiday and was offered the opportunity to earn commission by attracting British clients to a new camp in Calvi then under discussion. Attracted by the idea, he thought 'what could be simpler? Charter a plane, put a couple of ads in the paper and the public would come rolling in'. He initially thought it could be done as a sideline to his job with Reuters. At that point, however, he had not reckoned with the reality of post-war British air transport regulation and the fact that, under the Civil Aviation Act of 1947 BEA had a state monopoly on European flights, even if they did not actually fly to Corsica. Raitz realized that it was no part-time job he was contemplating and he gave up his paid work to focus on the holiday charter dream – using £3000 left to him by a grandmother to form a company, Horizon Holidays, and finance the launch. It took from October 1949 until March 1950 for the Ministry of Civil Aviation to consider the request for a licence to fly charters to Corsica. The Ministry finally decided they would grant a licence, but imposed a severe restriction that Raitz was only allowed to carry students and teachers. This presumably was one of the origins of what later were known as 'affinity charters' that helped open the North Atlantic route to charter flights in the 1960s and 1970s. Such restrictions were used as a means to avoid direct competition with scheduled services open to the general public. The 'no frills' airline operations across the Atlantic pioneered by Freddie Laker in 1977, and the established carriers pricing tactics in response, would in due course overtake and replace affinity charters.

Raitz was fully committed by then and decided to proceed. He booked 16 charter flights for that summer, using 32-seater DC3 Dakotas to fly from Gatwick to the airfield at Calvi. The first brochure was just four pages long extolling the attractions of Calvi and the good deal on offer. His price for an inclusive week (transport, accommodation, three meals a day and wine) was £32.50. At the time the BEA return fare to Nice alone (as close as they went to Calvi) was £70. The first charter flights with paying passengers departed in May 1950 and marked what was effectively the birth of air inclusive package tours for the British.

Raitz reported that the first year hardly broke even, failing to meet the target of 350 passengers for the whole season. 1951 was better with 450 passengers, but more importantly a new Conservative Government with a programme to ease regulations created an Air Transport Advisory Council with a remit to be more responsive to new ideas in civil aviation. Accordingly, the restriction to teachers and students was lifted and Raitz applied for permission to fly to Palma in Mallorca as well as to Calvi and his request was granted in time for the 1952 season. From that time, although he was soon joined by competitors, his company grew rapidly for twenty years before falling victim to the vicious price war that accompanied the early 1970s oil crisis. His company was taken over by Clarksons in 1974 just before that company's collapse.

Raitz's career illustrates the full range of entrepreneurial action including:

- Rapid recognition of the market potential of a new opportunity, especially the attractiveness of Mediterranean holidays to the British market.

- Determination and risk taking in the face of a negative regulatory regime.
- Understanding the pull that low prices exert on market demand and achieving them through the purchasing power of charter operations and the appeal of inclusive tour pricing.
- Creation of a new tour-operating business model using chartered air transport and contracted bed spaces that would revolutionize British holiday taking over the next four decades.

Source: Bray, R. and Raitz, V. (2001) and the author's press clippings.

Resort Condominiums International – RCI

Timeshare is not a specifically British phenomenon and was not invented here. The concept originated in France in the 1960s but received a massive boost in the USA in the early 1970s before developing internationally, as noted below. By 2000, hundreds of thousands of British customers were timeshare owners; the market is still growing strongly and a number of resorts have been opened across the UK. RCI is included in this chapter because it is a powerful illustration of the influence of the global market-place that now exists for travel and tourism and because it is a business model that has changed the traditional ways of marketing holidays.

The concept of timeshare, also known as vacation or holiday ownership, typically offers purchasers the right to use a specified resort-based apartment or similar lodging for a specified number of days at the same time of year every year for a specified number of years. Annual maintenance fees are payable and ownership rights may be sold. Rights to property convey an agreed number of points – based on the size of the unit, time of year and location – and these points may be exchanged for use in other resorts. The purchaser may never need to visit the specific location/timing actually purchased. The resorts are typically carefully managed, modern, purpose-built self-contained centres in attractive destinations, providing a wide range of vacation facilities within enclosed boundaries.

The impetus for timeshare selling was generated in California and Florida in the USA when the world oil crisis in the early 1970s, and associated economic downturn, left many apartment block developers with properties that had been built but which they could not sell as entities in the depressed market conditions. These apartment blocks in vacation locations were known as condominiums in the USA and the selling of rights to temporary use at specified times – the timeshare model – was a way of achieving cash flow and capital returns to avoid bankruptcy at that difficult time. The concept was immediately attractive to the market and so successful for developers that what started as a short-term solution launched a new business model for holidays that had massive advantages and became a major vacation marketing strategy over the next quarter of a century.

It was quickly recognized that owners of timeshares would like to visit other resorts and exchange their ownership rights in one location for the equivalent right in other places. RCI was founded to facilitate and develop the exchange concept. The company does not develop and own resorts or sell timeshare ownership to customers. It was formed as a marketing agency that creates affiliations with the resorts that sign up to its strategies. It acts in many ways as a tour operator, facilitating the sale and exchange of weeks in selected resorts and arranging flights and other services as required. But it is more than that in the sense that its core business is to organize, market and develop a membership organization or club dedicated to facilitating the interests of its members. The members – timeshare owners – are a locked in 'captive audience' of which just about every relevant marketing detail is held on databases. They are loyal, repeat customers with a built in relationship with their supplier who has the opportunity to market a range of travel products and the means to measure closely how well they meet customers' needs.

Market volume growth for timeshare exchanges averaged over 15 per cent per annum over the 1990s – much faster than any other large volume form of vacation product with the possible exception of parts of the cruise ship market. By 2000, timeshare resorts were located in over 80 countries around the world with more than 4 million households in 175 countries of origin owning timeshare units in over 5000 holiday resorts. Timeshare in the UK was estimated to include some 250 000 households by 2000. RCI has some two thirds of this market and became a subsidiary of the Cendant Corporation in the USA in 1996, one of the world's foremost providers of consumer and business services. Cendant's travel related division is the leading franchiser of hotels and car rental agencies worldwide and, with its Alliance Marketing Division, it provides access to travel and related products to more than 73 million memberships worldwide, across more than twenty consumer service programmes. RCI as part of this corporation has a powerful network of synergy partners on which to draw.

Within Britain, apart from purpose-built timeshare resorts, a number of country house hotels (especially those set within large grounds) have utilized this business model to provide cottage/apartment style accommodation within their grounds. This may be marketed on a timeshare basis and draws on the hub facilities provided by the hotel. More relaxed planning permissions for rural areas have supported this development.

The success of RCI reflects:

- The entrepreneurial ability to turn what was initially a sales disaster into marketing success by changing the existing business model.
- The advantages of 'locked in' loyal customers providing the ideal base for direct marketing and 'relationship marketing'.

- Maintenance fees to ensure constant refurbishment and development of the product.
- Operation of quality assurance agreements with the resorts and monitoring of customer satisfaction to ensure that standards are maintained and developed.
- Low costs of promotion and distribution and near perfect circumstances for exploiting the marketing economies of the Internet. RCI developed its business using sophisticated customer call centres in the 1970s and 1980s but introduced its first website operations in 1998 with full transactional capacity in 2000.
- Achievement of some 90 per cent or more year-round occupancy for facilities.

Source: Middleton, V.T.C. and Clarke, J. (2001) and material supplied to the author by RCI Europe.

Ryanair and Easyjet

Since 1997, following completion of a ten-year deregulation process conducted under the ethos of the European Single Market, any airline holding a valid Air Operators Certificate in the EU cannot be prevented from operating on any route within the EU, including flights wholly within another country. This was a remarkable shift in regulation that made possible the development and expansion of 'no frills' budget airlines in the 1990s that has revolutionized the traditional practices of established scheduled airlines.

Ryanair

Ryanair started business in 1985 under the ebullient leadership of its owner Michael O'Leary, operating a 15-seater turboprop plane on a route from Waterford in Southeast Ireland to London Gatwick. A year later, Ryanair claimed to have 'smashed the Aer Lingus / British Airways high-fare cartel' (www.ryanair.com) on the Dublin–London route. That year Ryanair carried 82 000 passengers and bought two more planes to service the route.

By 1990–1991 Ryanair was succeeding in volume rather than profit terms and was refocused and relaunched as a 'low fares – no frills airline deliberately closely modelled on Southwest Airlines in the USA'. By 1995 it had grown to become the biggest passenger carrier on the Dublin–London route and carried 2.25 million passengers in the year. Ryanair was then well established and clearly well positioned to take advantage of the full effects of the EU deregulation of air transport that came into effect in 1997 and the airline expanded rapidly into mainland Europe. So confident were they of success that they placed a US $2 billion order for 45 new Boeing 737 aircraft in 1998. The airline was listed on Dublin and New York Stock Exchanges in 1997 and on the London Stock Exchange a year later.

Although dedicated to direct distribution to reduce costs, Ryanair were not the first to exploit the Internet and did not launch their booking website until 2000. Within little over a year, however, with full commitment to dedicated development, the Internet bookings accounted for 75 per cent of overall bookings and the airline had established European bases in Brussels Charleroi and Frankfurt-Hann. They were then looking to purchase up to 150 Boeings over an 8-year period to 2010. By 2003 further bases were established in Italy and Sweden. For the year ended March 2003 Ryanair declared passenger traffic up by 42 per cent to reach 15.7 million passengers, with revenues up 35 per cent and profit up by 59 per cent. By August 2003 Ryanair were flying 127 routes to cover 84 destinations in 16 countries and were more than half as big as British Airways with only a fraction of the staff costs. By way of comparison Southwest Airlines had a fleet of 355 aircraft in 2003 and were flying 64 million passengers to 58 US cities.

The Ryanair website claimed (May 2004) that 'Like Superman, we're going UP, UP, UP, and AWAY. Ryanair will be Europe's largest airline in the next 8 years.'

Easyjet

Created by Stelios Haji-Ioannou in 1995, Easyjet came onto the airline scene much later than Ryanair although its opportunistic low fares/no frills business model based on secondary rather than primary airports was very similar. The two airlines were soon competing head to head although they have been able to grow the total market massively with their aggressive low fare offers, as well as by taking share from established carriers. The early Easyjet aircraft carried the telephone number on one side of the fuselage and the website address on the other in the clearest possible statement that this was to be a direct marketing operation. It was not long before the telephone line was deleted.

Easyjet was an early adopter of e-marketing and launched its website in 1997 with first on-line bookings in 1998. By 1999 Internet bookings had exceeded one million and the telephone option was dropped. Easyjet carried its 10 millionth passenger in 2000 and was launched onto the Stock Exchange. Stelios stood down as Chairman in 2002 and is in the Guinness Book of Records as the youngest ever chairman of an international airline. He was just 28 when he founded Easyjet.

The careers of Michael O'Leary and Stelios Haji-Iannou both illustrate how it is still possible for market leading businesses to be developed from nothing to front runners in a short period of time. It is possible if the determination of leadership is strong enough, the service concept attracts the market and the business model delivers profit:

● Through identifying and exploiting new opportunities – in this case created by international airline deregulation decisions.

- By developing a successful low cost/low price business model with a highly successful approach to branding.
- Taking risks with the technology that has paid off.
- Creating or at least massively developing and popularizing a market for low cost travel abroad which had previously not existed for scheduled services.
- Effectively challenging the tour operator air charter business model that dominated outbound tourism from Britain for nearly 50 years from its origins at the start of the 1950s.

Although budget airlines are unequivocally engaged in mass production processes, their customers are willing, and enabled through travel websites, to create their own individual land-based travel packages, including the growing use of second homes. Mass production meets the demand for individual experiences in a neat twenty-first-century response to current consumer trends.

Source: Press cuttings kept by the author and the websites of the two companies in mid-2004.

Captain Stuart Townsend

In 1928 Stuart Townsend foresaw that although in its infancy at the time, car ownership was growing rapidly and that demand for motoring holidays to the Continent would expand and need much improved shipping services to facilitate the growth. At the time, the Southern Railway only operated Cross-Channel services between London and Channel ports in connection with Continental rail services and cars were not identified as an important sector of demand. Townsend decided that the market would provide him with a business opportunity and his first venture was to charter and convert a collier vessel, which could carry 15 cars, loaded by crane, and passengers between Dover and Calais.

In 1936, due to a strike of crane operators at Calais, Townsend's ship was berthed 'stern on' to the quay. As a makeshift arrangement to cope with the problems it was possible for the cars to be off-loaded over the stern. This was strictly a one-off temporary arrangement but it pointed the way ahead to what would become a roll-on/roll-off operation after the war. Other operators were having similar thoughts at the same time and later in 1936 Belgian Marine introduced a rebuilt ship with side doors and facilities for carrying 60 cars and passengers. By October 1936 three Anglo-French train ferries began to cater more effectively for motorists by offering space above the train deck for about 35 cars, which were loaded via a quayside ramp.

After the war, Townsend Ferries designed their own purpose-built link span facility used for stern loading to speed up the process of loading and unloading cars. This was the forerunner of roll-on/roll-off vessels (Ro Ro), although British Railways were the first with purpose-built ships in 1952.

The scene was then set for a new model of ferry operations that would facilitate the major increases in consumer demand for easy access to take cars across the channel for holiday and other purposes.

To exploit the growth market, Townsend Ferries merged with Thoresen Ferries in 1968 and the ensuing Townsend Thoresen Company prospered for nearly 20 years. The principal operators across the channel in the 1960s were in a state-owned consortium of British Rail with Belgian and French railway companies that dominated the market in volume terms. Townsend Thoresen ships offered a more consumer friendly, private sector service approach and product delivery; it provided effective competition on standards of service to the state-owned ferry operations. Later, influenced by what had been achieved, deregulation increasingly opened the way for greater competition on ferry routes.

Many now consider that the earlier roll-on/roll-off ferries were an accident waiting to happen because of the ship design and less than cautious procedures then used for operating the doors. The Townsend Thoreson ship, *Herald of Free Enterprise*, was to focus the issues in the disaster that occurred when the ship sank off Zeebrugge in 1987 with the loss of 193 lives. The ship, lying half submerged on its side at low water before it could be recovered, attracted massive negative national and international media attention. The fallout effectively ended the company's prospects under its own brand and it was taken over and absorbed into P&O.

Captain Townsend's career illustrates:

- The role of technology/innovation in changing the product concept and business model by altering the price and convenience that determines market growth.
- The role of private enterprise challenging dominant state companies.
- How luck and the fortunes of chance can both create and as easily destroy companies.

Source: Research by W.S. Richards for the draft contents of this book.

CHAPTER 7

National organization for tourism in Britain

Government's attitude to tourism in Britain for a large part of the fifty-year period has been one of benign neglect interspersed by a few short periods of substantial intervention usually linked to economic crisis.

L.J. Lickorish, draft chapter for this book, 2001

As noted in Chapter 1, Britain was by no means the first in the field of national tourist organizations, although it had its first officially recognized body in 1929. It has been and still is one of the relatively few countries in Europe in which the government has tended always to play a 'hands off' role using officially recognized or statutory agencies rather than establishing a government department for the purpose. There was a short-lived experiment with a government department in the 1940s but it was clearly not judged to be a success at the time and it lasted only three years. Another indication of the 'hands off' approach over the last fifty years is that, although the BTA was a strong supporter of the International Union of Official Travel Organizations (IUOTO), the UK Government consistently refused to join the successor body, the World Tourism Organization (WTO) when it formally became an inter-governmental body in 1975 and took over from the IUOTO. The UK finally joined the WTO in 2005.

Deciding the proper role of government in tourism is open to debate and it changes over time; there are no easy answers. Is tourism a matter for direct government intervention and control through a Department of Tourism, or is the work better done through a state-funded body with a Board appointed by government? Since it stands to benefit directly from a government role in tourism, what role should the private sector in tourism play? What role should national governments play in relation to regional and local government decisions? Related questions then revolve around the amount of funding that governments should provide and the allocation of that funding in supporting the functions undertaken by the national tourist organization. This chapter outlines the way that the British Government has responded to these questions over recent decades.

Government is the principal beneficiary of tourism activity

Writing in 1958, Lickorish and Kershaw commented that 'The role of government in the development of the travel trade is similar to that of an investor with most at stake' (Lickorish and Kershaw, 1958, p. 244). An economic activity that is generating some £76 billion annually at the start of the twenty-first century in direct expenditure has immediate pay-offs to Central Government in particular measured in:

- VAT receipts
- Business taxes and national insurance payments (government and local authorities)
- Income tax (from some 2 million employees within tourism related sectors)
- Airport taxes and other taxes on passengers
- Petrol duty from tourist journeys.

Less obviously there are immediate government benefits in terms of balance of payments contributions and savings from *not* paying unemployment benefits and other subsidies that would be needed without tourism employment, and so on.

Obviously government (especially local government) incurs substantial costs in dealing with tourism. These range from providing roads and public transport infrastructure and subsidies for rail transport, to providing street cleaning, policing, public toilets and maintaining parks and gardens, etc., although most of these are also provided as much, or more, for residents as for visitors.

Rationale for government involvement with tourism

Over the years since 1945 one can identify seven main reasons why government is involved with tourism. They are summarized below. In every decade, however, as noted above, governments may choose to manage tourism directly or leave it more to accommodation, transport and attractions companies whose business lies in the tourism sector. Government choice changes over the years and it changes according to the political philosophy of the government in power at any point in time. As this chapter notes, Labour Governments tend to favour more direct intervention; Conservatives favour less intervention and withdrawal of funding wherever they consider it possible. The situation also changes according to the ambitions of different Ministers and Secretaries of State. As a result, governments' treatment of tourism and the tourist boards they fund is in a state of constant flux. The troops, so to say, are formally reviewed every few years and marched first up and then down the hill in a process that defies all industry logic and provides no benefit to tourism. It appears unlikely that this will change.

Moreover, government involvement with tourism in the UK has not been for the benefit of the sector as such but rather to use the sector in order to achieve broader government objectives for which tourism has been seen to be a useful tool. Without exception the rationale in the points below reflect broader government requirements. These were most bluntly stated when Lord Young in the Thatcher Government of 1985 agreed to take on the Employment Department as long as he could have tourism in it 'to provide some good news stories'. When that purpose was served, interest in tourism rapidly cooled.

1. *Balance of payments.* Whenever the economy imports more than it exports as a trend, governments have to be concerned with all forms of economic activity that generate overseas earnings. Inbound tourism generates income paid for in foreign currencies and in that sense it is an export industry no different from overseas trade in manufactured goods or earnings generated by the financial services of the City of London. Balance of payments arguments are still very relevant but were most dominant in the pre-war period of the 1930s and the post-war austerity and recovery eras into the 1960s. They have become important again in the twenty-first century as the British spend more abroad each year than inbound visitors contribute.

2. *Promotional support and co-ordination.* Responding to the need to support those who generate foreign earnings, this is the classic route into tourism organization for most governments. Historically, this is how the UK Government first accepted a tourism role and it is still perceived to be the most important task and the one that dominates total tourist board spending. As promotional spending attracts the support of large organizations such as airlines, hotels and railway companies, it is especially attractive to governments seeking to offload as much spending as possible onto the private sector. Such companies are typically most concerned with inbound rather than domestic tourism and it helps to explain why domestic tourism in England has always been treated as something of a Cinderella in UK tourism.

3. *Economic and social engineering.* As in most countries, wealth creation in the UK is unevenly spread and in many parts of Scotland, Wales, Northern Ireland and in the North, the Midlands and South West England there is a powerful need to support any significant economic activity that can create and sustain employment. Because some form of tourism can thrive in almost any part of the UK, governments at

national, regional and local levels welcome tourism development as a way to solve the otherwise intractable issues of economic decline as traditional industries are shifted to low cost countries abroad. Employment concerns were clearly being expressed by the late 1960s and have remained a key concern ever since. More than any other reason this powerful motivation helps to explain why Scotland, Wales and Northern Ireland spend far more per head of their population on their tourism sector than is the case in England (see later in the chapter). Allied to this reason are the various forms of government financial incentives to tourism developers that have been utilized in the UK over the last fifty years. At the end of the 1990s, tourism was seen as an ideal vehicle for delivering parts of the New Labour social engineering mantras of *Access for All* and *For the Many not the Few*.

4. *Market failure.* A rather more recent argument, reflecting the fact that tourism provision on the ground is dominated by tens of thousands of small and very small businesses, is that Government (or its agencies) must be involved in tourism to help compensate for the fact that tourism is not an industry in the normal economic sense of the word. Tourism cannot act in any cohesive or collective way to formulate its own policies and strategies – or indeed to gauge its successes or failures. However attractive the idea may be to governments, *laissez faire* is not an efficient process to secure wise tourism growth. Trade bodies for hotels, self-catering, attractions and transport have existed for decades to support and develop strategies for their members. But there have always been too many such bodies with narrow and often competing sectoral interests that cannot represent the 'industry' effectively. In their classic outline of UK tourism published in 1958, for example, Lickorish and Kershaw listed 46 separate national organizations concerned with tourism into and within the UK (Lickorish and Kershaw, 1958, p. 320). There would have been many more if the regional dimension had been included. In any case, most small businesses in tourism do not belong to trade associations. The 'market failure' argument surfaced in the 1980s and has been a concern ever since. The UK now has a CBI led 'Tourism Alliance' (since 1999), but it is not yet clear how effective as a lobby it will be when the inevitable sectoral tensions arise.

5. *Sustainable development.* Although the BTA held its first conference on sustainability issues in 1972, it was the Rio Earth Summit twenty years later that put the notions of sustainable or 'wise' development onto the political agenda. It was, and is, a concern originating internationally rather than in the UK. As the probabilities of global warming become more evident, it is necessary for governments to consider and promote sustainability in all its forms. In a tourism sense the government's active interest really dates from its Tourism Strategy of 1997 and is outwith our review period in this chapter (see Chapter 9).

6. *Industry co-ordination.* In response to ideas of 'market failure,' all national tourist boards typically identify the following activities as part of their logical remit. It does not follow that tourist boards have to undertake all these activities directly, but it does mean that they need to ensure that they take place in a co-ordinated way in the national interest.

- Devising and promoting policy directions in collaboration with leading players in the industry (with government agreement and in some cases direction).
- Research and intelligence (tourism in the end is not an industry but what is measured).
- Provision of tourist information to assist potential and actual travellers including website provision since the late 1990s.
- Quality assurance programmes, usually focused on hotel classification and grading, with logical extension to other forms of accommodation and to attractions. Such programmes typically include inspection and may extend to licensing procedures.
- Education and training programmes to promote quality and facilitate training activity nationally.

Each of these co-ordination activities tends to have regional as well as national dimensions for their effective implementation, and the history of official tourism organization over the last fifty years reflects both regional as well as national dimensions.

7. *To manage and channel industry lobbying.* Once created, national tourist boards naturally take on the role of champion for the tourism sector. They are more effective in this if they develop and maintain close liaison with key players in the relevant industry sectors. Governments do not always welcome this, of course, generally preferring uncritical approval of their actions. In recent years in the UK governments have manipulated the tourism organizations they support in order to ensure that they obey directions of their own choosing, rather than pursue ends based primarily on tourism sector logic. For example, in 1997 the UK Government abandoned the core promotional role of the former English Tourist Board (which it wound up) in order to focus on strategic and co-ordinating roles for a new body called the English Tourism Council. In a classical political U-turn in 2003 the English Tourism Council and its associated strategic and co-ordinating roles were duly wound up and the promotional role reinstated, albeit the responsibility of yet another organization.

Government role interpreted as an organizational issue

In the UK, at least, government dealings with the tourism sector have been interpreted over the last fifty years as a matter for organization at national and regional level. The conventional wisdom of tourism involvement has meant that changing organizational structures and granting more or less funding, with more or less direct control over policy directions, has become the only real focus of government action. Obviously governments also deal with transport interests, planning regulations, local government responsibilities, heritage support and so on, but typically as separate issues, and not in ways that reflect the interests of the tourism sector. The story of this chapter, therefore, inevitably focuses on national tourism organization and its regional implications.

From 1945 to 1955

Before World War II, as noted in Chapter 1, trade interests, especially those of hoteliers in London, prompted the government of the day (through its Board of Trade) to recognize and help fund the *Travel Industry Association of Britain and Ireland* in 1929. At £5000 per annum it was more a symbol of support than a major commitment and the Association's main functions were to undertake promotion and attract foreign visitors. Almost immediately, the new Association was in some difficulty as the impact of the 1930s world recession cut tourism flows across the Atlantic by some 50 per cent or more in the immediate aftermath of the crisis.

The available evidence suggests that governments in other European countries, notably France and Italy, were more sympathetic to their tourism trades and provided greater support than the UK, not only in funds for promotion but also in subsidies for the key sectors such as transport and hotels. For example France invested massively in the liner *France* in the early 1930s as an act of faith, while the UK Government cut the budget of its fledgling travel association by 25 per cent. It stopped all work on the *Queen Mary*, pulling its investment so that no work was done until the mid-1930s. It is an interesting historical irony that the new *Queen Mary*, launched 70 years later in 2003 was built in a French yard, there no longer being a ship building industry in Britain capable of such a project.

Apart from the prosecution of the war, the early 1940s were a period of intense planning activity for post-war development. In Education, Health and Social Security, as well as for major industries such as transport and the docks, and for countryside access via national parks (the 1949 Act), the foundations were laid for what would become the welfare state and nationalization in the post-war era.

The Attlee Government elected in 1945 was committed to state ownership and control, believing that centralized planning and nationalized industries would provide the most efficient way to organize the country's economic and other affairs. During the war, there being virtually no tourism, the Travel Association (its full title at the time was 'The Travel and Industrial Development Association of Great Britain and Ireland') operated only on a care and maintenance basis. It turned its attention to post-war recovery by participating in an evaluation of post-war options. In 1942, an

Interdepartmental Committee (was this a forerunner of 'joined up govern-ment' proclaimed as 'new' over fifty years later?) was set up with represen-tatives from the Treasury, Board of Trade, British Council and the Travel Association. It published a report in 1944 containing recommendations for post-war organization and action. Produced by a Mr R.G. Pinney and often referred to as the *Pinney Memorandum*, the title of the report was 'Britain, Destination of Tourists?'. This was a very far-sighted piece of work in the context of wartime Britain. It clearly anticipated the potential impact of air travel on tourism in the 1950s and 1960s and it called on government to establish an official tourism organization as a statutory body and accept financial responsibility. Lord Derby, then President of the Travel Association, wrote 'This Memorandum tells the story of our neglected tourist industry and suggests how it could be developed into one of our principal sources of income on international account after the war . . .' (Pinney Report, 1944, Foreword).

Also in 1944, the Catering Wages Commission reported on future tourism activity, recommending the establishment of a government body (or division of the Board of Trade) with four departments: Tourism; Hotels; Catering; and Domestic Holidays. In 1946 the government appointed Lord Inman as adviser on tourism and the Board of Trade duly created a British Tourist and Holidays Board (BTHB) with the recom-mended four divisions. But it was never formally established as a govern-ment department. Lickorish, who joined the Travel Association in 1946, reported that the new Board was in effect an appendage of the Board of Trade, staffed by seconded civil servants including its Chief Executive and Financial Officer. They were unlikely to have been the high-flyers of their day. 'The Travel Association was appointed to act as the Board's Tourist Division but the working relationships were neither clear nor harmonious and the Board had a wide range of ill-defined functions and few staff with any experience of the industry sectors and trades involved' (Lickorish, 2001, draft chapter).

The Travel Association, which at that time was a membership organi-zation for the travel trades, had developed strong links with the leading players in tourism and it had expertise in overseas promotional activities. In 1947, Harold Wilson (subsequently Prime Minister but then President of the Board of Trade) granted substantial additional funding to support the Association's work abroad. Lickorish noted that 'the general opinion and press comment at the time considered that efforts to attract foreign visitors were foolish at a time of shortages, food rationing and the general dull and drab appearance of often bomb damaged cities, towns and resorts'. Lickorish also widely quoted a leading article at that time to the effect that 'no foreigner in his senses would come to this damp and dismal island'. The exact source is not recorded but it is understood to have been a piece in *The Economist*.

Across Western Europe the American Marshall Aid Plan provided fund-ing for the reconstruction of war-devastated economies. The potential of tourism was recognized by governments in France and Italy as a growth sector in the post-war economy and US resources were adapted and utilized for that purpose, but not in Britain. In an era of austerity and rationing, the idea of leisure travel and fun were considered rather trivial, not serious, and triviality did not sit easily on serious shoulders bent to (or by) the wheel of the welfare state.

In 1951, the first post-war review of tourism changed the title of the Travel Association to British Travel and Holidays Association and terminated the short-lived BTHB within the Board of Trade. The BTHA was to be a non-profit-making company limited by guarantee and, in return for its continued grant-in-aid, the government retained its direct influence as eight of the 20 Board members, including the chairman, were to be nominated by the President of the Board of Trade. Seven of the Board were to be elected by the members of the Association and three seats were allocated to the Scottish, Wales and Northern Ireland Tourist Boards. Sir Alexander Maxwell, who had been chairman of the now superseded BTHB, was made first chairman of BTHA. Interestingly, the President of the Board of Trade charged him in a letter with responsibility for 'bringing overseas visitors to this country and ensuring that they as well as home holidaymakers are well received and accommodated and have the best facilities that can be provided'. Although the BTA would lose its domestic tourism responsibilities in the 1960s, they would return to the successor organization 'VisitBritain' in the twenty-first century, albeit only for England.

It was further required in 1951 that 'it will be for the Association to keep a close watch on the efficiency and development of all those [tourism] trades and services and do its best by persuasion and voluntary action to co-ordinate their activities'. Further objectives were to advise the government on framing of policy and assist in its execution; provide information on tourism for the traveller and the trades; and impress on the public and those employed in the industry the importance of tourism for the national economy (BTA 1929–1969, p. 22).

Visitor numbers from overseas were estimated at 618 000 in 1950 and the first ever national holiday survey of the tourism habits of the British population in 1951 revealed some interesting figures (see Table 7.1).

Whatever else this post-war period reveals, it offers some indicators that are relevant and reappear over the next fifty years. These include:

- Some bold and imaginative thinking (by Pinney and those who foresaw a future of growth).
- A broadly supportive government, not entirely sure of how best to handle tourism and changing the organization after only five years (the short lived Board).
- The importance of representing the travel industry – at that time possible through a membership body.
- The significance and market power of the English-speaking market and the Empire Diaspora.

Table 7.1 Overall tourism data to 1955

Year	Visits from abroad	UK holidays
1937	488 000	15 000 000*
1946	203 000	n/a
1950	618 000	25 000 000
1955	1 037 000	25 000 000

Note: statistics of this era are not reliable but they are at least indicative. The domestic data is for holidays of four or more nights. All data are rounded up.
*Brunner (1945)

A formula for a government influenced and supported membership body for tourism rather than a government department was endorsed and would remain in place until 1969 with a clear remit that embraced most of the rationale set out at the start of this chapter. Separate boards for Scotland, Wales and Northern Ireland were established and their links with the BTHA, which also embraced local government interests in membership, were tied into the structure. The public/private sector balance was thus resolved realistically at that time and a proactive foundation laid for the growth years. For developments in Scotland and Wales, see pages 151–66.

Less fortunately, although understandably, tourism appears to have been generally identified as 'holidays' in the post-war period. This helped create a political and popular understanding of the two terms that would still be relevant in the 1990s when even a reputable journal, such as *The Economist* would introduce its survey of world travel and tourism with the sub-title, 'The Leisure Principle' and illustrate the piece with holiday images (*The Economist*, March 1991). Similarly, the use of the term 'travel trades' was popular at the time, reflecting the common official usage as in The Board of Trade. But it sowed linguistic confusion as *travel trade* (as in travel trade press) has ever since been commonly used to identify the sector of holidays abroad handled by travel agents and tour operators and their transport partners in the business.

From 1955 to 1969

In market terms, obvious with the benefit of hindsight, Britain had some massive advantages for inbound travel, although they were not widely realized back in the early 1950s. Britain had excellent relationships with the USA as victorious allies in the recent war; Churchill was feted in America and the Royal Family enjoyed massive – and positive – coverage. The days of the Empire were drawing to a close, but the kith and kin and common language links with Canada, Australia and New Zealand, and with South Africa and India were powerful assets as soon as travel was facilitated by air transport developments. Mainland Europe was still recovering from the war and travel by individuals was still relatively depressed in this period. In the

Table 7.2 Tourism data from 1955 to 1969

Year	Visits from abroad [*]	UK holidays domestic [**]	UK holidays abroad [***]
1955	1 037 000	25 000 000	1 500 000
1960	1 669 000	31 500 000	3 500 000
1965	3 597 000	30 000 000	5 000 000
1969	5 821 000	30 500 000	5 750 000

[*]visits lasting one night or more (all purposes)
[**]holidays lasting four nights or more
[***]includes holidays of one plus nights – few in volume at this time
For sources see Appendix V

domestic market seaside resorts were nearing their twentieth-century peak of popularity although enterprising tour operators were already developing the market to destinations abroad and forcing changes in air transport regulation to achieve it.

The dramatic rise in inbound visitor numbers and their revenue contribution shifted the perception of the government to be more favourable in principle and to see the benefits that tourism could bring.

As a membership body, the British Travel Association achieved some 5000 members. This could not have been more than a tiny minority, or less than 1 in 20 of the businesses involved in tourism. Yet it represented most of the bigger players as individuals as well as businesses and it provided a significant base of influence for dealing with the government and putting an industry view. Perhaps reflecting the smaller size of the tourism sector at that time, it appears that the private sector had more influence over the directions of tourism policy in the 1960s than it has today.

By 1968 the UK had a new Labour Government under Harold Wilson, with an agenda for economic regeneration and developing regional initiatives (Department for Regional Affairs headed by George Brown). It was a government committed to intervention and in a few years had legislated for QUANGOS to cover the Arts, Sports, Museums, Countryside, Waterways and Countryside and Forest recreation. Tourism was relevant to all of these and it was a logical climate in which to include it within the greater control of the State. At the time there was growing recognition of the contribution of tourism but also of the deficiencies in the product supply side that needed to be addressed. The arrival of the first jumbo jets was just over the horizon with implications for rapid growth that focused on the problems with London hotel capacity. Moreover, tourism was helpful to the main thrust of government objectives such as balance of payments, economic growth and employment, regional regeneration and the need to encourage domestic tourism development to help offset the rapid switch of the UK market to destinations abroad.

The mood of the time was for intervention in the market, with financial incentives available through a Hotel Development Incentives scheme (HDI) and equivalent funding (on a much smaller scale) for other tourism product developments. The problem was how could these be seen to be managed with due financial probity by a non-statutory membership body? Scotland and Wales already had their own tourist boards for almost the same length of time as Britain but with limited powers. As Labour Government strongholds, the mood in Scotland and Wales was to take more control over their tourism rather than accept the views of the British Travel Association, which could be criticized as having a London centric focus on inbound tourism.

Consideration of these issues led to the first ever White Paper dealing with the future for tourism in 1968. In 1969, the Development of Tourism Act was passed. The White Paper envisaged statutory boards for Scotland and Wales with a new statutory Board to take over the role of the British Travel Association, incorporating an English Tourist Board with authority over England and having full responsibility for overseas promotion. Scotland was opposed to this as providing too much power for the BTA and a number of English MPs took the view that England should have its own Board. A last minute change was adopted to provide for an English Tourist Board as a separate legal entity alongside those for Scotland and Wales (Northern Ireland had its own legislation and was not part of the 1969 Act). It is possible that the strong opposition to these changes from the established Travel Association, fearing for loss of its powers, to some extent encouraged the government to make the changes more radical than they otherwise might have been.

Whatever the political calculations, Britain ended up in 1969 with four co-equal national tourist boards, each charged with essentially identical powers (including advice to government on tourism matters). The only exception at the time was that promotion of the UK abroad would be the exclusive role for the new BTA (British Tourist Authority). The three national boards would be the channels for any investment programmes that were funded within their boundaries.

Part 1, Clause 6 of the Development of Tourism Act 1969 contained a splendidly anodyne exhortation that 'in discharging its functions . . . each Tourist Board shall have regard to the desirability of undertaking appropriate consultation with the other Tourist Boards . . .'. The Act itself made no provision whatever for a co-ordination mechanism between the Boards and in practice, although this was not acknowledged formally until the various reviews of the 1980s, the terms of the Act quickly became a recipe for organizational infighting. This was not an easy time as England had responsibility for over 80 per cent of the product that the BTA was responsible for promoting and also had to establish its own authority as a new body with no membership guidance. The Act was criticized in the House of Commons and Enoch Powell memorably stated 'It would be a pity if this Bill were to leave the House without at least one Member laying his curse upon it....It has all the classic features of a socialist measure. It establishes bureaucratic boards in order to perceive commercial opportunities and promote commercial operations' (Jeffries, 2001, p. 86).

All the Board Members of all four bodies were henceforth to be political appointees including the chairmen of the Scotland, Wales and England tourist boards who also had seats on the new BTA Board; Northern Ireland was invited to participate in order to provide a UK perspective. There were endeavours to reach a workable demarcation of efforts but the net effect was that, while the BTA was able for a period to retain its exclusive role abroad, it had to accept what in practice was exclusion from domestic tourism and all forms of product development. Some would say that a divide was opened up between promotion and product development and delivery that in other industry sectors would be regarded as disastrous.

England, Scotland and Wales focused on domestic tourism and the development of the product, drawing on their new investment funding and created their own regional bodies to support their endeavours. The BTA was given powers to 'encourage the provision and improvement of tourist amenities and facilities in Great Britain' but it was not in control of funding for this purpose and was never able to exercise these powers. Over the next two decades both Scotland and Wales achieved ways to make inroads into the BTA's initial 'exclusive' control of overseas promotion. Ironically, jumping ahead, the English Tourist Board was axed in 1997 to be replaced by the English Tourism Council, which in its turn was abolished in 2002 to become part of VisitBritain, the successor body to the BTA. The original intention of the 1968 White Paper appears to have been implemented – for the time being.

Although his view was not entirely unbiased, it was Lickorish's view of the 1969 Act that 'the result was an unwieldy and impracticable whole with much duplication and inefficiency in the domestic field'. For example, England's regions, which ironically were created on a membership model not dissimilar to the pre-1969 BTA, attracted both private sector businesses and local authorities. They were not under the direct control of the English Tourist Board (ETB), however, and they increasingly and successfully over the years lobbied government for greater devolution of the ETB's funding, thus weakening the central influence (Jeffries, 2001, pp. 92–3). They could also join with the BTA in overseas marketing programmes from which the ETB was excluded. Over the years each of the national boards developed their own bespoke systems for accommodation classification and grading. However, considerable progress has been made toward harmonization since 2003. A Quality Review Group, chaired by Alan Britten, negotiated agreement in 2006 of common standards for England, Scotland, Wales and the AA, for full implementation in 2008. The Hotel Development Incentive scheme included in the 1969 Act, which many criticized as opening the gates for public spending after the private sector had already got the message, overspent by ten times what the government envisaged in 1968, as hoteliers rushed to take advantage of the money on offer.

On the other hand, many hotel projects outside London were given a boost that made possible the subsequent growth of tourism. Overall, over 100 000 new bed spaces were grant aided in England by 1974. Since the great majority of these were of a much higher standard than before, the national tourist board could properly claim success for the programme. Through the provision of investment funding under Section 4 of the 1969 Act many smaller attractions and other projects were funded in Scotland, Wales and England that would otherwise not have been built.

Overall, the net effect of 1969, however, was to divide those responsible for developing key sectors of market demand from those responsible for product supply and it disenfranchised the leading tourist industry players at national level as none of the new bodies had a membership base. Needless to say, all the boards were committed to consultation and reviews, but a *them* and *us* feeling between politicians and industry was created that remains to some extent to the present day. It also created a form of market interference by public sector officials that many in the private sector resented as unfair competition. Although this was probably not intentional, the creation of statutory funded tourist boards directly responsible to a sponsoring Ministry also meant that real responsibility for tourism policy and strategy would be gradually, but effectively, transferred to Ministers and civil servants for whom industry knowledge, experience or any form of industry accountability was not a requirement. That created scope for constant interference with the industry and tilted the balance of power in tourism strongly toward the public sector – a pendulum shift that would be an issue for the rest of the century.

1979 to 1995 The review years

The years following the 1969 Act were turbulent for UK tourism, albeit there was significant growth and change overall. Major economic crises were experienced including:

- The oil crisis in 1973 which led to Britain's 3-day week and fears for a time of petrol rationing (coupons were issued but never used).
- A second world energy crisis in 1979 and deep economic recession in the UK.
- The Falklands War and Miners' Strike, 1982–83.
- International economic crisis in 1990/91 which led to a collapse in the price of houses.
- The first Gulf war with its impact on international travel.
- Inflation rocketing in 1992 as the UK was forced out of the Exchange Rate Mechanism.

The private sector, as we note in Chapters 4 and 5, coped remarkably well with the years of fluctuations and market changes that occurred as a result of all this economic and political turbulence. There were famous casualties in this period such as Laker and Harry Goodman's Intasun, and less obvious casualties in England's coastal holiday resorts and the tens of thousands of guesthouses that had once dominated holiday supply. There were also some

Table 7.3 Tourism data from 1979 to 1995

Year	Visits from abroad [*]	UK holidays domestic [**]	UK holidays abroad [***]
1977	12 281 000	36 000 000	7 750 000
1989	17 290 000	31 500 000	21 000 000
1992	18 535 000	32 000 000	21 750 000
1995	23 700 000	33 000 000	26 000 000

[*]Visits lasting one night or more (all purposes)
[**]Holidays lasting four nights or more
[***]Includes holidays of less than four nights
For sources see Appendix V

remarkable success stories as tourism grew in rural areas, towns and cities and chains such as Post Houses, Travelodges and Travel Inns responded to new tourism movements. There was an explosion in visitor attractions in the 1980s, well before Lottery Funding was available in the mid-1990s. Center Parcs changed the traditional model for resort-based domestic holidays and the short break phenomenon in hotels and self-catering grew rapidly. Charter airlines expanded to respond to and develop the UK tourism market as British residents switched the bulk of their holiday spending abroad. The growth of day visits by an increasingly mobile population in the UK changed the nature of much of domestic tourism provision.

In terms of the official organization for tourism, it was soon obvious that, whatever the intentions of the 1969 Act, it was not effective in practice for reasons indicated above. Yet meddling with the official organization for tourism was seen politically throughout this period as an adequate surrogate for government action in support of the 'industry'. The various sectors that comprise the tourism industry got on with their business, while there ensued a bewildering and seemingly continuous range of Whitehall reviews of tourism and consultation processes. In these the government, especially the Conservative administrations of 1979 to 1997, proclaimed ever-increasing commitment to tourism development while simultaneously seeking justification and ways to reduce its already limited expenditure via tourist boards. Devolution pressures, which surfaced under the Labour Governments of the 1960s and 1970s meant that Scotland and Wales were increasingly left to manage their own interests in tourism, whilst the UK Government talked 'national' but focused mainly on inbound tourism and England.

From the late 1970s onwards, in a rather unlovely and costly gavotte, an ever-changing cast of ministers, civil servants, chairmen and senior board officials grappled with 'reviews' for the best part of twenty years. A review took place every three to five years and tourism responsibility was shifted from Trade to Trade and Industry, to Employment, to National Heritage and at the end of the period to Culture, Media and Sport. Consultancies did well out of the process while Ministers and civil servants came and went through their revolving doors with alarming frequency. For the most part, all of the review activity was conducted secretly within government and none of the detailed reviews were ever released to scrutiny by the industry. Pronouncements were made, often in response to planted questions in Parliament, but the evidence for them was never revealed. As Middleton put it following the 1989 review: 'After 12 months of deliberation it is not good enough that an industry generating £19 billion turnover, and in which government is a player as well as referee, should be treated with so little apparent respect for its intelligence' (Travel GBI, September 1989). For many observers this exclusive focus on organization matters and so-called strategies was unhealthy and time wasting. It provided little of consequence in supporting the competitiveness and development of the tourism industry.

The evaluation of this review process is sufficiently complex to be worthy of a PhD thesis but for the purposes of this chapter the following four reviews are typical of the genre. The issues were invariably the same – how, simultaneously, to voice and claim more recognition and support for tourism by spending less. Many in the 'industry' experienced repetitive consultation fatigue that continued unabated when a new Labour Government took office in 1997. It is sad to report that the issues that concerned the long forgotten Sproat et al. are still under review and consultation in 2006.

The Sproat/Lamont review 1982/83

There had been a review by government departments in 1979 just before a major economic crisis and change of government. By the late 1970s the Labour Government of the day was directing the Boards to give more prominence to the promotion of England's economically depressed regions rather than London. But it was Mr Sproat, as Minister for Tourism under the new Conservative Government who set in hand the first major review of the 1969 Act. It immediately focused on the duplications between the ETB and BTA and their finances. The tone of this and other reviews is encapsulated in a press comment at the time by Malcolm Wood, then Marketing Director for ETB: 'The fate of the English Tourist Board seems to lie between at best dismemberment and at worst total disappearance depending on which "informed" source is to be believed' (Wood, 1982). The comment was prophetic although it took another twenty years before it happened.

In commenting on his review (in Scotland in March 1983) Mr Sproat said 'it is about time tourism shed its Maypole and Morris dancing image and was recognized for what it really is – one of Britain's major growth industries with a capacity to attract massive foreign earnings and revitalize many of our towns'. He went on to note that 'a substantial reallocation of resources is involved for both agencies (ETB and BTA) with the object of cutting out waste, duplication and non-productive activities generally, and ensuring that the maximum amount of money and effort is concentrated at the sharp end of their operations – the active promotion of tourism' (Dept of Trade Press Notice, March 1983).

There was fulsome support in the review for the achievements of tourism and a hint at a possible tourism tax that did not materialize. The practical outcome was that the budget of the BTA was cut for 1983/84 for the first time since 1969; the budget of the ETB was significantly reduced. A partial merger between the BTA and ETB was implemented, with one chairman from 1984 for both bodies housed in the same building in Hammersmith, and common administrative and other services involving some 60 per cent of staff, freeing up two separate prime central London office locations. The ETB was directed to provide more support for its regional bodies, a theme based on the perceived economic regeneration power of tourism that has featured ever since in the Westminster view by both parties.

In 1986, however, the Select Committee for Trade and Industry carried out a review of tourism and was clearly not impressed by the Sproat/Lamont changes. It noted that the legislative framework (the 1969 Act) 'means there is no overall policy applied to developing tourism in the UK as a whole ... no co-ordination of funding ... no cohesion between the strategies pursued by the boards'. The committee called for one new statutory board for British tourism reporting to one minister to ensure co-ordination. But that was never likely to be acceptable to Scotland or Wales and the recommendation was ignored.

The Lord Young review: Leisure Pleasure and Jobs – the business of tourism in 1985

By 1985, with unemployment around two million, the government needed some employment initiatives to help justify its policies. Lord Young headed an inter-departmental review of tourism, which resulted in what many consider to be the most influential and positive report of all the review processes, *Leisure Pleasure and Jobs*, published in 1985. Lord Young was subsequently chosen by Mrs Thatcher to handle the Employment brief and he agreed to do so provided he could take tourism into his department in order 'to have some success stories'.

The report produced under his aegis provided the most positive messages about tourism to date under the headline of 'Action for Jobs'. It said little about tourism's contribution to exports or foreign exchange but it did focus clearly on enterprise and employment issues as a tangible contribution of tourism that most people could readily understand. The unequivocal association of tourism with leisure and pleasure was unfortunate in the sense that it confirmed long held prejudices but it also identified tourism with a buoyant leisure sector, and jobs and the positive actions that flowed from it were helpful for the industry.

Although Lord Young was not a man for intervention in industry affairs he did identify the need for joined up government action and instituted an annual review whereby all the departments concerned with tourism should review their responsibilities and overlaps systematically. His tenure encompassed action on a wide front such as liberalization of licensing laws, improved signposting and a green light for education and training developments. The shift to Employment as the Department responsible for tourism was the first move from Trade and Industry since the 1920s. Coincidentally, tourism in the Department of Employment was at that time linked with government interests in small businesses and Lord Young firmly believed that 'the way to reduce unemployment is through more businesses, more self employment and greater wealth creation, all leading to more jobs' (Action for Jobs, 1986). At that time the link did not produce any significant development for the tourism industry and a major opportunity for new thinking on the tourism role of small tourism businesses was lost.

The Fowler review 1989

With the economy booming by 1989 (the 'Lawson boom') and a confident government committed to private enterprise and cutting back the state sector, there was felt to be less need to support tourism financially. The review of 1989, therefore, was intended to produce a radical downsizing in the role and funding of the ETB. In 1988, under Lord Young's successor, investment for tourism provided for under Section IV of the 1969 Development of Tourism Act was withdrawn in England, although not in Scotland and Wales.

Under the Fowler review, ETB staffing was cut by around half and the Board instructed to devolve more of its functions and (reduced) funding to the regions. Its ability to co-ordinate in the national interest was effectively undermined in ways that just over a decade later would lead to its demise. The BTA was instructed to devolve more functions to its offices overseas but its budget survived more or less intact because of the perceived contribution to the national economy. Across the UK there was a massive resurgence of private sector investment in the 1980s for leisure, entertainment, recreational, accommodation and catering facilities associated with rising income per capita. These boom investment years were shortly to come to an abrupt end but would resume by the mid-1990s when the effects of the 1991–93 recession were overcome.

The Fowler review formalized views of 'market failure' as part of its rationale for achieving the continuing support of the Treasury. It was defined as 'acting where intervention will be effective, improving deficiencies, and identifying gaps unfilled by the market'. Students of government language will recognize that none of these can be defined with any precision so that only ministers and their civil servants can decide how best to act and whether or not they succeeded. Since governments do not reveal their thinking to the tourism industry, 'market failure' is probably more useful as a smoke screen than as a strategy for action.

Department of National Heritage review 1992

By the early 1990s, the government was well aware that other countries were reducing their grants to national tourism bodies. It was in the midst of the deepest economic recession since the 1930s and desperate to cut back wherever possible. The stage was set for another round of cuts in real spending on the official organization. The justification claimed was that 'Tourism in England is now a mature industry' with all the implications that it could safely be left to its own devices. Under the new Major Government, responsibility for tourism was transferred to the newly created Department of National Heritage. Although the English Tourist Board now got back its own chairman it was a seriously weakened organization by comparison with Scotland and Wales. Control of tourism policy was increasingly taken over by the government department, as noted below. More positively, the heritage links would prove to be generally very beneficial in terms of providing more investment in British visitor facilities than at any other time in twentieth-century tourism – via the Heritage Lottery Fund and Millennium Funding Commission established under the Act of 1993.

Government management of tourism

Although tourism policy was nominally in the hands of national tourist boards from 1969, the series of government review processes that followed the 1969 Act produced formal policy guidelines initiated by government departments that Boards were required to follow. From 1992 onwards the ETB, for example, was required to work to Medium Term Corporate Plans initiated by civil servants. The first English Tourism Industry Forum was created and Jeffries noted that by the late 1990s 'the mainstream civil service would appear to have taken over gradually much of the role of the BTA, whose old Committee Structure had once been the main conduit for dialogue between government and industry as a whole' (Jeffries, 2001).

The Department for Culture, Media and Sport (DCMS) developed the Industry Forum to meet two or three times a year at the end of the 1990s but the agenda was always firmly controlled by government. There were some 21 civil servants dealing with tourism within DCMS by 2000 and increasingly they dictated and controlled the tourist board agenda. By 2003, government decided it could do without a consultation Forum and it was simply discontinued (in its form at that time), although no announcement to this effect was made.

The effects on the funding of tourist boards that resulted from the review processes make significant reading. Table 7.4 was provided for a Select Committee Report of 2003 that was critical of government policy and implementation.

Table 7.4 Government grant in aid for tourist boards in Great Britain

Data for 1979/80 to 1994/95 at 1979 (constant) prices. Data for 2002/03 at current prices.

Year	BTA £ million	England £ million	£ per head of pop[*]	Scotland £ million	£ per head of pop[*]	Wales £ million	£ per head of pop[*]
1979/80	£12.8	£10.3	£0.29	£4.3	£1.11	£3.7	£1.75
1984/85	£11.3	£11.6	£0.32	£6.6	£1.67	£4.2	£1.94
1989/90	£12.8	£10.9	£0.29	£6.0	£1.50	£5.0	£2.23
1994/95	£13.3	£4.5	£0.12	£7.0	£1.74	£5.8	£2.55
2002/03[**]	£30.0	£11.6	£0.24	£28.0	£5.50	£22.6	£8.10

[*]Pence or pounds per head of population aged 16+ in each country
[**]Estimate in House of Commons Research Paper 03/73 of September 2003
Source: Estimates provided by DCMS in Culture, Media and Sport Select Committee Report in Feb 2003.

Summary

By the late 1990s, it was increasingly clear to many involved in tourism in England, that Westminster Governments did not understand and were essentially disinterested in tourism in England other than its role in generating contributions to the balance of payments and providing employment in the regions. (This was not the case in Scotland and Wales – see Chapter 8.) Its role in local and area economic regeneration was certainly recognized but interpreted as a case for devolving central spending to the regions – a process strongly encouraged and promoted under the New Labour Government's plans for devolution when it took over in 1997. The Treasury clearly did not believe the data summarizing the contribution of tourism in England and denied the Government's role as the main beneficiary of tourism activity through taxation (or considered it a constant and useful windfall with no commitment).

By 1999, expenditure by national governments on tourism (amount of annual spending allocated to tourist boards divided by the number of visitors) was:

England	£0.20 per visitor
Scotland	£3.76 per visitor
Wales	£4.99 per visitor

Source: Tourism Society (Jeffries, 2001, p. 192)

These are not the same data as those shown in the table provided for the Select Committee shown above but the orders of magnitude make the same point. There is no logical reason for parity between these figures but a disparity of this magnitude speaks volumes for the lack of effective analysis and policy consideration.

Three quotes seem to be more eloquent than a formal conclusion.

In February 1997, with a foreword by the then Prime Minister John Major stressing that 'tourism is one of our foremost industries', the government launched '*Success through Partnership*'. Drawing perhaps on his cricketing interests, Mr Major set out his wish that the tourism industry be 'a world class player in a global game' and declared his Government's commitment to achieving that goal. Complete with vision and action plan, this document was the Conservative Government's last tourism document before it fell to New Labour.

New Labour immediately set in hand its own detailed strategic review. When it emerged, complete with politically correct illustrations under the title '*Tomorrow's Tourism*' in 1999, the new Prime Minister Tony Blair declared in his foreword 'the challenge facing us now is to create a competitive world-class industry in Britain...'. As so often in the past, the aspirations were not matched by any Westminster commitments to increase funding in real terms, and the English Tourist Board was wound up in 2000 to be replaced by the English Tourism Council. Three years later the English Tourism Council was wound up and the merry-go-round at national level continued.

In 2004, the outgoing chairman of VisitBritain, with wide experience of tourism at regional and national level in England (and nothing to lose by his comments), noted: 'Unfortunately, I do not know a Government in the last 20 years that has believed in tourism... They don't see it as an industry. They can't feel it, touch it. There are no cars coming off the production line and most politicians will only respond to crises. They will not invest or think of the future' (Sir Michael Lickiss to members of Cumbria Tourist Board, September 2004).

Scotland, Wales and Northern Ireland

Throughout the last fifty years, Scotland, Wales and Northern Ireland have had their own tourist boards at national and regional levels. They have pursued tourism policies that had regard to developments in England and the role of the BTA, collaborating as they judged appropriate according to the circumstances within their national boundaries. Scotland and Wales were included in the 1969 Development of Tourism Act and their Boards gained statutory status at that time, but their policies have since developed in ways agreed with their own Secretaries of State and their tourism sectors rather than according to Westminster decisions and plans. Since devolution in the late 1990s, both countries are now directly responsible for tourism through an elected Parliament (Scotland) and Assembly (Wales). Both have powers to promote themselves abroad as well as through VisitBritain, and the processes for UK-wide agreement and co-ordination on tourism policies are now left to voluntary agreements and are unclear in 2006. See also Chapter 8.

The Scottish and Wales Tourist Boards

The history and development of the Scottish Tourist Board

Dr Brian Hay

Origins of the Scottish Tourist Board (STB)

Tourism is a significant industry in Scotland; in 1970 there were 5.12 million tourists (4.42 million UK, 0.7 million overseas tourists) and by 2005 tourism accounted for 17.3 million tourists (14.9 million UK tourists, 2.4 million overseas tourists), with a spend of over £4214 million (£3006 million from UK, £1208 million overseas). In 1970–71 the STB grant-in-aid was £0.4 million, plus £1.1 million for the Hotel Development Scheme (HDS); by 2005–06 it had risen to £43.3 million.

Although the 1969 Development of Tourism Act formally established the Scottish Tourist Board (STB) as a statutory, funded body, its beginnings can be traced back to the late 1920s. At that time a 'Come to Scotland' organization existed but, as Johnston (1952) stated, 'it existed – just and no more' and received no central government funding. The Scottish Office proposed a new organization, the 'Scottish Tourism Development Association', funded through the Scottish Office. The first grant in 1930 was almost £346, but this was gradually reduced until by 1939 it was only £250. As the Second World War drew to a close, the Scottish Council on Industry established a

Committee of Enquiry on Tourism and in 1945 an independent Scottish Tourist Board was established.

Although in the 1940s STB received some funding from the Scottish Office, most of its income came through contributions from the private sector, with some local authorities also providing financial support. In the late 1940s early signs of stress between the STB and the UK Government began to show; by 1948 the STB were questioning why they were providing £6000 of the Board's voluntary funds to the UK for overseas marketing. By 1950 more conflict became apparent when the STB applied for membership of the United Nations International Union of Official Travel Organisations; perhaps not surprisingly, the British Travel and Holiday Association (BTHA) objected. However, in the same year the STB was officially invited to join the BTHA.

In an early indication of the special needs of the Scottish regions, especially the Highlands and Islands, in 1950 the STB established a Highlands Tourism Advisory Committee, and by 1955 the STB expressed a need to develop tourism in the 'backward areas in Scotland'. By the late 1950s there were difficulties in obtaining finance for tourism developments and in 1960 the STB received a special grant from the Scottish Office of £15 000 a year for three years, to assist with tourism in the Highlands.

In the 1960s, perhaps reflecting its independent status, the STB took a strong stand on issues that affected tourism. They opposed many of the railway closures proposed by Lord Beeching; supported the creation of a tourism tax of 6d (2.5p) per sleeper night; and opposed the development of National Parks in Scotland, as well local planning applications which would adversely affect tourism. They also called for the setting up of tourism courses at universities and colleges, along with the establishment of national tourism training centres. They supported the Countryside and Tourism Amenities (Scotland) Bill, which was withdrawn from Parliament because of political pressure, and the development of a National Tourism Plan for Scotland, but the Scottish Office did not publish it. In fact it was to be another 30 years before the first plan was unveiled.

As the 1969 Tourism Act was being drafted the STB made a strong case for a separate board, as there were concerns that one UK-wide board might be established. In another indication of the tensions that were to appear in later years, the STB Board minutes of 1967 noted that Scotland's tourism 'must be the exclusive business of the Scottish Authority and must not be subject to London control and direction'.

Relationships with the British Tourist Authority (BTA)/VisitBritain (VB)

Ever since the formation of the STB in 1969 and, indeed, in the preceding years, the relationship between the STB and the BTA has been rather like a dysfunctional family – can't live with them, can't live without them! However, there was also a feeling that more could be achieved by working together than by not working together. In the years before the 1984 Act (which gave the STB overseas marketing powers) the STB not only was dependent on the BTA for overseas marketing but was also not responsible for tourism marketing for the Highlands; both these restrictions contributed to the view that the STB was not functioning as a full-service tourist board. Following the 1984 Act the STB and the BTA developed their first memorandum of understanding, which set out the principles as to how the two Boards would work together.

By the 1980s the issue of overseas marketing powers for the STB had become a politically sensitive issue and in 1983 it was announced in Parliament that the STB was to appoint its first Director of Overseas Marketing. Gradually, during the 1980s each organization began to understand their strengths. The STB thought that the BTA should focus on developing new markets for Scotland, whilst the STB would undertake further development of existing markets, by supplementing the work of the BTA. The inability of the STB to operate by itself in overseas markets continued to limit its activities and, as a compromise in the late 1980s the STB undertook to fund staff posts in BTA offices in Germany and France.

After the 1998 Scottish Devolution Act, the STB developed a new memorandum of understanding with the BTA, which recognized that STB had the skills to develop its own overseas marketing activities. This, along with external developments such as the Scottish Executive's Route Development Fund to introduce more direct flights to Scotland, the free-market forces of the budget airlines and the development of probably the world's first fully integrated tourism organization, helped to develop a clearer relationship between the STB and the BTA.

Over the years, the relationship between the two Boards was like a rebellious teenager (STB/VS) and parent (BTA/VB) and this attempt at parental control was not appreciated by the STB. The 1984 Act could be analogous to the teenager leaving home and their first taste of freedom. Now that the STB has grown into an adult, the relationship has developed between two equal partners.

Local tourism associations and changing organizational structures

The STB has always experienced tensions within the formal organizational structures between the STB and the BTA, and between the STB and local area organizations, especially in the Highlands with the Highland & Islands Development Board (HIDB). Although in 1950 the STB established a Highlands Tourism Advisory Committee, it was not until the 1969 Act that there was the first serious attempt at working with the local tourism associations. This was through the seven newly STB established Regional Tourism Associations (RTOs), whose functions were to promote tourism in their area and to provide information for their visitors. In 1970 the HIDB, which was responsible for tourism in its area, established Area Tourism Associations (ATOs), each with their own office and TICs.

As a result of the Local Government Act of 1973, both the new Regional Authorities and the District Councils could exercise tourism powers, but by 1975 it was clear that most of the Regional Authorities were not willing to support the RTOs. In an effort to encourage the development of RTOs, the STB continued to develop their own network of TICs and by 1978 operated seven TICs. The duplication of tourism responsibilities by both the Regions and Districts continued to cause difficulties and the 1986 Local Government Act placed the sole responsibility for tourism development with the District and the Islands authorities, and removed tourism powers from the Regional authorities. The Act gave the local authorities only discretionary powers to undertake tourism, but it paved the way for the development of 16 Area Tourist Boards (ATBs) in the STB area of Scotland and 17 ATOs in the HIDB area. Some local authorities with few tourism products decided not to form ATBs and two (Moray and Edinburgh) made the decision to exercise this function at their own hands, rather than to form ATBs. The ATBs were to be funded through membership fees, commercial income and the STB, with one third of their funds from each.

The STB tried to co-ordinate the marketing activities of the ATBs through a series of joint advertising campaigns, whilst the ATOs, along with the HIDB, developed their own separate joint advertising campaigns, including overseas marketing. In the early 1980s the STB was in the unusual position whereby a Regional Development Agency (HIDB) could undertake overseas marketing in its own right, but the STB could not. In 1993, following a major review of tourism by the Scottish Office, the tourism functions of the HIDB were transferred to the STB and the ATOs were re-formed into ATBs and directly funded by the STB.

In order to co-ordinate tourism in 1988 the Scottish Office formed the Scottish Tourism Coordinating Group (STCG) which included the Scottish Office, STB, HIDB, Scottish Development Agency (SDA) and the BTA. Membership of the group gradually expanded to bring in a number of other agencies, as well as private sector groups such as the Scottish Tourism Forum. Over time, this group emerged as the Tourism Strategy Group, dominated by private sector organizations, in whose name the 2006 National Tourism Strategy was issued.

By the 1990s it was clear that for a small country, operating a network of 34 ATBs was not an efficient use of public money, especially as tourists pay little attention to local authority boundaries. The 1994 Act not only required that ATBs be set-up across the whole of Scotland, but it also reduced the number of ATBs to 14. Eventually, with the reorganization of VisitScotland (VS) in 2005, they disappeared altogether and their activities and staff were transferred to VS.

Changes continued to take place, and in 2006 both Glasgow and Edinburgh set up Special Purpose vehicles (SPV) to manage the functions carried out by their Convention Bureaus. VS formed a National Convention on Tourism with all 32 Local Authorities in Scotland.

Quality assurance schemes

In 1961 the STB first called for a scheme to grade hotels in Scotland, one which would be operated by its own inspectors 'who would be above suspicion'. By 1966 they had established an Accommodation Registration and Assessment Scheme to provide advice to the industry on the standards of accommodation.

In 1971 proposals were introduced to develop an accommodation registration scheme operating through the Post Office using a scheme of self-registration at a cost of £3 per establishment; the scheme had a limited success. However, as the Hotel Development Scheme (HDS) came to an end in 1973, the STB was keen to maintain standards of the facilities it had recently funded and in 1972 put forward to the Scottish Office a scheme for the compulsory registration of accommodation. This was rejected so in co-operation with the English and Wales Tourist Boards, the STB developed a voluntary registration scheme for accommodation, recognizing that it was unlikely to be comprehensive. By 1974 the STB had set out the minimum standards for accommodation, to be operated on a voluntary basis; accommodation meeting these minimum standards were given a distinctive symbol in STB publications. Some 6000 serviced and self-catering establishments were registered.

By 1978 membership of the scheme had declined to about 39 per cent of known establishments and a joint STB/WTB/ETB working party was set up to make further recommendations to the UK Government. Professor Beavis from the Scottish Hotel School was appointed to investigate the case for a statutory registration scheme for accommodation. The STB also established the Sneddon Committee to provide a Scottish input to the Beavis review. The Beavis Committee recommendations were published in 1981 and a new voluntary, self-classification scheme for hotels and guesthouses was introduced in 1982.

In the Highlands and Islands the HIDB introduced a three-number classification scheme in 1983. 1983 also saw the start of the Thistle Commendation scheme for the caravan sector and for the first time 'qualified inspectors' were employed to inspect the properties. Following the development of the caravan park scheme, the STB started discussions for a self-catering scheme and, at the request of the caravan-site operators, for a caravan park grading scheme.

Following the Department of Trade and Industry's (DTI) rejection of a compulsory scheme – again for reasons of not wishing to impose burdens on the industry – the STB suggested that standards could be raised by a team of verifiers checking that establishments met the criteria claimed by the operators and that they abided by the STB code of conduct. These checks would not apply to existing establishments, but only to new ones. The STB replaced the three-category classification scheme with a single-category system denoted by a national symbol. In 1985 the first team of verification and grading officers were appointed, and scheme members could opt to be either classified or classified and graded. By 1987 classification and grading had developed into two components, where grading was an assessment by STB officers of the quality of facilities and welcome; this grading was complemented by a classification system of 'listed' and one through to five crowns.

In 1992 the STB expanded the top end of the scheme by introducing a 'Deluxe' grade, and in 1995 the STB began to again push the quality agenda by questioning why should they still be supporting non-graded accommodation by listing them in their publications, so they decided to promote only scheme members in all STB publications. After another major review of the scheme in 1997 the STB adopted a new five-star scheme, along with a series of designators (e.g. hotels, self-catering, etc.) to reflect consumers' understanding of the quality of service.

Since 2000, recognizing that the quality assurance schemes focused only on accommodation and not on other elements of the tourist experience, the STB has gradually expanded the scope of the schemes covering hotels, serviced accommodation, campus accommodation, self-catering, camping and caravan parks, hostels, and visitor attractions to other aspects: The Green Tourism Business Scheme, Ancestral Tourists Welcome, Walkers and Cyclists Welcome and Eat Scotland (a food grading scheme), and an inspection scheme for wheelchair accessibility are all part of the portfolio of the quality assurance schemes.

As the scheme developed new categories were added; for example hotel designators now include not just 'hotel' but also Country House Hotel, Small Hotel, Town House Hotel and Metro Hotel. In 2006 the success of the scheme is reflected in the following membership: 1104 attractions, 4064 serviced accommodation, 7724 self-catering units (3454 providers), 290 holiday parks, 168 hostels and 523 in the Green Business scheme.

Product development

The 1969 Development of Tourism Act included provision for capital grants and loans through the Hotel Development Scheme (HDS) for the development of hotels for a short period up to 1973. This scheme resulted in an investment of £28 million, including direct grants of £5.3 million from the STB (1975 prices) spread over some 470 projects. It funded 80 new hotels, 180 hotel extensions and some 5500 new hotel bedrooms and represented the biggest boost in hotel development since the great Victorian resorts hotels of the 1890s. There were, however, shortcomings in the scheme; it covered only hotels and not other forms of accommodation and it had little impact on the rural areas. For example, only 60 new hotel bedrooms were built in the Borders, but there were 1600 in Glasgow. As part of its new advisory role in 1975 the STB established at Strathclyde University a development advisory service which had provided support to over 4700 businesses by the time the service ended in 1981.

When the HDS ended, the STB funded development projects through its Section 4 (S4) grants. Over the years 1974–93 there was continuing investment across the tourism product not only in hotels, but also to other forms of accommodation and attractions. The S4 programme began to diversify into larger projects and in 1986 awarded its largest ever grant of £1.2 million to Bultin's in Ayr in a profit-sharing deal. In the 1990s, recognizing the importance of its advisory/policy role, the STB established a Product Development unit which produced a series of development guides and undertook some major studies. By 1991 the STB was investing £4.9 million a year through its S4 grants.

The 1993 Tourism Review recognized that support from both Local Enterprise Companies (LECs) – established in 1991 by Scottish Enterprise – and the STB for tourism development projects was not an efficient use of public funds. S4 funding ceased in 1993 and the responsibility for funding tourism projects was transferred to the LECs.

By the mid-2000s the Product Development unit had changed its focus to Sector Development in order to avoid confusion with the functions carried out by the LECs. It now undertook three main activities, namely: development of new sectors such as culinary tourism; development of new products such as the Adventure Pass; and development of existing products. The development function had come a full circle; it had started out as an advisory service, managed the HDS, expanded through the S4 scheme, then focused on delivery of national projects – and it is now again an advisory/supportive service.

Looking ahead

As indicated above, STB, now VisitScotland since 2001, has transformed its role and functions beyond recognition in the thirty years since the 1969 Development of Tourism Act. In April 2005, VisitScotland became a single, country-wide comprehensive organization managing all 120 TICs in Scotland, with 14 areas offices and its own offices in London, Edinburgh and Inverness. It is probably the world's first fully integrated tourist board, providing a single contact point for tourists and for tourism businesses.

This transformation evolved over the years in an ever-competitive marketplace, in which a small country has to endeavour to manage its scarce marketing resources better than other destinations do. The reorganization was driven in part by the major changes in the marketplace and the need to stay ahead of the game. Given the constraints in public funding, VS has recognized that it could not undertake all the activities it wished, and in recent years has aimed to join in partnership with other organizations, for example in its national website operations for prospective visitors and for supporting Scottish businesses.

In the early 2000s VS conducted extensive brand research on the changing marketplace and three key words emerged, namely: *Enduring, Dramatic and Human*. The result of this was the development of a major new themed marketing campaign 'Live it, Visit Scotland' setting the tone for visits to Scotland in the first decade of this century.

Chronological listing of the main tourism legislation/reviews in Scotland

1964 *Countryside and Tourist Amenities (Scotland Bill).* This bill met strong opposition from the BTHA and was withdrawn. It proposed to establish a separate 'Scottish Tourist Fund' created from a tax of 6d per sleeper night and the establishment of local regional tourist associations.

1965 Establishment of the Highlands & Islands Development Board with powers to undertake tourism marketing both in the UK and overseas.

1969 *Development of Tourism Act.* Established the STB with funds direct from the UK Government. STB to be responsible for tourism policy for all of Scotland, but only for marketing and development outwith the HIDB area.

1973 *Local Government Act.* This provided concurrent powers for the new Regional Authorities and District Councils to undertake tourism marketing, provided that their activities were supported by the STB.

1984 *The Overseas (Tourism Promotion) (Scotland) Act.* This, for the first time, allowed the STB to market itself overseas.

1986 *Local Government and Planning (Scotland) Act.* This provided discretionary powers for the District Authorities to participate in tourism activities and enabled them to set up Area Tourist Boards.

1990 *Enterprise and New Towns (Scotland) Act.* Established Scottish Enterprise, Highlands & Islands Enterprise and the Local Enterprise Companies with tourism development functions.

1993 *Tourism Review.* STB established as the lead agency for all Scottish tourism marketing, the Local Enterprise Companies being given sole responsibility for funding tourism development. HIE lost its tourism marketing powers, but STB opened an office in Inverness.

1994 *Scottish Tourism Strategic Plan,* published by the Scottish Tourism Coordinating Group/Scottish Office Industry Department.

1994 *Local Government (Scotland) Act.* This reduced to 14 the number of ATBs across Scotland.

1998 (Following the 1997 Referendum) *Scotland Devolution Act.* Established a Scottish Executive and Parliament in July 1999, with the STB now reporting to the Scottish Parliament.

2000/1 *New Strategy for Scottish Tourism,* published by the Scottish Executive and STB required to undertake a management review of its staffing and functions. The Chief Executive and all the Directors left; a new management team was appointed and STB began trading as *VisitScotland.*

2002 *Tourism Framework for Action 2003–2005,* published by the Scottish Executive.

2005/6 *VisitScotland* network came into being, a single organization with 14 area offices and over 1000 staff. Publication in 2006 by the Scottish Executive of *Scottish Tourism: The Next Decade.*

The history and development of the Wales Tourist Board

Professor Elwyn Owen

Origins of the Wales Tourist Board (WTB) – the early days

In Wales the first national tourism organization was created on 27th October 1948, when the preliminary meeting was held of the nascent Welsh Tourist and Holidays Board. Today it seems surprising that the meeting took place at the Shire Hall, Shrewsbury – chosen, no doubt, because participants from different parts of Wales could get there by train. Although the Board of Trade facilitated that development – with its President, Harold Wilson, playing an active part in the process – there was no government funding for this new venture.

As in Scotland, the initiative for establishing the Board came largely from local government and tourism businesses. In keeping with the traditions of Welsh public life, the new organization had an elaborate committee structure but very few resources, and the fact that it survived at all says much about the vision, perseverance and ingenuity of the pioneers. Indeed, it was not until 1965 that the newly established Welsh Office made its first grant of £2550 to the voluntary Board – in support of the £9515 from local authorities, £10 868 from the British Travel and Holidays Association, £3471 from commercial sources and £3768 from advertising revenue and sales (Howell, 1988).

During its early years the Board was based at Llandrindod Wells. In 1955 the office was re-located to Cardiff and the organization's headquarters would remain within the capital city until 2006. Partnership working featured very strongly in the Board's philosophy from the very start – not least because it needed the support of others in order to survive – enabling the organization to develop close links with local authorities and the industry from the outset. Although relationships with these key stakeholder groups would occasionally become more fractious in later years, the tourism sector undoubtedly benefited from the small scale of Wales and the (general) willingness of its institutions to work together.

The post 1969 period

With the passing of the Development of Tourism Act, the Wales Tourist Board was established as an independent statutory body, sponsored by and accountable to the Welsh Office, through the Secretary of State for Wales. Between 1969 and 1999, eight persons held that office and it was their responsibility to appoint chairs and board members; to set key funding and staffing parameters; and to receive annual and other reports from the

Board. In 1999 the National Assembly for Wales came into being, inheriting devolved powers and responsibilities from the Secretary of State and assuming the role of sponsor department for the Wales Tourist Board and other public bodies in Wales. It was now the responsibility of the First Minister to appoint chairmen and board members, and a more transparent approach was adopted in relation to governance, accountability and scrutiny.

The establishment of the statutory WTB coincided with a period of painful structural change in Wales as the economy and society struggled to come to terms with the loss of traditional extractive and heavy industries. Although the tourism sector would also have to adapt to change, there was a pressing need to diversify the Welsh economy and successive Secretaries of State looked to tourism as a key option for regeneration. As a consequence, the Board enjoyed a continuity of support from the Welsh Office and subsequently the Welsh Assembly Government, which engendered confidence and encouraged initiative. This contrasted sharply with the situation in England, where ministerial commitment to tourism was far more fickle and where successive reviews and reorganizations led to confusion and loss of influence.

In 1976 the Wales Tourist Board produced the first in a series of medium-term strategies. Unusually for the time this was issued as a consultative document, to enable the tourism industry, local authorities and official bodies to express their views on the future thrust of WTB policy, and it established a precedent for all future WTB strategies (see for example 1988, 1994 and 2000).

For a period of thirty-five years WTB was the only Board established under the Development of Tourism Act to retain all its powers, acquire additional responsibilities and continue to operate under the same name. Dramatic change came in July 2004 when the First Minister, Rhodri Morgan AM, made a surprise statement to the National Assembly for Wales, heralding a far-reaching change in governance whose shock waves are still being felt. The Wales Tourist Board was to be merged with its sponsor Department and become part of the Welsh Assembly Government. In 2006 the staff of the Wales Tourist Board became civil servants, working mainly with the newly created Department for Enterprise, Innovation and Networks (DEIN) which inherited responsibility for the relevant duties and powers prescribed by the Development of Tourism Act 1969 and other legislation. Thus the Wales Tourist Board became history and the name *Visit Wales (Croeso Cymru)* was adopted to identify the tourism team within the Welsh Assembly Government and for marketing purposes.

Regional structures in Wales

As elsewhere in Britain, the Wales Tourist Board recognized the importance of establishing a regional presence. The main motivations for doing so were to provide a forum for discussing matters of common concern within the tourism sector; to generate financial support for WTB programmes; and to facilitate service delivery at local level. Over the years, the approach to regional service delivery in Wales changed considerably, again echoing what happened in England and Scotland, bringing in its wake a deal of confusion and not a little acrimony.

At its first meeting, the Wales Tourist Board resolved to create Regional Tourism Councils for North, Mid and South Wales, with a small core staff appointed and funded by WTB. They received financial support from local authorities and tourism businesses, to be spent within the region, primarily on local information services. Each Regional Council appointed its own Executive Committee, consisting of a balance of elected representatives from funding local authorities and business subscribers. From the outset the chairs of the Regional Tourism Councils were invited to attend meeting of the Wales Tourist Board, in a non-voting capacity.

The Regional Tourism Councils were successful in mobilizing local authority and trade support. They provided a useful forum for seeking policy advice and were instrumental in establishing a network of information centres. However, their constitutional and operational relationship with the Board was ill-defined and this became a source of contention. In an effort to rationalize the situation, the Board facilitated a programme of consultation which culminated in the establishment in 1991 of three Regional Tourism Companies, limited by guarantee. These were managed by a Board of Directors, half of whom were elected by the trade and half by local authorities. They received core funding from WTB and they also received membership fees from the trade and local authorities. With the encouragement of WTB, they raised money to fund local marketing initiatives and they also sought to supplement their income by setting up stand-alone trading companies.

The Regional Tourism Companies benefited from being formally constituted entities and provided a range of services for their tourism sectors. They occupied difficult territory, however, and their place within the tourism hierarchy was not always clear. Funded by WTB, local authorities and businesses, they served several masters, and whilst they themselves saw benefit in being membership organizations, the Wales Tourist Board and the Government began to view this as a source of conflicts of interest. A further complication arose from the fact that the boundaries of the Regional Tourism Companies were not coterminous with the Government's four economic development regions. In 1999 a working party was established to review the situation again – although, not surprisingly, it was not easy to secure consensus among bodies whose interests and priorities differed. Having sought independent consultancy advice, the Board announced a radical new approach that would create four new Regional Tourism Partnerships. These would be the conduit for substantially enhanced regional funding but would not themselves be membership organizations. With the creation of these new Partnerships, core funding from WTB of the existing three Regional Tourism Companies would cease. This was a contentious proposal as WTB's regional stakeholders sought to understand precisely what it would mean for them. The ferocity of that debate can be judged by the Board Statement that:

From all quarters, the message has been clear – there is concern, disquiet and confusion surrounding the introduction of the four new regional partnerships.

*The communication could certainly have been better and more structured and,
in the absence of detailed information, the vacuum has been filled – by some
legitimate concerns and in other cases by inaccurate speculation.*

(Wales Tourist Board, 2001)

The Regional Tourism Partnerships (RTPs) came into being in April 2002.
Each is constituted as a not-for-profit Company limited by guarantee, whose
Board consists of directors elected by businesses and local authorities. Until
March 2006 the RTPs received core funding from WTB; now it comes
directly from the Welsh Assembly Government. Their role is to act as
enabling and commissioning bodies, which work through others to achieve
their stated objectives. Although the three Regional Tourism Companies
ceased to be in receipt of WTB core funding in 2002, they were free to operate as independent companies. One of them (Tourism South and West
Wales) went into voluntary liquidation shortly afterwards, but North Wales
Tourism and Mid Wales Tourism continue to operate as membership organizations. At the time of writing, it remains to be seen how the Regional
Tourism Partnerships will fare following the assimilation of the Wales
Tourist Board into the Welsh Assembly Government.

Telling the world about Wales

From its formation in 1969, marketing was a cornerstone of the work of the
Wales Tourist Board. During the early years the terms of the 1969 Act were
accepted without question in Wales: WTB was still finding its feet as a statutory
organization, and had neither the inclination nor the confidence to campaign
for a broader remit. The Board's marketing sights were set firmly on the domestic market, which at that time generated the lion's share of tourism to Wales,
and a major preoccupation was to protect the traditional resorts, which were
catering primarily for the British long-holiday market. Although there was an
aspiration to increase the number of overseas visitors to Wales, this was not yet
considered to be a priority and, despite any latent misgivings about how well
the interests of Wales were being represented by the British Tourist Authority,
the existing arrangements were thought to be logical and workable.

During the 1970s and 1980s, the Board focused its marketing efforts on
response-generating advertising, aimed specifically at the UK holiday market.
The results were very encouraging – at least in terms of number of enquiries
and cost per response – but it became increasingly apparent that traditional
response-orientated techniques lacked the precision needed in a more sophisticated marketing environment. Patterns of tourism demand were changing
and there were fears that traditional techniques meant preaching to the converted, rather than facing up to the more difficult challenge of winning new
business. Thus, greater reliance was placed on using targeted direct mail techniques to generate interest and brochure enquiries, and to spread marketing
effort more evenly through the year. WTB was amongst the pioneers in apply-
ing database-marketing techniques to tourism marketing.

Response-based marketing techniques were not best equipped to tackle the important task of creating a distinctive image for Wales and winning new converts. Research confirmed that Wales' scenic attractiveness was widely recognized amongst British people, as was the potential to engage in a variety of activities – but these attributes did not set Wales apart from other competing areas within Britain. Although culture and heritage have traditionally been used to highlight the distinctiveness of tourism destinations, research showed that this was not a good option for Wales in the 1970s and 1980s, at least within the domestic market. A significant proportion of British (mainly English) residents tended to respond negatively to the language and culture of Wales, and those who had not spent a holiday there wondered whether they would be made welcome. For this reason, when seeking to position Wales within the domestic market, WTB focused more on such positively perceived assets as the natural environment, activity products and proximity to key markets. The Board's image-building advertising became more important and evolved over time, winning praise for its high production values, dramatic imagery and inventive copy. With the emergence of a greater sense of Welsh identity, the break-up of the traditional model of 'Britishness' and the creation of new devolved political structures, WTB espoused a more confident approach to the use of cultural and linguistic imagery in its domestic marketing activity, which proved very successful.

By the 1980s WTB understood the need for an integrated and cost effective approach to overseas marketing but it was also concerned about Wales' very small share of this important and lucrative market. It was determined to gain a bigger foothold overseas to help reduce reliance on traditional domestic holiday markets now in decline. In addition, WTB wanted to put its own stamp on the way Wales was being promoted abroad, and to counter what it saw as an overly Anglo-centric approach.

WTB decided to open its first office in London in 1982 to encourage footloose overseas visitors staying in Britain's major destination to spend at least some time in Wales. Soon afterwards the post of Overseas Marketing Director was created, delivering a strong message that attracting more overseas visitors was now a major priority for the organization. When the Scottish Tourist Board won the power to engage in overseas marketing in 1984, WTB chose not to press for similar legislation – although with hindsight it was a mistake not to have done so.

There now existed an anomalous situation in Wales where organizations such as the Welsh Development Agency could engage in tourism-related marketing operations outside Britain, while the lead agency for tourism was debarred from doing so. Although the British Tourist Authority now began to earmark an annual budget for marketing activities specific to Wales, pressure grew for legislative action to be taken. After sustained pressure from WTB and its partners, the Tourism (Overseas Promotion) (Wales) Act 1992 finally gave WTB the power to undertake overseas marketing activity to supplement the work of the British Tourist Authority.

The 1992 legislation took much of the heat out of the politics of overseas marketing. Wales now had far greater bargaining power and was able to devote its own resources to cost effective initiatives focusing on products and markets especially important to Wales. Greatly enhanced funding from Europe and from the Welsh Assembly Government enabled the Board to develop its overseas marketing work substantially. Greater confidence within the nation and the emergence of facilities, performance venues and events of world standing were important in helping Wales to face up to the challenges of a more competitive and uncertain post-9/11 world.

Product development

The Board took very seriously its remit under the Development of Tourism Act 'to encourage the provision and improvement of tourism facilities'. The Act made provision for two schemes of financial assistance – the Hotel Development Incentive Scheme (HDIS) and the Special Tourism Projects Scheme (popularly termed the Section 4 or S4 scheme).

HDIS was a time-limited programme, administered during the first five years of the statutory Board's life. Its effects were immediate and significant, enabling hotel development and improvement in Wales to achieve a momentum not previously experienced during the twentieth century. As a consequence, 4161 new bedrooms were created in Wales, increasing hotel stock by 10%.

Unlike HDIS, the S4 scheme was a discretionary one and it enabled financial assistance by way of grant or loan to be offered towards the capital cost of any project which the Board considered would provide or improve tourism facilities or amenities. The S4 budget was relatively small in absolute terms and other official agencies such as the Welsh Development Agency and the Development Board for Rural Wales were also able to invest significant sums in tourism related projects. In addition, the Welsh Office and later the Welsh Assembly Government also administered specific grant aid schemes with a bearing upon tourism, as did local authorities. In its original form the S4 scheme was linked to regional development policy and confined to certain designated Assisted Areas, but in 1980 the scheme was extended to the whole of Wales.

As time passed continuation of the S4 scheme was questioned, particularly when equivalent schemes in England and Scotland were withdrawn. WTB mounted a vigorous defence of the scheme, assisted by proactive local authorities and tourism businesses. As a consequence, the S4 scheme remained a key development tool in Wales, and successive WTB medium term strategies featured a series of imaginatively designed programmes targeted geographically and sectorally, to be implemented with partner organizations. Thus, for example, during the six years ending 31 March 2006, WTB invested £13 million into tourism growth areas and £44 million into sectoral initiatives. These sums were enhanced significantly by ERDF funding from Objectives 1 and 2 programmes and Welsh Assembly Government match funds. This helped to facilitate an estimated total capital investment of £275 million in just over 1000 projects leading to the creation/safeguarding of almost 4200 jobs.

The quest for quality

In tourism as in other highly competitive industries the notion of quality is very important. It soon became apparent to WTB that there was much to be gained from working with business leaders who were prepared to invest in superior quality facilities, and commendation schemes were seen as a valuable tool for doing so. Such schemes allowed operators meeting specified standards to use and display a readily identifiable symbol which served as a badge of achievement that could underpin marketing and, over time, encourage other operators to raise their own standards.

WTB's first commendation initiatives related to the static caravan sector – which was very important to Wales and striving to adapt to changing consumer tastes. The Dragon Award Scheme, launched in 1976, set out to encourage higher standards for caravan units and the appearance of caravan parks, thereby challenging existing perceptions and breaking new ground in Britain. The Farmhouse and Guest House Award was another good example of an early WTB initiative to drive up product and service quality – this time in an emerging sector whose operators stood to benefit from encouragement and training in product development, customer care and marketing.

During the mid-1970s accommodation enterprises featuring in WTB publications were required to signify that their facilities met certain prescribed standards – although no inspections were undertaken to confirm that fact. The next major development came in 1980 when, after consultation with the trade, WTB introduced a pilot scheme to inspect accommodation establishments in order to verify that the basic information about facilities was correct. The scheme was subsequently extended to all serviced accommodation enterprises that wished to be included in WTB literature. Although this remained a voluntary system, its implications were significant and at the time it was a brave step, which was criticized by some for being exclusive. Nevertheless it was supported by the majority of operators and heralded a new approach that would also be espoused in England and Scotland.

Over the years all the statutory tourist boards worked hard to improve and rationalize their accommodation accreditation schemes – not always agreeing on the best way forward. In 1987 the accommodation guides published by the English, Scottish and Wales Tourist Boards incorporated the new harmonized Crown Classification standards for the first time and within a couple of years new grading-based schemes were introduced. WTB also became heavily involved in developing accreditation schemes for the activity holidays sector, beating out a new path which other boards would follow.

From the outset the Wales Tourist Board had been a consistent advocate of statutory registration of tourism accommodation, at first in the face of strong criticism from some trade quarters. Over time trade resistance to statutory registration dwindled and the Board began to court support from the newly established National Assembly for Wales. In 2002 WTB's proposals put forward for a system of statutory registration in Wales, backed by independent inspection, were accepted in principle by the Welsh Assembly Government, although not yet implemented.

Looking ahead

The decision to merge the Wales Tourist Board with other public bodies within the Welsh Assembly Government was a controversial one. Ministers saw this as an opportunity to honour a long-standing promise to increase accountability, improve the delivery of public services and reduce duplication of effort. Critics of the decision, on the other hand, considered that WTB had a proud record of exemplary service and that the mechanisms needed to ensure probity and accountability were already in place. They foresaw problems from merging public bodies charged with policy delivery with the central government department charged with policy formulation and scrutiny, and they feared that an organizational culture would emerge characterized by aversion to risk and political expediency, rather than enterprise, enthusiasm and innovation.

The merger has now taken place, and those working within the new structure need to be allowed to settle down into their new roles. The outcome of this bold experiment will be followed very closely, not just in Wales.

References

Howell, Lyn (1988): *The Wales Tourist Board – the Early Years*. Wales Tourist Board; Cardiff.

Owen, Elwyn and Owen, Lyn (2007): *From Candy Floss to Mountain Bikes: A View of the Wales Tourist Board 1969–2006*; University of Wales Institute; Cardiff.

Wales Tourist Board (1976): *Tourism in Wales – A Plan for the Future.*

Wales Tourist Board (1988): *Tourism in Wales – Developing the Potential.*

Wales Tourist Board (1994): *Tourism 2000 – A Strategy for Wales.*

Wales Tourist Board (2000): *Achieving our Potential – A Tourism Strategy for Wales.*

Wales Tourist Board (2001): *The Regional Tourism Partnerships – the Way Forward for Tourism in Wales.*

Welsh Assembly Government (2006) *Achieving our Potential 2006–2013 – Tourism Strategy for Wales, Mid Term Review.*

CHAPTER 9

The story looking ahead in the twenty-first century

Writing in the 1940s, Pimlott looked backwards to comment:

> *There have been few important changes [to holiday taking] during the present century, which could not have been foreseen by a careful observer in 1900. The main trends were settled. Annual holidays were spreading from the middle class to the better-paid manual workers . . . The major seaside resorts of today were firmly established . . . The motorcar was ceasing to be a joke and a nuisance, and the bicycle had reopened the countryside to the people from the towns. If the general standard of life continued to rise, all the ingredients were present for a vast expansion in the number of holiday-makers.*

> (Pimlott, 1947, p. 212)

In the early twenty-first century, the future is rather harder for the careful observer to foresee because we are looking at a mature market and a mature supply in which global forces, not domestic holiday trends are the main driving forces. Tourism in the broad sense in which it is now interpreted at international level (UN Statistical Commission definitions of 1993) is a far wider concept than holidays, which have become only a minor element of total British tourism. Tourism appears to be at a crossroads where the directions for development are far from clear. Paradoxically, such directions may be more, rather than less, likely to be influenced by government action and decisions than hitherto.

The late 1990s witnessed some major discontinuities in tourism such as the emergence of the Internet as a dominant marketing tool; deregulation of European airlines; real concerns for the impacts of global warming;

recognition of traffic congestion; and road pricing. Other shifting factors were an emerging commitment, at least in principle, to sustainable development and government determination to devolve tourism decisions to regions in England – along lines already adopted for Scotland and Wales. All of these will be in play over the next quarter century and the outcomes are hard to predict.

Specific predictions are always likely to be wrong with hindsight because they tend to be dominated by recent events. A classic example is from 1979 when the advance of technology and energy crises led people to believe that massive unemployment and job sharing would be the inevitable future of work in the UK. Clive Jenkins and Barrie Sherman published *In place of work*, in which they confidently predicted that 'the new microelectronic technology is developing so rapidly that a society with many millions of people permanently unemployed is not only inevitable but imminent'. The same authors later published *Leisure Shock* (1981) to develop the theme of predicted massive unemployment in the 1990s and the urgent need for government intervention to cope with massively expanded leisure time. It did not happen. By 2004 unemployment, as measured, was at its lowest level for decades and most people had less, not more disposable leisure time.

At least we can identify the main context of change as reflecting society's response to the post-industrial era of the twenty-first century. 'In post-industrial societies, travel and tourism and mobility generally are no longer a pleasure periphery but an integral and structural part of modern societies and will continue to grow in line with economic progress in all parts of the world. The Zeitgeist of the new age, liberated by the "new economy", is aggressive individualism largely unconstrained by any concepts of collective restraint' (Middleton, 2002, p. 457). 'Integral and structural' provides some confidence that tourism is likely to survive, wherever the winds of change may blow.

12 trends, which are discussed in this chapter

1. Over the last half-century frequent repeat movement away from home on a day or staying basis for business, social and leisure purposes has developed to become part of the way we live and the quality of life for over 95 per cent of the British population. Holidays are now just a minor part of such movement.
2. As a consequence, tourism and leisure have become a core part of the post-industrial and post-agricultural economy (the so-called 'new economy') of just about every urban and rural community from Land's End to John o'Groats.
3. Market maturity and the growth in supply of domestic and international products are forcing the pace of competition and producing losers as

well as winners. Maturity and competition signal an end to so-called mass tourism.

4. In the second half of the twentieth century the winners in the tourism industry were generally large branded businesses that found new ways to meet consumer demand at the lowest possible cost through economies of scale and efficient marketing that ironed out traditional seasonality. Many smaller seasonal businesses disappeared, unable to compete.

5. Facilitated by ICT and especially the commercial development of the Internet, efficient large businesses, some operating on a global scale, will continue to dominate key aspects of transport and accommodation operations in the first decades of the twenty-first century. But low cost ICT and the Internet have liberated efficient small businesses from their traditional market isolation heralding an important shift in market power to small businesses at destinations.

6. For most of the latter part of the twentieth century a long-term shift toward deregulation and privatization has liberated public transport from state ownership and/or control; licensing laws and retailing regulation have been lightened. A countervailing regulatory movement now seems likely to remake the case for closer regulation of tourism in the interests of environmental protection, better destination management and setting limits to growth.

7. Sustainable issues and quality management will increasingly dominate the tourism agenda within the next decade. These are matters for destination management at local level, albeit with national and regional agreements.

8. Destination management – management activities designed to influence visitor volume, visitor types and behaviour at local authority level – has been overlooked and taken for granted in most of the UK for decades. Trends now evident will force greater attention on what happens at local level.

9. Attractive rural areas, heritage landscapes and heritage town centres have been among the strong growth sectors of British tourism over recent decades. All are now under threat from unsympathetic planning and development and some will decline as British seaside resorts did in the last quarter of a century.

10. As a global phenomenon of immense economic significance, tourism – the world's largest industry – has become a logical target for international terrorist movements seeking to achieve disruption and chaos to further their own ends. As the 9/11 carnage so vividly illustrated, tourists are highly vulnerable to organized terror, especially where suicide bombing is the chosen medium. Further violence against travellers is inevitable.

11. The twentieth-century growth of tourism was powered by the activities of remarkable individuals who challenged and overturned the established business models that dominated the tourism industry.

There is every reason to expect the same will be true in the twenty-first century.

12. Given the breadth of what is now covered in the modern tourism definition, the simplistic concept of a 'tourism industry' appears to be working against better understanding and management of the sector.

Frequent repeat movement away from home on a day or staying basis for business, social and leisure purposes has become part of the way we live

Fifty years ago, after the Second World War, tourism was understood to be mainly a matter of annual holidays by the British in Britain. Elizabeth Brunner's (1945) classic analysis of the industry at the end of the war was entitled *Holiday Making and the Holiday Trades*. The model for what we now call tourism was still that of the 1930s – with a rather wider franchise as the economy recovered from the war and holidays with pay took effect. Inbound tourism was comparatively insignificant in volume and apart from essential business and visits to London, it was primarily a matter of visits to friends and relatives from English speaking countries (USA and the former Empire connections).

Today and looking ahead, tourism around the world is the frequent repeat movement from home on a day or staying basis for the whole variety of reasons that an affluent, mobile population considers a normal part of daily lives. Annual holidays are still important but now only a minor part of all tourism movement. Travel by choice, for a few hours or a few days, in Britain, the rest of Europe and internationally is now part of the perceived quality of life for over 95 per cent of the British population. From cradle to grave, apart from those too old or too ill to be able to travel and others incarcerated at Her Majesty's Pleasure, modern Europeans are on the move and consider national boundaries irrelevant to travel.

The more affluent the population of a country becomes, the more likely people are to want to engage in travel of all kinds. In 2005, what has become a daily routine activity for most people in developed societies is still an aspiration elsewhere in the world. Hundreds of millions in India and China as well as in the former Eastern European States and Soviet Russia will have exactly the same ambition just as soon as their economic circumstances permit it. In that sense, at least, we can predict growth in a global sense as Pimlott did for Britain in the 1940s (Pimlott, 1947).

Political and media attitudes, however, continue to reflect old stereotypes. Just as the word 'German' still generally signifies jack-boots to the popular British press, so the word 'tourist' conjures up instant negative images of hordes, grockles, and lemmings killing a golden goose around every corner. No metaphor is too mixed to describe tourism in the popular press; no cliché too overworked. After 50 years of efforts by tourist boards and private sector interests, the positive contribution of modern tourism is increasingly recognized in Scotland and Wales and by local authorities and the new regional authorities in England. This, no doubt, is progress. But tourism is still generally perceived in the media and by most in Parliament as a relatively homogeneous business of leisure and holidays.

Whatever else, modern tourism is not homogeneous. The word 'tourist' is a meaningless term, about as useful for understanding and management purposes as the word 'motorist'. It hangs like a dead albatross around a vibrant sector of the British economy. Modern tourism has become a massively complex movement with economic, social and environmental implications that are not yet understood.

Looking ahead, the implications of *hyper-mobility* as a derogatory expression for modern tourism movement will become more important. There are now clearly emerging implications of limits to further movement imposed, for example, by urban and motorway traffic congestion domestically and by the environmental pollution of airplanes internationally. The volume of demand for personal mobility will continue as the less well-off increase their incomes, but governments are urging the case for price regulation through the imposition of 'green taxes', congestion charges and road tolls. If feasible under international agreements, a fuel tax for airlines is likely to follow. Already we have a Government committed to further tourism growth in principle even as it seeks to evade the implications on the ground. The balance will surely become more difficult to resolve.

Tourism and leisure have become a core part of the post-industrial and post-agricultural economy

Increasingly dubbed 'the visitor economy', for just about every urban and rural community in Britain, from Land's End to John o'Groats, the consequences of modern tourism have brought an economic regeneration lifeline. This consists of hotels, other accommodation and attractions, of course, but also shops, museums, art galleries, heritage attractions, theatres, festivals, theme pubs and clubs, cafes and restaurants, golf clubs, sporting facilities, speciality retail and events of every kind. Combined these have generated and sustained demand from growing visitor numbers whose expenditure has helped to compensate for the decline and loss of traditional nineteenth and mid-twentieth-century industries. Driven primarily by the need to create and sustain employment, the classic British examples of urban regeneration to which visitors are vital are Glasgow, Cardiff, Leeds, Liverpool and Birmingham but there is hardly a village or town that has not identified its heritage and culture as a key element in its economic future. Glasgow, for example, had over 35 000 employed in shipbuilding and marine engineering in the post-war period – and around 1000 hotel beds. After the Garden Festival (1988) and City of

Culture (1990), Glasgow had some 12 000 hotel beds and some 55 000 jobs supported by tourism at the start of the twenty-first century (Radio 4 Programme, 9 September 2004).

Economic regeneration has been supported in many places in the last two decades by access to EU funding for less developed regions. Many more areas have benefited from urban regeneration funding provided by Central Government and more recently by regional policies. Many have had access to millennium and heritage lottery funding to support their tourism ambitions. Offsetting this positive development, however, farming is no longer an economically viable activity in the scenically attractive uplands of Britain, while rural communities and market towns have lost most of their rural roots and lifelines. What is widely regarded and cherished as the traditional countryside seems certain to change its appearance in the next two decades unless the existing tentative links between conservation, farming, visitors, cultural landscapes and sustainable development are given much greater energy and 'investment'. The countryside is threatened by insensitive commercial developments in the name of 'vibrant rural communities'. It is further threatened, even in national parks, by hundreds of towering industrial wind farms dominating heritage landscapes. Such industry may appease government consciences about the unsustainable use of energy and global warming but it will also undermine key aspects of an already fragile tourism resource base. Foot and mouth disease in 2001 revealed just how important tourism is to the rural economy in Britain and it is dangerous to assume that what attracts visitors is not at serious risk of damage.

Market maturity forces the pace of change – the era of mass tourism is over

The 1950s inherited a mainly Victorian infrastructure of tourism supply and enjoyed what was, in effect, a captive holiday market. One might argue that the resorts squandered that inheritance by neglect and comfortable assumptions that the future would be like the past. For most of the half-century since, it was the case internationally that the demand for much of tourism generally exceeded supply. Demand drew entrepreneurs into resort development, airlines and tour operation and their energies have made tourism the fastest growing sector in many countries. New destinations and new countries have been opened up to tap the demand. So great was the demand that mass marketing for mass tourism at lowest achievable prices was the dominant sales approach long after other major consumer industries such as housing, alcohol, motor cars and white goods were developing much more sophisticated marketing techniques based on much better consumer research.

'If it ain't broke', so the argument ran in relation to saleable tourism products 'don't fix it'. British seaside resorts pursued the policy until it was too late for many to change. One may speculate that many rural areas will follow the same trajectory for the same reasons as history repeats itself once more.

The collectivist, mass leisure era of the early to mid-twentieth century (see Chapters 1 and 2) in many ways died in the 1960s and 1970s as more demanding and more knowledgeable consumers exercised their individual choices. Tour operation, the dominant British form for holidays abroad, was a curious exception made possible only by the excess of demand over supply. But the Internet revolution opened other opportunities for customer access after 1995 and sounded the death knell of traditional mass marketing. Even so, it seems astonishing that it was only in 1999 that Thomson, the leading British tour operator for some 30 years, declared that it had finally moved away from the 'one size fits all' approach that had characterized its marketing over the years (*Travel Trade Gazette* 26.07.1999).

It is a basic rule of economics that growth markets always attract new supply and tourism supply has been increasing faster than the growth of demand as countries around the world have identified the economic benefits of tourism as a means of growth in the twenty-first century. More supply means more competition and it produces losers as well as winners.

In the second half of the twentieth century the winners in the tourism industry were generally large branded businesses

As the overall tourism market grew and developed internationally it was logical for big companies to grow bigger. Since the 1980s, international, multinational and global tourism companies have emerged and grown so that their brands and logos are internationally known. Hilton, Marriott, Intercontinental, Disney, British Airways and TUI are almost as well known as Nike, Coca-Cola and Toyota. Although larger size does not always equate with lower costs, the economies of scale achievable by bulk purchasing, bulk marketing, bulk distribution and providing multiple services to customers have driven down the unit costs of production and, therefore, consumer prices. Since the 1980s this process has been immensely aided by developments of ICT that facilitate the control and marketing of unsold capacity and the manipulation of prices to achieve sales on a minute by minute basis. Able to dominate and utilize the power of the Internet since the late 1990s, large companies have been the dominant force in modern tourism.

Efficient large companies with low cost operations have and will continue to drive out inefficient smaller businesses in their sectors, just as the giants of the supermarket world make it impossible for smaller rivals to match them on price, quality and choice. In Britain, hundreds of traditionally built two and three star hotels, many small guesthouses, smaller caravan parks and many self-catering apartments in holiday resorts have been driven out of the market in the last two decades. They were simply unable to compete.

Looking ahead, there seems every reason to suppose that large corporations will continue to dominate supply in hotels and much of self-catering accommodation, in air transport and in much of the catering and allied hospitality provision. But they will not replace the importance of smaller businesses dealing face to face with visitors at destinations for reasons noted below.

Paradoxically, there will be a shift of marketing power to efficient small businesses at visited destinations

Since the dawn of modern tourism in the nineteenth century, the sector has been comprised mainly of small operators. In 1900, the only big companies were railway and shipping companies, a handful of tour operators such as Thomas Cook, and the grand hotels in cities and at railway termini. For the whole of the twentieth century, with the few exceptions of holiday camps and other privately run resorts, such as Center Parcs, tourists were mostly catered for and looked after at the destination by small businesses. Notwithstanding the growth of big businesses in tourism including hotels and catering operations, at the destination visitors are still looked after primarily by small and very small businesses in the twenty-first century.

In EU parlance, SMEs (small and medium sized enterprises) have less than 250 employees. A small enterprise has less than 50 employees. But 50 employees is a very large tourism business at most destinations in Britain and tourism is dominated by enterprises with less than 10 employees (also known as micro enterprises). Many businesses have less than that, of course, being operated by a male or female proprietor, often on a part-time basis. Guesthouses, farm houses, cottages for rent, B&Bs, cafes, taxi drivers, shops, bars, many caravan and camping sites and even small attractions are typically run by a full-time staff of one or two, including the proprietor.

Such small enterprises are vital for tourism. They comprise all that most visitors, especially visitors coming from a distance, will ever encounter of the local population in the places visited. The best of small businesses have personality, character related to the destination, reflect local customs and traditions including local architecture, and they speak with a local dialect. They exude pride of place, often utilize locally produced supplies and deal personally with visitors by phone and letter as well as e-mail. They meet visitors on an equal basis and offer a source of advice and help in relation to what a destination offers. They do not force customers to deal with automated call centres and they have to be people centred and friendly in order to survive.

By contrast big companies are increasingly impersonal, deal only via automated websites and call centres, and employ anonymous staff trained only in their set procedures. They often have to employ staff who are not from the local area or necessarily of the same nation as the residents of the destination. Such staff may not be competent in speaking the local language. Big companies are typically efficient, if impersonal, in dealing with customers who have no problems, but are at their worst when customers have questions or encounter difficulties and wish to complain or have assistance. Airlines can fly people cheaply to destinations and budget hotels can cheaply accommodate their physical needs for rooms and food – but neither provides the emotional quality of the relationship with the destination that only small locally based and orientated businesses can supply. Memorable experiences are unlikely to be provided by budget hotels and budget airlines or by airport terminal shops and branded catering outlets. The better smaller operators, dealing face to face with visitors on their premises, provide the human warmth and local touch that satisfy service expectations and provide real contact with the visited destination. Market trends suggest these qualities are likely to be in higher demand over the next decade.

Since the 1990s, falling costs of ICT, phone costs and the availability of the Internet and gateway providers have revolutionized the marketing potential of efficient small businesses. The majority of customers in Britain are already computer literate and, looking ahead, the future looks very bright for small businesses providing friendly service, value for money and what customers perceive as good quality – effectively marketed through the Internet.

Regulation, deregulation, regulation again

In Britain, under the Labour controlled eras of the 1940s and 1960s, but decades before the advent of European legislation, the political thrust was to regulate industry and businesses in the interests of social, labour and welfare objectives. A combination of state ownership, state-appointed agencies or Quangos and a raft of regulatory provisions covered transport provision (see Chapter 4). Accommodation and visitor attractions were considered too unimportant to warrant their own regulation, such as registration and licensing, although they were embraced in general business regulation.

There was even a short-lived initiative to establish an official government department for tourism in the 1940s and government intervention was especially evident in exchange controls to inhibit British visits abroad, in planning regulations and the creation of national tourist boards and their regional counterparts. In the early 1970s, after the 1969 Development of Tourism Act, tourist boards in England probably reached the peak of their powers and government support. Despite frequent calls over the decades for the statutory licensing and classification of hotels, often coupled with other calls for a tourist tax, especially for London, neither of these options was taken up although the issues do not go away and seem certain to return, doubtless in 'modern' forms.

The regulatory pendulum swung the other way in the 1950s and more markedly in the 1980s and 1990s, especially under the Conservative Governments of Mrs Thatcher. In the 1980s state ownership and regulation were anathema to the Government, although many critics have pointed to the way that centralist powers controlled by Westminster grew in other sectors such as education and local government. British Airways was privatized, investment programmes for tourism were stopped (in England although not in Scotland and Wales), and private enterprise and market forces were the watchwords.

The process of less involved government probably reached its peak just before the Maastricht Treaty. While the then British Tourist Authority continued to receive government support for its role in promoting inbound tourism, the English Tourist Board was effectively emasculated by successive cuts in its budget and more or less ineffective attempts to create economies of scale in its operations in collaboration with the BTA. As noted in Chapter 7, it was at this time in the early 1990s and subsequently that real control of national tourism organizations was quietly shifted into the hands of civil servants in the Department of National Heritage and its successor, the Department for Culture, Media and Sport.

The pendulum swing back to greater regulation probably dates from when the Maastrich Treaty was signed and was given more impetus after the election of the new Labour Government in 1997. Regulatory powers influencing tourism businesses increased, especially in health and safety issues and environmental controls, and these and a raft of social legislation affecting tourism employees were increasingly transferred to Brussels. The UK Government has looked to small businesses to act as its agent in taxing employees and delivering some of its employment benefits. But there was also a powerful deregulation movement for airlines under the competition rules endorsed by the EU. Although the deregulatory debate and initial steps had been going on for over a decade in Europe, it was almost 20 years after President Carter deregulated domestic airlines in the USA in 1978, that Brussels was implementing the same principles in its policies for airlines.

Seeking to bolster the powers available to its new Regional Development Agencies in England, the Government found it easy to dismantle the English Tourism Council in 2003. Responsibility for marketing domestic tourism for England was transferred to a new department within VisitBritain while abandoning vital processes of national co-ordination across the UK as a whole and within England in particular.

Looking ahead, although the tourism implications seem very likely to be lost or subsumed within a focus on specifically defined problems such as global warming or traffic congestion, in which tourism plays only a minor part, more regulation and control, including fiscal measures, look inevitable. There is the need to influence the environmental impacts of a hyper-mobile society. Thus, we may see a greater level of taxation in one form or another imposed on air travellers (to help combat global warming), on car travellers (to avoid gridlock) and on users of the countryside (to mitigate visitor pressures on fragile natural environments). 1996 – the year that the first airport taxes were levied – and 2003 when the Central London Traffic Congestion Charge was implemented are likely to be significant dates for the future of British tourism. At the time of writing, the regulatory pendulum affecting tourism interests appears to be in full swing back toward the 1960s.

The Treasury is understandably worried that Britain has been spending more each year abroad than overseas visitors spend here, with the deficit rising every year since 1996 to a record level of some £17 billion a year in 2003. If it follows its own precedents, the Treasury will probably increase the budget of the BTA and ignore the easier and far more substantive future gains to be had from domestic tourism through supporting the provision of better reasons to stay in Britain than travel abroad. Lack of government interest in domestic tourism is also reflected in the fact that British local authorities have never had a statutory requirement to deal with visitors within their boundaries (see below). In 2005, most do have some policies and programmes in place, increasingly as an arm of local economic regeneration. But local tourism budgets in England are severely squeezed by pressure from Westminster to allocate funds to targets that Government chooses and in 2006 they do not include support for domestic tourism.

Sustainable tourism will dominate the agenda for the next decade

Concerns about the unsustainable activities of mankind can be traced back through history. They surfaced more pointedly and in global form in the 1960s, 1970s and 1980s as over-intensive agriculture and fishing, global warming, ozone layer depletion, acid rain, loss of rain forests, marine pollution and the loss of many species were identified and became more measurable with new technology developments such as satellite photography. But as a subject for government strategy and action at international, national, regional and local level, and as an action programme intended to embrace the private sector, sustainable development did not emerge until the Rio Earth Summit of 1992. For a brief period the world's attention was drawn to the need to reduce, reuse and recycle (and the many variants on the theme). Attention focused on trying to limit at least some of the pressures of a rising world population and the environmental damage caused by economic development and consumer pressures. The United Nations took a lead and, urged by an astonishing array of NGOs and green lobby interests, many governments began to respond. The European Union is clearly committed to the ideas, not least in its current agricultural policy and payments, for example, and in its environmental regulation generally.

Entrenched political and industry attitudes, however, and established economic systems and human behaviour patterns are not amenable to rapid change. The ideas of sustainable development are massively complex. The implications of attempting to move toward global equity (the rights of developing nations to the same levels of finite resources and pollution as already enjoyed by developed nations) and to achieve social and inter-generational equity may prove self-defeating. Countries and global industries do not respond to calls for common sense and much of the Rio hopes and aspirations have not been realized. *Agenda 21* (the so-called 'blue print' for sustainable development) agreed at the Rio Summit was always more pious hope than practical programme. On the other hand, the fact that it was agreed at all reflected an important milestone along a route that seems likely to become much more important in the twenty-first century.

Internationally, it has taken over a decade for the ideas of sustainability to be translated from idealistic concepts, with which no-one can disagree, into the beginnings of action programmes which are acceptable to competing interest groups. For tourism there is no coherent action consensus yet. Around the world, from the initial, often misguided dalliance with so-called eco-tourism, to wider tourism response in the actions and recommendations for action by the World Tourism Organization and the World Travel and Tourism Council, one can identify a process that will develop. But sustainable programmes are still at an early stage of development and despite a massive shift in general consciousness over a decade, they have barely scratched the surface of popular tourism and visitor behaviour. Countries such as Australia and New Zealand have taken the issues more seriously than most – not least because so much of their tourism offer reflects the promise of pristine environments, which they therefore have to protect. In Britain in 2005, although the ideas of sustainability are generally adopted in the endless unread public sector 'visions and strategies' that now surround tourism, most of it is no more than lip service.

There are two main directions for sustainable tourism. One is the management of the physical, economic, social and cultural environment at the destination (destination management as noted below) and the other is the planned programme of actions that businesses in tourism can take to reduce their environmental impact and communicate with their customers. These range from reducing energy and water consumption, to local sourcing of food and other supplies, and promoting sustainable ideas in their marketing. In 2005 such programmes are being implemented in some larger tourism organizations and a far-sighted minority of smaller businesses, although they have had only minor impact yet on the tens of thousands of small businesses that will continue to dominate tourism provision.

In 2005, however, there are schemes in all parts of the UK that are now actively promoting such programmes. In 2003/04 a government sponsored national scheme to recognize best practice for local authorities (the Beacon Council Scheme) recognized tourism for the first time. It included 'Promoting Sustainable Tourism' as one of its themes and attracted over 30 entries from across England. This is not much more than 5 per cent of all eligible authorities but it is a start.

Looking ahead one can fairly confidently predict that airline prices will be forced to rise either through carbon trading schemes or through the imposition of significant fuel taxes that will finally overtake the Chicago Convention agreements of 1944. Such taxes will have to be justified internationally on environmental pollution grounds. Motorway and urban road pricing is already a reality and is likely to extend greatly in a deliberate attempt to curtail mobility. Wider action, such as a combination of fiscal incentives and penalties to reward businesses that adopt more sustainable practices can also be predicted. More contentiously, because it would oppose the current Government's views of a 'vibrant rural economy,' we may see more effective local planning controls to prevent overdevelopment/inappropriate development in scenic areas attractive to visitors and to support better destination management practice.

Over the next decade it does not seem too optimistic to hope that good sustainable practice will become an assessed core part of product quality evaluation schemes for accommodation, attractions and destinations. One may predict that growing numbers of consumers will recognize the worth of such evaluations and be willing to opt for higher graded, more sustainable products as an indicator of the quality of the experience provided and value for money. The implications for change among UK local authorities, noted in the next section, seem likely to facilitate that process.

Destination management – a neglected art in the twentieth century

As outlined in Chapter 7, the government approach to tourism in the UK for over sixty years has tended to focus on organizational issues at the national and regional level. Local authorities have been consulted to embrace them at least nominally within the new regional structures created in the last three years but usually with the comfortable assumption that local authorities can be cajoled or compelled to implement whatever visions, strategies and policies are agreed. Since 2002, the national (England) agenda has been for regional devolution of tourism responsibilities to new Regional Development Agencies (RDAs), and the former English Tourism Council was abolished to facilitate the regional shift of emphasis. RDAs are, of course, 'strategic' rather than action bodies and look to others on the ground to implement whatever action is called for.

Experience and evidence suggests to many on the ground at local level that Westminster preoccupation with the national and regional level has become less relevant in tourism and may be counter productive. Many believe that 'the local destination is the only logical basis for understanding the specific impact of tourism and for developing the tools of visitor management needed for sustainable development' (Middleton and Hawkins, 1998, p. 82). Destinations mean specific places, such as cities, towns, countryside and seaside locations, the majority of which are the direct responsibility of elected local authorities in the UK. It is widely acknowledged that tourism success depends on the quality of the experience that visitors receive when they visit places. Promotion typically focuses on the attractive images that each destination affords. These include heritage architecture, townscapes and landscapes and the special characteristics of place for which local authorities carry responsibility. The logic of this is that *destination management*, the buzzword of modern tourism, is essentially a matter for local authorities although they have no acknowledged role as such under the new Regional organizational arrangements in England.

Interestingly, this local perspective was better understood both before and after the First World War when seaside towns were being developed by entrepreneurs working with municipal authorities. Seaside authorities fought for and gained parliamentary support in the 1920s and 1930s to use locally generated rates for tourism promotional purposes and facilities. History was forgotten, however, when local government was reorganized in the early 1970s and wider boundaries were drawn in which most resorts were typically only one element within a wider area economy. Permission to engage voluntarily in tourism activities was included in the 1972 legislation and participation in the regional tourist boards created under the 1969 Act was a very positive step for many local authorities. But there was no requirement or statutory duty to engage in support for tourism or in destination management. With few exceptions, over the 1970s to 1990s, such as access through membership to regional tourist boards, the local dimension of tourism was subjected to frequent exhortation but largely left to its own devices.

Successful tourism destination management requires that local authorities have to be involved with supporting the visitor experience on the ground because – in essence – they control the look and the overall ambience of visited places. An attractive place to visit means that a local authority has exercised its planning and development controls, provides and maintains key infrastructure such as promenades, street furniture, landscaping and parks and gardens, and often owns or subsidizes theatres, museums, art galleries, monuments and heritage objects and collections. Local authorities are also responsible for the provision of public toilets, street cleansing and car parking. Where alternative transport to the use of cars exists, it is usually provided or subsidized by a local authority. As soon as they are committed to any form of tourism action, local authorities naturally and unavoidably consult with local tourism businesses and seek to engage their participation in the design and implementation of plans. Through the actions of the Tourism Management Institute (formed in 1995) and the first issue of the *Destination Management Handbook*, which that body devised in 2003 with the former English Tourism Council, there is now a basis for progress. The government sponsored Beacon Council Award Scheme in 2003/04 identified ample evidence of good practice in partnerships with local businesses, which augurs well for the future.

In England, throughout the period covered by this book, tourism has been a non-statutory activity for local authorities, meaning that they have no legal requirement to take any destination management actions in support of tourism. For decades until the 1980s, apart from leading seaside resorts and cities, most did little other than provide and operate parks and gardens and subsidize museums and the arts and public lavatories. Since the 1980s, as noted earlier, tourism has been widely identified for its potential contribution to the local economy and tourism personnel are now frequently to be found reporting to the economic development department within a council. The economic focus provides tourism interests with far more influence within council decisions than they ever had under departments for leisure or parks and gardens. Even more significant for the longer run, most local authorities are now required to focus efforts on achieving a high quality of life for local residents. In many ways, apart from added traffic, quality of life for residents is often the same as quality of experience for visitors and the new linkages of economic development, sustainable development and quality of life within local authorities have benign implications for the future management of tourism.

Unfortunately, until the mid-1990s, although all local authorities have the necessary planning and other tools to manage tourism, very few local authorities had any means of estimating the volume and value of their tourism and the changing characteristics of the visitors they receive. Effective destination management in the absence of adequate management information is, of course, impossible. Although surrogate, low cost means of estimating volume and value were introduced in the 1990s, such UK resources as are available to devote to the statistics of tourism have been expended at national and regional level; the local level has been left to fend for itself as best it can.

Looking ahead, the requirements of a mature industry, the implications of achieving greater sustainability and the need to enhance quality and succeed in an ever more competitive marketplace seems certain to put greater emphasis on the proactive role that local authorities will have to play in the next decade. After decades of focus on the national and regional level, this implies either an unlikely increase in government spending on tourism or a shift of resources from the national and regional level to the local level. This would amount to a beneficial revolution in UK tourism although there are few signs in 2005 that the fundamental requirement for better destination management at local level has any substantive recognition in Government. Currently, under immense pressure from ratepayers as a result of coping with rising costs and Central Government requirements for their statutory functions, most local authorities are being forced to cut back on all 'nonessential spending'. For many that includes public toilets and other tourism related provision and some have closed established tourism departments to help balance their accounts. For destination management to have meaning, local government tourism interests need far better understanding and national lobbying than they have today.

Tourism and terrorism

The free and unrestricted movement of people of different nationalities around the world with minimum processing through check-in procedures and border controls was a post-war dream after two world wars. It came close to reality in much of the West in the 1960s. But such freedom of movement attracts and provides endless opportunities to those who seek the attention of the world's media. Hijacking of airplanes has been a logical target for terrorists for over 30 years since Palestinians first staged a four-plane hijack in 1970. Terrorist groups seeking political goals have subjected the UK and many other parts of the world to bombings and other destruction of lives and property. Such activity reached its apogee (to date) on 9/11 when terrorists hijacked four planes in 2001 and two were flown into the World Trade Centre in New York and one into the Pentagon. There is a terrible and lasting symbolism in the globally transmitted pictures of aircraft, global icons of modern tourism, being flown into the twin towers with their passengers using mobile phones to inform others of their imminent death. The media exposure at the time and for years afterwards provided the 'oxygen of publicity' for the perpetrators at a level perhaps even they did not anticipate.

It is too soon to be sure whether there is any way back from the mounting tide of security that now attends public places, especially domestic and international flights. The fact that the 9/11 hijackers had been checked and passed through security at US airports does not suggest that it will be easy. In Britain, with their expertise honed in Northern Ireland, the IRA bombed London in 1973 and other English cities later, establishing a similar rule that places of easy access to all nationalities provide the needed cover for terrorist operations. The more recent escalation of terror utilizing suicide bombers raises the security issues still further.

Looking ahead, international terrorism and international tourism seem likely to go hand in hand. Security devices will improve but so will the ingenuity and planning of the attackers and the clear implication is that costs will rise for customers and convenience will fall, trapped in queues and security procedures. Major incidents already trigger major turndowns in tourism flows and the full impact of the fear factor is hard to evaluate.

Multiple visions – through a glass, darkly

Over the last fifty years tourism has been subjected to hundreds of what are now long forgotten, never realized government and agency pronouncements about its future. In one sense, therefore, the output of strategies and policy statements is not new. On the other hand, there has been a veritable explosion in strategic output since the mid-1990s. It has been massively expanded by the demands of the present Government and the emphasis throughout the public sector on various forms of 'top-down' targets and objectives based on grandiose visions, strategies and policy statements. The process has been grasped and further elaborated by the new regional authorities; each determined to mark its influence. Each document has its attendant consultants, consultancy phases and multiple drafts, and takes up thousands of hours of meetings and staff time, not to mention trees and document shredders. Facilitated by ever more efficient word processors, websites and e-mail communication, strategies have become a national obsession in twenty-first-century tourism in Britain. At best, such strategies are outline action programmes; mostly they are complicated time and money wasting surrogates for action on the ground, which is invariably allocated to or assumed to be the responsibility of other bodies, especially local authorities.

As a result, the tourism world in 2005 is awash with national, regional and local 'visions' at every turn that few but their mainly public sector authors will ever read, and which will have little or no impact at all on the ground. Apologists will claim that the 'key issues have been addressed', which presumably absolves the authors from blame or personal responsibility when action fails to materialize. Few policy statements last more than a year or two at most before circumstances change (or political masters change), the authors move on and the whole crazy process is repeated. In 2005, information overload and the production of strategies has become an occupational hazard.

Looking ahead, it seems safe to predict that the tidal wave of policies swamping tourism development will increase further until a government has the courage to recognize the local destination realities of modern tourism, target the 'bottom-up' approach and reward achievements on the ground rather than wordage in strategy documents. One should not hold one's breath.

Rapid expansion of tourism as a subject for study

Prior to 1968, tourism was not a separate subject for study in Higher Education in the UK although it was established in a small number of colleges and universities in mainland Europe. It grew initially from courses leading to qualifications for the hotel and catering industry, which had been established mostly after the Second World War. Following the Robbins Report of 1963 and the creation of new universities out of the former Polytechnics/Colleges of Advanced Technology, the University of Surrey created its first degrees in hotel and catering management in which, from 1968, tourism was first taught and examined as an optional subject.

Influenced by the leadership of Professor Rik Medlik in the 1960s, tourism studies leading to degrees commenced at postgraduate level in 1972 at the new Universities of Surrey and Strathclyde (Scottish Hotel School). These were followed by the first undergraduate degrees at what was then Bournemouth College of Higher Education in 1986. Other courses quickly followed, boosted by the decision to create the next wave of new universities in the early 1990s. Expansion reflected both student interest and demand and the drive by governments to expand vocational participation in higher education. It is less obvious that the commercial sector played a role in the growth of provision.

In the UK, degree course provision had grown since the 1970s to some 100 degree level courses in over 50 institutions by 2000 (see data in Appendix V). In addition, many schools and colleges of further education are now also offering courses, many as part of the National Vocational Qualifications process (NVQs). Internationally, in the first years of the twenty-first century, although there is no official registration as such, some 582 academic institutions in 92 countries were known to be offering courses in aspects of tourism, leisure, hospitality, outdoor recreation and sport. Some 2700 individual researchers/authors in the field were recorded in 101 countries. Some 122 000 books, articles and reports were also listed (Centre International de Recherches et d'Etudes Touristiques). These are certainly minimum estimates, as entries have to identify themselves to the Centre.

Influenced by the development of tourism studies and the need to promote and facilitate greater professionalism in tourism, the UK Tourism Society was formed in 1977 for individuals engaged in all the private and public sectors that contribute to the tourism economy. The Society celebrated its twenty-first year in 1998.

Is the idea of a 'tourism industry' counter productive in the twenty-first century?

Just as the word 'tourist' has continued to generate stereotypes of visitor movement that are fifty years or more out of date, so the term 'tourism industry', into which so much lobbying went in the last quarter century, now appears to be increasingly less useful in the twenty-first century.

From the 1960s, at least until the 1990s, there was a good case in the UK for identifying visitor related services as 'the tourism industry'. It helped to focus political minds on a sector of the economy that deserved recognition and treatment *pari passu* with other major sectors, such as the finance industry, information and communications technology or shipbuilding. It helped to forge links between disparate sectors. It was a way of saying that a sector generating some £75 billion a year in direct spending should be considered and appropriately supported by government. Barely a ministerial speech has been uttered in the last decade that did not start with overall 'industry' estimates of tourism expenditure and employment.

It is still not known with any accuracy, of course, how many people are actually employed in the 'tourist industry', but that does not prevent 'guesstimates' being used on every occasion and no doubt ignorance is helpful when the data are to be manipulated for political reasons. Some indication of the current acceptance of the term can be seen in the Foreword to the 3rd Annual Report of the Tourism Alliance over the signature of Digby Jones, then Director General of the CBI. In his short statement, the term 'tourism industry' appears no less than ten times in 21 lines of text (July, 2004).

Paradoxically, as tourism and thus the sectors of economic activity it sustains become more and more diverse and more recognizably significant in their own right, it becomes counter productive to attempt to lump them together as a single 'industry'. As explained in Appendix III, tourism is not an industry in any of the normal senses identified by economists. There is no doubt that local and regional government understands the importance of tourism; they do not have to be convinced. There has been an All Party Tourism Committee in the House of Commons for decades and after extensive lobbying there is understanding that tourism matters even if the level of knowledge does not appear to go much deeper.

At government level, the first Department of National Heritage was established at Westminster in 1992 to include responsibility for tourism matters; it was renamed the Department for Culture, Media and Sport in 1997. In this sense one might argue that Government and politicians do now take the 'industry' seriously, at least in the ceaseless political wordsmith chatter of national and regional visions and strategic pronunciations.

The Treasury, however, which matters most, appears unconvinced. To the Treasury, inbound tourism is what matters because it represents invisible exports that offset what the British spend abroad. The more British visitors spend abroad, the more the Treasury is concerned about the 'balance of payments effects'. The Treasury is not concerned with domestic tourism (four-fifths or more of the total expenditure attributed to tourism) because it considers that domestic tourism spending represents money moving around within the UK economy, not new money generated, as is the case with inbound visits. It looks very different in regional and local economic terms, of course, but it fails to convince the Treasury.

The real problem for the twenty-first century is that the business of tourism has become just too diverse to be treated as if it were a single industry. For most practical purposes, such as planning and regulations, marketing, development support and incentives or fiscal impositions, each of the sectors in tourism is different. The air transport sector, for example, strongly influences the volume and routes of travel flows but airlines have few commercial interests in common with railways, cruise ships or motorcars against which they compete. Farmhouse B&Bs have nothing in common with budget hotels in cities; theme parks have little in common with cathedrals or zoos, and the ethos and objectives of Club 18–30 are somewhat different from those of the Saga Group. Glyndebourne and Aldeburgh have little obvious affiliation with nightclubbers in Wolverhampton or Blackpool, but all of these are aspects of the 'tourism industry' under the agreed definition of tourism. More importantly, local authorities are leading players in the tourism 'industry', but the concept of industry does not fit happily at all with their role.

Looking ahead, although progress is as always bedevilled by the inadequate measurement of tourism, one may hope that the idea of a 'visitor economy' or tourism sector as a cross-cutting theme for government will replace misleading simplistic notions of an 'industry'. Perhaps, on that basis, the Treasury may be rather more convinced. Government has already abandoned one national tourist board and passed the baton to the regions in England. One may speculate that there is now a case for abandoning the increasingly superfluous level of regional tourist boards in favour of more proactive links directly between regions and local authorities, either individually or in visitor logical destination area groupings.

Whether or not the RDAs acquire elected regional assemblies as the present Government wishes, the case for better links between regions and local authorities remains powerful. There will still be a vital case for national co-ordination, for example on research, website operations, visitor information and accommodation grading, but it is not obvious that there will be a role for the existing tier of regional tourist boards that were created after the 1969 Act. Some have already been dismantled. Perhaps 'modernization' will sweep them all away to follow the Board that created them.

Into the future

To pull together the main threads discussed in this chapter, two developments are striking when looking ahead in the context of what happened in the last fifty years. They suggest a third consideration of a radical shift in current government approaches to tourism in the UK.

First is the recognition that tourism, which in the 1950s was for most people a once a year seasonal demand for domestic holidays and not available to all, has grown into a radically different phenomenon over the last fifty years. Now involving frequent, year-round day as well as staying visits to international and domestic destinations, tourism has evolved to become an integral part of modern living. Tourism is now for the many, not the few, and it is inclusive of virtually all in society.

Second, because of the first point, it becomes increasingly clear that supplying visitor needs has become an important part of private and public sector service provision and employment in nearly every local community. For most urban, coastal and rural localities, modern tourism is now a significant influence on the local economy, a key element in economic regeneration, influences the look and feel of public spaces and is part of the quality of life of local communities. Equally important, it can play a significant role in sustaining the qualities of the local environment. Although they have no statutory obligations for tourism development and management, few UK local authorities can afford to ignore such a pervasive aspect of local life.

These two points on demand and supply represent a revolutionary change in British tourism in little over 50 years. Such change must surely have an impact on the way that tourism is managed in Britain. Historically, as outlined in Chapter 7, it seemed reasonable and logical that tourism, in so far as any form of national policy and intervention was needed, should be managed by national tourist boards, funded by and reporting to Central Government. Regional tourist boards were a logical extension of that approach and were seen as the way to engage with local authorities.

Devolution of tourism to Scotland and Wales in the 1990s and then to English regional development agencies takes the same case forward. It is logical in principle, of course, but it is also very much a top-down approach to tourism that was arguably justified by the circumstances of the tourism sector and its stage of growth up to the 1990s. It is also an approach dominated by politicians and civil servants with little if any direct experience of the tourism business. It is an approach that creates layers of bureaucracy devising strategies and setting targets for each other while contributing little of value at local level where tourism takes place. Whenever tourism in Britain appears to be an item for government consideration, the Government has invariably focused not on the tourism sector's needs but on yet more tinkering with the top-down organizational structure and the allocation of funding and nominal responsibilities between the layers.

The third consideration arises, therefore, because of the further growth of tourism and its far-reaching influences in the twenty-first century. The consideration is whether or not top-down national, regional and now sub-regional 'policies' are still the best approach for Britain or whether time has overtaken this form of governance. The alternative is deliberately to shift the present emphasis on the national and regional toward the local level where tourism actually makes its impact, whether it be central London, Cardiff, Gloucester, Llandudno, Manchester, North Yorkshire, Edinburgh, Thurso or most places in between. This would require a revolutionary bottom-up focus that would necessarily embrace local authorities and local businesses as key partners in any decision-making processes. Where local authorities choose to work together within a broader area, such groupings should be welcomed. This approach would not have been possible before the modern era of near universal availability of management information systems and Internet communications, but it must be an option over the next decade.

This book is not the place to outline how the bottom-up approach would work. It would clearly require close public and private sector collaboration. But a shift of this type would be a radical, modernizing step indeed. It would necessarily echo and take forward into the new century the best of the public/private sector approach that existed in the UK before 1970. It would make more sense and offer better prospects of collaboration than the mess of the past and present top-down layering of the governance of tourism constructed since the 1960s and summarized in Chapter 7.

The contribution
of the late L. J. Lickorish
CBE, 1922 to 2002

Invariably known as Len, Leonard Lickorish graduated in Economics at University College, London in 1941. He served as a Royal Air Force pilot from 1941 to 1946, latterly flying twin-engined Mosquitoes in which he developed navigational skills he was later to use onboard racing yachts off the Essex coast.

He joined the British Travel and Holidays Association immediately after the war in 1946. It was then Britain's official tourist organization with a staff of just six and he set up its research department. He was with the Association as it developed its role in the early 1950s becoming General Manager in 1962. When the Association became the British Tourist Authority under the 1969 Development of Tourism Act, Len was appointed its first Chief Executive Officer, becoming Director General in 1972, a post in which he served until his retirement in 1986. His well-deserved CBE was awarded in 1975. He was earlier made an Officer of the Crown of Belgium in 1967 in recognition of his work to develop tourism within Europe. He was a Fellow of the UK Tourism Society.

Colleagues report that he was a demanding boss and set high standards for himself and his staff. Punctilious, although frequently unpunctual, he was small in stature but big in spirit and a man of clear visions that he worked to achieve. Calm in crisis, of which he saw many, he rarely got rattled. He was stubborn when he was convinced he was right, which was often, and his combination of conviction and determination not infrequently put him into disagreement with government and officials with responsibility for the tourism portfolio. Very much a night owl, he did much of his work in his office between 6pm and 10 pm. For those who were privileged to know him well, he had a vitality and good humour with a sense of the ridiculous that made him special. Suitably primed with a glass of whisky in the cockpit of a sailing boat or by his own fireside, he had a remarkable fund of stories that he told with memorable wit and warmth. Not the easiest of men to get to know, he was invariably courteous, caring and loyal to his friends, including several former employees of the BTA who held him in the highest regard.

As part of overseeing the remarkable growth of inbound tourism from 203 000 visits in 1946 to just under 14 million in 1986, when he retired, Len extended the BTA's activities overseas to over twenty countries. He was well known to all the leading players in UK tourism through the BTA's system of committees and through other bodies via which he pursued the policies of growth. In addition, Len served on numerous international committees and was a strong believer in Europe, as the appreciation from William Burnett shows (see below). He worked in Europe in the 1940s to help re-establish the International Union of Official Travel Organizations (IUOTO) that later became the World Tourism Organization. Over the years he was variously Chairman of the European Travel Commission and European Tourism Action Group. From his retirement in 1986 until not long before his death, Len remained active in Britain and in Europe in numerous voluntary capacities. These included being a member of the Advisory Council of the World Travel Market, a Trustee of the British Travel Educational Trust, a Council Member of the Royal Overseas League and his role as a Visiting Professor at the University of Strathclyde.

Len was an active author since his first book in 1958 with A. Kershaw, *The Travel Trade* (Lickorish and Kershaw, 1958) through *Tourism Marketing* with Alan Jefferson (Lickorish and Jefferson) and *Developing Tourism Destinations* with Kit Jenkins and Jonathan Bodlender. He contributed numerous articles on tourism to journals and in the press. It was Len's idea in the mid-1990s to write a book on the story of tourism from 1945 to 1995, covering the half-century of his own direct involvement. The book, in collaboration with W. S. Richards was in draft form, although far from complete when he died. Many of the ideas and the material in this book draw on these early drafts.

Len died in May 2002 at the age of 80. If anyone in the last half-century deserved recognition for his remarkable personal contribution to the growth of British tourism, it was surely Len Lickorish. He served his country well; he served tourism well.

An appreciation from a European perspective

by William Burnett MBE – European Union of Tourist Officers (EUTO), President 1986–89, Secretary General 1993–2000

Len was the only person from outside its membership ranks to be accorded the status of Honorary Member by the European Union of Tourist Officers (EUTO). Such was the esteem and high regard with which he was held by those who work at the grass roots of the tourism family network. The honour, accorded in 1993, was conferred not solely in recognition of his tremendous achievements professionally, but also to acknowledge a kind and very human person.

EUTO, primarily through various national associations, brings together some 1800 individual professional tourist officers, mainly employed in the public or public/private sector partnerships of local, regional or national tourism organizations. Geographically they are spread from Finland in the north, to Italy in the south and from Iceland in the west, to Austria in the east. As Len frequently remarked, it was the tourist officers working in a city, resort or spa that were the real heroes of the industry, as it was they with whom the tourist came into direct contact, unlike those in the loftier echelons of the national tourist organizations. 'No national tourist office ever served as much as a cup of tea to a tourist' was his often-used remark. Such recognition meant a lot to the humble tourist officer, especially as it was uttered with sincerity by someone who was recognized as being one of the outstanding figures of world tourism.

Tourist officers from a number of European countries gathered in the Swiss resort of Montreux to create EUTO in 1975. The foundations had been laid much earlier, however, in 1963 when tourist officers from Austria, France, Germany, the Netherlands and Switzerland met in Salzburg and established the Europäische Arbeitsgemeinschaft (EAG). Soon afterwards the EAG extended an invitation to colleagues in other European countries to join. One of them was a UK body; known then as the Association of Resort Publicity Officers (ARPO), which subsequently became the British Association of Tourist Officers (BATO) and was the forerunner of today's Tourism Management Institute (TMI). ARPO sought advice from Len Lickorish, then General Manager of the British Travel and Holidays Association, who was strongly supportive of the role of the local government publicity officer (the word 'tourism' did not exist then). He was also, even in the 1960s, pro-Europe. Len's advice was to join EAG and commenced British tourist officers' involvement in a pan European body of like-minded professionals.

A fledgling EUTO continued to receive Len's encouragement and support and BATO, with modest financial assistance from BTA, was able to host the first UK EUTO Annual Convention in Cardiff in 1977. When the paucity of BATO's budget put its continuing membership of EUTO in some jeopardy, rumour has it that Len, because of his belief that the UK should be active in things European, offered an acceptable solution to the problem.

The European Tourism Action Group (ETAG) was undoubtedly the brainchild of Len. He was well aware that the European Travel Commission, of which he had been a dynamic chairman, was a marketing co-operative of government funded national tourist offices. He felt it needed to have a forum that embraced far more widely the voice of the industry; the players that went to make up the tourism product. EUTO considered that the voice of the professional tourist officer, someone who came in direct contact with both the tourist and within their localities, the industry, should be heard within the structures of ETAG. Initially, and for some years after its creation, there were those within its membership who did not consider that the tourist officer was a meaningful element of the product and that therefore EUTO should not have a place within the ranks of ETAG. Len was not one who shared such a view. On each occasion when EUTO sought to be admitted to ETAG, Len, by then its secretary, argued its cause. For some years his argument failed to carry the day. Ultimately his tenacity prevailed and EUTO became, what is now acknowledged, a rightful and active member of ETAG. However, without Len championing its case it is doubtful the relationship would have ever come about.

An element in strengthening the contribution that members of EUTO could make to the work of ETAG was achieved by Len becoming a regular guest at the EUTO Annual Seminar and Convention. The first time he was able to accept the invitation was in 1987, when the Danish association acted as hosts, in Odense. Keen to be involved from the outset, Len sought guidance as to how the British delegation would be travelling to Denmark. When he learnt that the majority intended to cross the North Sea by ferry he asked to be included in the group. During the twenty-hour crossing he demonstrated that a skill in ballroom dancing was amongst his little known hidden talents! The attendance lists of EUTO's annual gathering indicate that in his capacity as secretary of ETAG he was present on eight occasions. His last appearance was as an Honorary Member at the Silver Jubilee convention, staged in Trieste in September 2000.

It was some time in the mid-1980s that the various institutions of the European Union – the Parliament, Commission, etc.– woke up to the fact that tourism was one of the major economic, social and employment activities of Europe. Some twenty years on, many consider that it still does not receive the recognition and support that it warrants from such institutions. Len would certainly share such sentiments. He was a tireless campaigner, a champion of the tourism cause within the Brussels and Strasbourg corridors of power. If, at the conclusion of a meeting, there was still an ear around to be bent, with a further telling point still to be made, Len would never let such an opportunity pass by, even at severe risk of missing the last flight or train home.

Surely one day someone will write the definitive history of European tourism. Such a tome will undoubtedly contain much by way of facts and figures. However, given that tourism is very much a 'people' business, its pages are bound to honour the names of the many personalities who have made a contribution to the present day status that it enjoys. Without a doubt, at the forefront of any such list will be the name of Leonard J. Lickorish.

The British Travel Educational Trust, 1970 to 2004

The British Travel Educational Trust (BTET) was an educational charity formed in 1970 with funds contributed by the travel industry to the former British Travel Association. Under the Development of Tourism Act of 1969, the British Travel Association, which had been Britain's national tourist organization with funds contributed by travel industry members as well as by Government, was wound up. It was replaced by the British Tourist Authority as a statutory body funded by Government (see Chapter 7).

Len Lickorish, who had been Director General of the Association, was appointed the first Director General of the new authority, and the Trust was his brainchild. He recognized an opportunity to promote education in tourism in its widest context at a time when the educational and training needs of the tourism sector were scarcely recognized outside the new universities.

On his retirement in 1986, Len Lickorish became a trustee of BTET, then under the chairmanship of Lord Montagu of Beaulieu and administration of the Trust continued to be funded by the British Tourist Authority.

The Trust provided funding for international research projects undertaken by individuals and projects related to tourism education undertaken by organizations. Priority was given to projects that would be of clear benefit to the British tourism industry and which could not be funded from other sources or where there were opportunities for partnership funding.

Recent projects include:

- A study of the balance of payments and the travel account.
- Support for the National Liaison Group for Higher Education in the UK.
- Support for the development of the GNVQ in Leisure and Tourism.
- A study of the organization and funding of visitor and convention bureaux in the USA.

In the case of international tourism research projects the Trust provided grants to cover travel and accommodation expenses and also met report publication costs.

Projects to enhance tourism education and training included research and development activities, the organization of conferences and seminars, projects to promote best practice and tourism award schemes.

However, in the early years of the new century it became clear that the income generated by the initial funding of the Trust was insufficient to make a significant contribution to the education and training requirements of the travel and hospitality industries. Both were now operating on a scale which could scarcely have been envisaged in 1970 when the Trust was created.

The trustees decided that the best use of the funds could be made through the Springboard Charitable Trust, the objectives of which were closely similar to those of BTET. Agreement was reached in 2004 for the funds to be transferred and that the Springboard Charitable Trust would, together with other activities aligned to BTET priorities, establish a new annual award for excellence in tourism education, which will commemorate Len Lickorish and BTET.

BTET originally agreed to help fund the publication of this book (see Preface) and as one of its last decisions, support was provided to Victor Middleton in 2004 to enable him to complete the story of British tourism initially drafted by Len Lickorish and Bill Richards.

Defining and measuring tourism and the tourism industry

This appendix notes in basic outline what is meant by 'tourism industry' and why it has proved so difficult to measure tourism with any accuracy over the last half-century. It helps explain why politicians and public sector policy makers have found it so hard to comprehend the sector and respond effectively.

The basic definition on which understanding of the tourism industry is based

In 1938, just before the Second World War, the Committee of Statistical Experts of the League of Nations addressed itself to tourism. The Committee produced an influential definition that continued to affect the understanding and measurement of tourism around the world for the next fifty years or so after the institution was swept away in the war. It determined that the term 'tourist' should mean:

> Any person travelling for a period of 24 hours or more in a country other than that in which he [sic] usually resides.

In other words, the guidance given to government statisticians was that, although travel purposes were deemed to embrace business meetings, health and social purposes as well as pleasure and holidays, measurement was confined officially to international tourism only. Domestic tourism was not included; day visits were not recognized at all. To the present day, the statistics provided by the World Tourism Organization are for international tourism and still based primarily on the 1938 definition.

In 1994, following widespread international consultation led by the World Tourism Organization, the United Nations Statistical Commission adopted revised definitions of tourism in 1994, stating that:

> Tourism comprises the activities of persons travelling to and staying in places outside their usual environment for not more than one consecutive year for leisure, business or any other purpose.

Endorsed by the Organization for Economic Co-operation and Development (OECD), this is the definition that operates in Britain as in other parts of the world in 2005 and it covers visits for most purposes, domestic as well as international tourism, and day visits. It indicates the distance that international understanding of tourism has travelled since the Second World War.

Measuring tourism and the tourism industry

One of the first people to attempt to review tourism systematically in the 1930s was Professor Ogilvie. He quickly appreciated the problems and noted that 'This Island . . . the classic hive of tourists and journey's end for tourists from all the world over, is . . . to the astonishment of foreign observers, in deep ignorance of the extent of the movement to and from its shores' (Ogilvie, 1933).

During the war in 1944, the Pinney Memorandum was published, evaluating the rationale for the establishment of an official national tourism organization after the war (see Chapter 7). In listing its proposed functions, it is interesting to note that Pinney, who was well aware of data deficiencies, recommended that the first function should be: 'The making of a preliminary and a periodical survey of all matters affecting the prospects of the national tourist industry and the collection and publication of statistical and other data' (Pinney Memorandum, 1944, Chapter 8).

Since 1944, the national tourist organizations of the day in the UK have been given responsibility for data collection and evaluation. The responsibility was formally included within the 1969 legislation (see Chapter 7). It is a matter for judgement that, although all have addressed and made some progress in this matter, the effectiveness of UK tourism data has been and still is a source of constant frustration and disappointment to observers of the industry. The tourism sector has grown faster than the means of attempting to measure it. Measurement has never been given the priority necessary for a sector with no other means of defining national, regional and local goals and evaluating progress. In a world increasingly dominated with targets and indicators, this is a major failure that has seriously hampered the industry for half a century so far. It is not resolved yet, although it was addressed again in 2003/04. As always, progress will depend on the Government agreeing the funding to overcome the 'data deficit'.

A tourism industry that is not an industry – a recipe for confusion

With the arrogance of present times, it is widely supposed that endeavours to estimate the importance of tourism is a new idea. It is not. The two quotes above indicate that the thorny path to measurement has been trodden for over 70 years. What is astonishing, perhaps, is that progress has been so slow. Evaluations of tourism, with arguably greater scholarship and credibility than can be found in the last 25 years, took place in the 1930s and 1940s (see Chapter 1). An impressive study for Nuffield College published in 1945 by Elizabeth Brunner got directly to the heart of the matter as noted below. (Although, in the light of the 1940s, Brunner identifies tourism as 'holiday trades', the analysis is as perceptive now as it was then.) She wrote:

> The holiday trades were divided into two classes for estimation purposes.
>
> • Firstly there were the primary holiday trades or the direct consumptive trades of Entertainments, Sport and Personal Service, which cater directly for the holidaymaker in his role as one who has money to spend on leisure and luxuries.
> • The secondary class consists of the trades of building, decorating and contracting, gas, water and electricity, transport and communications, and the distributive trades. These latter are the trades stimulated by tourist traffic rather than the tourist industry itself; they provide the means to the end rather than the end of holidaymaking.
>
> (Pimlott, 1947, p. 241)

As noted in the Preface to this book, long after Miss Brunner's work has been forgotten, it has become conventional wisdom in recent years to speak glibly of 'the tourism industry', as though it were a neatly identifiable group of businesses (supply) serving a particular market (demand). In reality it is not an industry at all but an aggregation of many different markets comprising an almost infinite variety of consumer demand that can only be measured as consumption patterns. It is best understood as a sector of the economy that provides services and the activities undertaken by a mobile population away from home, whose presence and especially spending has a major impact on the destination visited. Such spending has both primary and secondary effects as Miss Brunner identified.

As forms of demand or consumption, the meaning of tourism is inevitably dependent on what is actually measured in surveys. Absurd as it may seem, government statisticians are the ultimate arbiters of what we understand by 'the world's largest industry'. Tourism is, as it was in 1945, a statistical concept measured by available affordable survey techniques working to the agreed definitions of the demand at any particular time. If you change the definition, you change the 'industry'.

For most of the second half of the twentieth century, general understanding of tourism around the world was established by the definition coined by the League of Nations in 1938 noted above. It was agreed that the term 'tourist' should mean international visits. In the 1950s to 1960s as domestic tourism increased in importance, there was a broad consensus in Europe, led by British survey practice of the time, that domestic tourism was a business of holidays comprising four nights or more away from home. Holidays in Britain were first measured on that basis in 1951 and such measures have continued for over 50 years. Although holidays of four plus nights was always a measurement of convenience, not a formally agreed definition, it was still being peddled, for example, as an adequate definition of tourism in the initial discussions that led to the EC Statistical Directive for Tourism of 1995. By 1995, it was subsumed within the UN Statistical Commission Agreement of 1994.

It took nearly 60 years after the League of Nations agreed its definition before the World Tourism Organization (WTO) and the United Nations Statistical Commission adopted revised definitions in 1994 quoted at the head of this Appendix. The 1994 definition has been endorsed by OECD and the EU. It is no longer restricted to international movements and there is no restriction in it on the time spent outside the usual environment, so that both day and staying visits are included. For statistical purposes a tourism day visit is assumed within the UK to last at least 3 hours away from home, although that is a measure of convenience and is not adopted in all countries. All types of traveller engaged in tourism are described as visitors, and therefore the visitor now represents the one basic concept common to all forms of tourism.

When in Britain it was decided to measure domestic tourism on the broader basis of all purposes, and for one or more nights from home, a new survey was introduced in 1972, although it continued to separate 'trips' of one to three nights from 'trips' of four or more nights. The word 'trip', associated as it is with 'trippers' has been part of the reason why tourism stereotypes in the media still associate visitors with candy floss images. Day visitors (inevitably measured as 'day trippers') were not formally measured nationally in Britain until 1994. Although business purposes (not commuting) are included within the UN definition, the UK measures only leisure day trips. The notion of business 'trippers' has so far been a trip too far.

In 2005 it is still the case that most countries, including the UK, cannot measure all the categories of the definition they nominally agree to in the official definition. In Britain, visits are still described as 'trips' in most data reports.

Caveat emptor

Ignoring all the long established criteria and codes of practice for presenting data, tourism data are often presented and quoted with no clarification of what is actually included and it is always essential to know:

- Do the data cover international or domestic visits (or both)?
- Do the data include day visits?
- Do the data include visits to friends and relatives and to non-serviced accommodation or are they based on visits to the registered hotel sector only? Does the 'hotel' sector include self-catering establishments?
- If holidays are measured, are the data restricted only to holidays of four or more nights or do they measure holidays of one to three nights?
- Do the estimates of expenditure measure only what is spent by visitors or do they include allowance for the way that secondary tourism spending works its way through an economy via what is known as the 'multiplier effect'? (For example, for every 1000 full-time employees providing services to visitors, there are typically another 500 employees whose jobs depend *to some extent* on the way the income from visitors is spent – from laundry workers, makers of cameras and the food industry to hairdressers and policemen.)

The economic impact of tourism in the UK is massive – but how big?

The major economic impacts of tourism have never been taken formally into account in the UK Government statistics of general economic indicators or in the system of national accounts based on industry output. Difficulties of definition and description arise because tourism is basically different from most other major sectors of the economy, which are described and measured from the basis of supply or output. Agriculture, fishing, mining, steel or car manufacturers are relatively easily described by their products, turnover, value added and capital investment. But tourism is not and never was a single industry. It comprises the output of at least two dozen different sectors and to make matters more difficult the services providing for visitors' main needs, such as transport, accommodation, catering, retail and entertainment, also serve a residential population to a greater or lesser extent. For example, the catering industry serves visitors, but it also serves larger sectors of demand such as local residents, local community needs in offices, factories, schools and hospitals, etc., which together account for a major part of that sector's total output.

The World Travel and Tourism Council (WTTC), representing the major travel and tourism companies in the world, states: 'Travel and Tourism plays a major role in growth and job creation. It is woven into the fabric of domestic and international commerce, its components such as transport, accommodation, catering, entertainment and travel services are closely linked to other industries and are a catalyst for their goods and services' (WTTC, 1996).

As an illustration of the current problems, the World Tourism Organization reports world tourism spending (based on international travel) of over US$400 bn for 1995, a figure widely quoted as authoritative. For the same year, the World Travel and Tourism Council (based on the UN definition) calculated total tourism sector outputs (primary and secondary spending) of US$3000 bn. Which to believe? Both figures are purporting to offer decision-makers the same piece of information. Caveat emptor.

Satellite accounting for tourism

In the last decade, finally recognizing the difficulties of traditional attempts to measure tourism, the WTO and the OECD (representing the industrialized countries of the world) have developed and agreed an extension of the internationally agreed national accounting systems that will measure the economic impact of tourism in a comprehensive and consistent way. Known as satellite accounting (because it is a spin off from the main national accounts) the process is highly technical and expensive to implement. It was pioneered in Canada and is being developed in some European countries but it is not yet available for the UK nationally, although the first pilot work was undertaken in 2004 in collaboration between government and tourist boards. The work has provided indicators of what *could be* produced. The concepts have been enthusiastically embraced by many in UK tourism as the best way ahead for measurement.

The drawback with satellite accounting procedures is that they require statistically reliable survey data on the detailed expenditure of visitors. If such data is available, satellite accounts could measure the total activity of the tourism industry for the first time and could feature in government economic indicators, which are at the centre of policymaking. Most importantly, it would be possible to measure tourism more or less comparably with other industries for the first time. When it happens, the data will facilitate the understanding of the complex demand and supply for tourism in ways that were first identified as needed in the 1930s and 1940s. Unfortunately in the UK, data on visitor expenditure are not adequate and reliable.

In 2004, a report to Government (DCMS) unequivocally stated that: *'Existing [data] sources are no longer fit for purpose and the potential economic, social and environmental contributions of the tourism sector will only be realized if priority is allocated to better measurement'* (National Statistics Quality Review Series, Report no. 33, 2004, p. 4). These are the data sources that are the vital input for reliable satellite accounting procedures. At the time of writing there was no indication that Government would respond to the recommended data priorities.

Chronology of general events affecting the UK and influencing tourism patterns between 1945 and 1995

1945	Election of Labour Government committed to nationalization
1946	7500 TV licences sold
1948	Blockage of Berlin – Berlin Airlift
1949	Mao Zedung proclaimed the Communist People's Republic of China
1951	Festival of Britain
	Election of Conservative Government committed to denationalization and deregulation – in power until 1964
1953	Coronation of Queen Elizabeth II
1954	Wartime food rationing finally ended
1955	Independent (commercial) TV launched
	First Wimpy Bar (fast food burger chain) opens
1956	Suez Canal military expedition against Egypt
1957	Treaty of Rome – foundation of the Common Market and later the European Union
1958	First section of British motorway opens (M6 Preston bypass)
1959	M1 linking London and Birmingham opened with first motorway service station (Forte)

1961	Contraception pills commercially available for first time
	Beatles first LP released
1962	Rachel Carson's *Silent Spring* published
1964	Labour Government elected headed by Harold Wilson – to 1970
1965	Civic Trust Survey *Planning for Leisure* highlights the need to plan for a more affluent, car owning, more mobile society and the pressures on the countryside in particular
1966	Barclay Card issued the first 'hole-in-the-wall' customer credit cards and launched a revolution in consumer spending and credit habits
	The Times changed its historic front-page format
1967	*Torrey Canyon* tanker on the rocks of Land's End – 13 000 tons of oil pollute 80 miles of coastline. RAF called in to bomb the wreck and burn the oil
1968	US space craft orbits the moon
	Creation of Sport, Countryside and Arts QUANGOs
	New universities (1963 Robbins Report) granted charters to make possible massive expansion in higher education
1969	Maiden flight by Concorde. First Boeing 747 flies into London
	Development of Tourism Act
1970	Conservative Government led by Ted Heath elected
	Palestinian hijackers attempt a four-plane hijack
1971	Decimalization of UK coinage
1972	'Bloody Sunday' in Northern Ireland
	UK Miners' Strike
1973	First IRA bombing in London
1974	British accession to the Common Market
	Oil prices quadruple in first international energy crisis that plunges UK economy into crisis
1975	Three-day week/threat of petrol rationing/Heath Government falls and is replaced by Harold Wilson and then (1976) James Callaghan
	First McDonald's restaurant opens in Britain (Woolwich)
1976	First North Sea oil piped ashore
1977	First Laker Skytrain flies the Atlantic
	Tourism Society formed for professional people in tourism
1978	Deregulation of airlines in the USA changes the post-war approach to airline regulation and influences Atlantic traffic and later EU decisions
	Shah of Iran deposed and replaced by a fundamentalist Ayatollah
1978/9	'Winter of Discontent' leads to fall of Callaghan Government and election of Conservatives led by Margaret Thatcher – committed to privatization and a smaller state sector
	Murder of Lord Mountbatten
1979	Second world energy crisis causes international economic downturn felt strongly in the UK

1981	First (IBM) Personal Computer on sale
	Brixton riots – associated with race and economic deprivation in inner urban areas
1984	IRA bomb the Grand Hotel in Brighton, narrowly missing the Prime Minister
1985	Damage to the ozone layer first identified as a major threat to worldwide economic sustainability
1986	Explosion and leakage of radiation at Chernobyl nuclear plant in Ukraine
	McDonald's restaurants extend to 200 in the UK
1987	*Herald of Free Enterprise* overturns off Zeebrugge – 193 people die
	Brundtland Report published
1988	Pan Am jet explodes over Lockerbie in major terrorist attack – 259 passengers and 11 on the ground killed
1989	Tiananmen Square protests in Beijing; Deng Xiaping sets China on route to quasi-capitalist economic development
	Berlin Wall removed, heralding the end of the post-war Soviet Empire
1990	East Germany reunited with West Germany
	Iraq invades Kuwait and triggers first Gulf war
	Mrs Thatcher forced to resign
	Britain joins the European Exchange Rate Mechanism (ERM)
1992	Maastricht Treaty signed. Single Market comes into being
	Britain forced out of the ERM ('Black Wednesday')
1993	China becomes a net oil importer for first time as its economy expands and puts growing pressure on global oil supplies.
	National Lottery Act passed
1994	National Lottery launched and Millennium Commission formed
	Sunday Trading Act passed
1995	TESCO Club card launched – first major store card for consumers
	First www commercial websites for travel appear on the Internet. E-marketing is launched

Selected statistics of UK tourism – with a health warning . . .

We have come to believe that there is no other sector in the UK economy as significant as tourism in which the key strategic and management decisions are so hampered by a lack of adequate data.

(DCMS, 2004)

As indicated in the Preface and Appendix III, the principal published statistics of British tourism are inadequate. Overall, orders of national magnitude taken over several years are generally realistic indicators, but regional data are not and the year-to-year measures are especially unreliable. Readers should be aware that whatever data they draw on it is likely to contain many traps for the unwary. The published statistics of tourism must be treated with great caution and taken with a large pinch of salt for the following reasons:

- Revisions to official data are frequent but often by a process that is seldom if ever explained to the user.
- Methodology changes, especially for the UK Tourism Survey (UKTS), which underwent major changes in 1989, 2000 and again in 2005. Data sets from 1995 to 2000 were simply changed without explanation. On the earlier methodology, for example, UK domestic tourism (visits for all purposes of one or more nights in 1995) were estimated at 121 million in 1995. Seven years later data back to 1995 state that there were 148 million such visits.
- So-called 'tourism data' are sometimes for holidays and sometimes for all tourism, which also includes business visits, and visits to friends and relatives.

- Tourism data may or may not include day visits, which in a British context, may almost double (or halve) any estimates of total 'tourism' expenditure.
- 'Holidays' sometimes means only 'long' holidays of four or more nights from home. Sometimes short holidays are included of one to three nights duration.
- Holidays by the British abroad are measured both by UKTS and by the International Passenger Survey (IPS). The two measures are quite different.
- Following the devolution of tourism in the late 1990s, the English, Scots and Welsh are in control of their own national data. For the main surveys they collaborate but there is always a need to check if data sets are for England only or include Scotland and Wales. UK data should include Northern Ireland but often cover Great Britain only.
- Expenditure data series published by tourist boards are usually stated in 'current prices'. This means that they ignore inflation, in part no doubt to make the growth in expenditure appear larger.

The selection of data in this section are offered warts and all, *de faut mieux*.

Section A – Pre-war statistics

Table AV.1 Estimates of visits to Britain from the USA, the Commonwealth and in total from 1921 to 1938

Year	USA	Commonwealth**	Total*
1921	56 483		174 099
1922	71 910		195 934
1923	69 000		205 268
1924	91 000		275 842
1925	100 550		270 623
1926	98 845		254 928
1927	111 528		291 878
1928	112 651		316 348
1929	113 466		331 404
1930	116 881		33 815
1931	82 672		275 901
1932	68 065		253 374
1933	54 671	70 000	330 520
1934	57 378	76 000	364 600
1935	65 588	76 000	391 760
1936	82 265	83 000	452 670
1937	102 840	85 000	488 150
1938	77 396	80 000	437 260

*The collection of official UK tourist statistics began in 1921
**Commonwealth tourist traffic to the UK was not measured between 1921 and 1933
Source: Home Office data – BTA History of Tourism.

Table AV.2 Passengers by air, United Kingdom to Continental Europe from 1923 to 1937

Year	Passengers	Year	Passengers
1923	6700	1931	22 400
1924	8300	1932	35 300
1925	9400	1933	45 400
1926	12 700	1934	62 100
1927	13 700	1935	75 700
1928	21 100	1936	86 600
1929	23 600	1937	92 200
1930	20 600		

Source: Board of Trade Journals.

Table AV.3 Passengers carried by the associated companies of Imperial Airways on Empire routes

Year	Passengers	Year	Passengers
1925	11 000	1932	48 200
1926	16 000	1933	79 100
1927	19 000	1934	135 000
1928	27 300	1935	200 000
1929	28 500	1936	236 300
1930	24 000	1937	244 400
1931	23 800	1938	222 000

Source: Wimperis, Aviation.

Section B – Domestic tourism statistics

Table AV.4 Currency allowances for British residents from 1946 to 1954

Year	Month	Allowance changed to:
1946	March	£75
1947	August	£35
1947	September	Allowance withdrawn completely
1948*	April	£35
1949	April	£50
1950	December	£100
1951	November	£50
1952	January	£25
1953	March	£40

Table AV.4 Currency allowances for British residents from 1946 to 1954 – (Continued)

Year	Month	Allowance changed to:
1953	November	£50
1954	November	£100
1966		£50**

*At the reintroduction of the travel allowance, it extended to all areas except the Dollar area which remained in force until July 1957.
**Exchange Control introduced for holiday travel, removed in 1970
Source: Lickorish and Kershaw, 1958; later data for 1966.

Table AV.5 Estimated number of holidays of 4+ nights taken by the British population in Britain and abroad from 1951 to 2003

Year	Britain (millions)	Abroad (millions)*	Total (millions)
1951	25.0	1.5	26.5
1955	25.0	2.0	27.0
1960	31.5	3.5	35.0
1965	30.0	5.00	35.00
1966	31.0	5.50	36.50
1967	30.0	5.00	35.00
1968	30.0	5.00	35.00
1969	30.5	5.75	36.25
1970	34.5	5.75	40.25
1971	34.0	7.25	41.25
1972	37.5	8.50	46.00
1973	40.5	8.25	48.75
1974	40.5	6.75	47.25
1975	40.0	8.00	48.00
1976	37.5	7.25	44.75
1977	36.0	7.75	43.75
1978	39.0	9.00	48.00
1979	38.5	10.25	48.75
1980	36.5	12.00	48.50
1981	36.5	13.25	49.75
1982	32.5	14.25	46.75
1983	33.5	14.50	48.00
1984	34.0	15.50	49.50
1985	33.0	15.75	48.75
1986	31.5	17.50	49.00
1987	28.5	20.00	48.50
1988	33.5	20.25	53.75
1989	31.5	21.00	52.50
1990	32.5	20.50	52.50
1991	34.0	20.00	54.25

(Continued)

Table AV.5 Estimated number of holidays of 4+ nights taken by the British population in Britain and abroad from 1951 to 2003 – (Continued)

Year	Britain (millions)	Abroad (millions)*	Total (millions)
1992	32.0	21.75	53.75
1993	32.5	23.50	56.00
1994	31.5	26.25	58.00
1995	33.0	26.00	59.00
1997	30.0	26.50	56.50
2000	28.0	30.50	58.50
2003	25.0	32.50	57.50

*Holidays in Britain are all 4+ nights. Shorter holidays are included in the abroad total
Source: British National Travel Survey (BNTS), and early figures in *The British Travel Association 1929–1969*, published by BTA in 1972.

Table AV.6 Estimated visits for all purposes by the British within Britain (latterly within the UK) from 1972 to 1995

Year	Total no. of trips (millions)	Tourist nights (millions)	Total expenditure (£ millions)
1972	132	605	1375
1973	132	590	1450
1974	114	535	1800
1975	117	550	2150
1976	121	545	2400
1977	121	545	2625
1978	119	530	3100
1979	118	525	3800
1980	130	550	4550
1981	126	520	4600
1982	123	505	4500
1983	131	545	5350
1984	140	565	5975
1985	126	500	6325
1986	128	510	7150
1987	132	495	6775
1988	130	505	7850
1989	110	443	10 865
1990	96	399	10 460
1991	94	396	10 470
1992	96	400	10 665
1993	91	376	12 430
1994	110	417	13 215
1995	121	450	12 775

Source: British Home Tourism Survey (BHTS), which became United Kingdom Survey of Tourism (UKTS) in 1989.

Table AV.7 Estimated visits for all purposes by the British within the UK from 1995 to 2000

(This is the extension to Table AV.6 above although the data have been revised back to 1995 by tourist boards to accommodate survey methodology changes in 2000)

Year	Total no. of visits (millions)	Holidays of 4+ nights (millions)	Holidays of 1–3 nights (millions)	Visits to friends and relatives (millions)
1995	148	40.5	53.0	29.7
1996	154	40.0	53.0	33.8
1997	162	41.6	60.1	34.7
1998	148	37.5	55.6	32.4
1999	173	40.8	64.7	39.6
2000	175	38.7	67.2	40.6

Source: UKTS (www.staruk.org.uk at May 2005).

Section C – Statistics of inbound tourism to the UK

Table AV.8 Visits and expenditure for all purposes – inbound tourism to the UK from 1946 to 2004

Year	Visits		Expenditure[**]	
	(000's)	% change	£ m	% change
1946	203		12	
1947	396	+95	21	+75
1948	504	+27	33	+57
1949	563	+12	43	+30
1950	618	+10	61	+42
1951	712	+15	75	+23
1952	733	+3	80	+7
1953	819	+12	88	+10
1954	902	+10	95	+8
1955	1037	+15	111	+17
1956	1107	+7	121	+9
1957	1180	+7	129	+7
1958	1259	+7	134	+4
1959	1395	+11	143	+7
1960	1669	+20	169	+18
1961	1824	+9	176	+4
1962	1955	+7	183	+4
1963	2159	+10	188	+3

(Continued)

Table AV.8 Visits and expenditure for all purposes – inbound tourism to the UK from 1946 to 2004 – (Continued)

Year	Visits		Expenditure[**]	
	(000's)	% change	£ m	% change
1964[*]	3257	+ 51	190	+ 1
1965	3597	+ 10	193	+ 2
1966	3967	+ 10	219	+ 13
1967	4289	+ 8	236	+ 8
1968	4828	+ 13	282	+ 19
1969	5821	+ 21	359	+ 27
1970	6692	+ 15	432	+ 20
1971	7131	+ 7	500	+ 16
1972	7459	+ 5	576	+ 15
1973	8167	+10	726	+ 26
1974	8543	+ 5	898	+ 24
1975	9490	+11	1218	+ 36
1976	10 808	+14	1768	+ 45
1977	12 281	+14	2352	+ 33
1978	12 646	+ 3	2507	+ 7
1979	12 486	− 1	2797	+ 12
1980	12 421	− 1	2961	+ 6
1981	11 452	− 8	2970	+ 0
1982	11 636	+ 2	3188	+ 7
1983	12 464	+ 7	4003	+ 26
1984	13 644	+ 9	4614	+ 15
1985	14 449	+ 6	5442	+ 18
1986	13 897	− 4	5553	+ 2
1987	15 566	+ 12	6260	+ 13
1988	15 799	+ 1	6184	− 1
1989	17 338	+ 10	6945	+ 12
1990	18 013	+ 4	7748	+ 12
1991	17 125	− 5	7386	− 5
1992	18 535	+ 8	7891	+ 7
1993	19 398	+ 7	9354	+ 19
1994	20 794	+ 7	9919	+ 6
1995	23 700	+ 14	11 900	+ 20
2000	25 200	−	12 805	−
2004	27 555	−	13 042	−

[*]From 1964 to 1995: includes residents of the Irish Republic
[**]At current prices
Source: Digest of Tourism Statistics, British Tourist Authority.

Table AV.9 Purpose of visit – inbound visitors to the UK

	1972 %	1976 %	1980 %	1984 %	1989 %	1994 %	2000 %
Independent holiday	36	35	33	23	21	21	23
Inclusive tour	12	14	11	9	8	9	10
Total holiday	48	49	44	32	30	30	33
Business	20	18	21	14	18	17	29
Visits to friends and relatives	19	17	19	13	14	14	26
Other	13	16	17	9	9	8	12

Source: *Digest of Tourism Statistics* and International Passenger Survey (IPS).

Table AV.10 Inbound tourism to the UK – country/area of residence

	1972 %	1976 %	1980 %	1984 %	1988 %	1992 %	1994 %
Area of residence							
North America	29	19	17	25	20	18	17
EEC	44	50	52	46	52	54	54
Rest of W. Europe	11	13	12	9	10	10	9
Rest of World	16	18	20	20	18	18	20

Source: *Digest of Tourism Statistics*.

Section D – Outbound tourism

Table AV.11 Total UK resident visits for all purposes to destinations abroad from 1951 to 2000

Year	Visits abroad (000's)	% change	Expenditure £ m	% change
1951	1500			
1955	2000	+ 33		
1960	3500	+ 75		
1961	4000	+ 14		
1962	4000	– 0		
1963	5000	+ 25		
1964	5897	+ 18	261	
1965	6472	+ 10	290	+ 11
1966	6918	+ 7	297	+ 2
1967	7202	+ 4	274	– 8
1968	7269	+ 1	271	– 1

(Continued)

Table AV.11 Total UK resident visits for all purposes to destinations abroad from 1951 to 2000 – (Continued)

Year	Visits abroad (000's)	% change	Expenditure £ m	% change
1969	8083	+ 11	324	+ 20
1970	8482	+ 5	382	+ 18
1971	9497	+ 12	442	+ 16
1972	10 695	+ 13	535	+ 21
1973	11 740	+ 10	695	+ 30
1974	10 783	− 8	703	+ 1
1975	11 992	+ 11	917	+ 30
1976	11 560	− 4	1068	+ 17
1977	11 525	− 0	1188	+ 11
1978	13 443	+ 17	1549	+ 31
1979	15 466	+ 15	2109	+ 36
1980	17 507	+ 13	2738	+ 30
1981	19 046	+ 9	3272	+ 20
1982	20 611	+ 8	3640	+ 11
1983	20 994	+ 2	4090	+ 12
1984	22 072	+ 5	4663	+ 14
1985	21 610	− 2	4871	+ 4
1986	24 949	+ 15	6083	+ 25
1987	27 446	+ 10	7280	+ 20
1988	28 828	+ 5	8216	+ 13
1989	31 030	+ 7	9357	+ 14
1990	31 150	− 0	9886	+ 6
1991	30 808	− 1	9951	+ 1
1992	33 836	+ 10	11 243	+ 13
1993	36 720	+ 6	12 705	+ 13
1994	39 630	+ 12	14 500	+ 14
1995	41 435	+ 5	15 683	+ 8
1997	45 957	–	18 652	–
2000	57 000	–	24 251	–

Source: Digest of Statistics; BTA and IPS.

Table AV.12 Visits from the UK to abroad – reason for travel

Purpose of travel	1972 %	1977 %	1980 %	1984 %	1990 %	1994 %	2000 %
Business	13	19	15	14	15	14	16
Independent holidays	26	27	31	28	31	31	29
Inclusive tours	44	32	36	41	36	38	36
VFR**	13	17	13	12	13	12	13
Other	4	5	5	5	5	5	6
Total visits (000's)	10 695	11 525	17 507	22 072	31 182	39 630	56 837
Growth ±		+ 8%	+ 52%	+ 26%	+ 41%	+ 27%	+ 43%

** Visits to friends and relatives
Source: *Digest of Tourism Statistics*.

Section E – other relevant data

Table AV.13 Main outputs of UK airports from 1961 to 2005

Year	Air transport movements (000's)	Terminal passengers (000's)
1961	449	13 793
1965	508	19 918
1970	607	31 606
1975	701	41 846
1980	954	57 823
1985	1097	70 434
1990	1420	102 418
1995	1612	129 586
2000	2045	179 885
2005	2406	228 214

Source: UK Airports (Annual Statement of Movements Passengers and Cargo 1995 – CAA, London).

Table AV.14 Number of motor vehicles registered in the UK

	Private cars (000's)	Public transport (includes taxis)
1930	1000	n/a
1939	2000	n/a
1946	1800	n/a
1950	2300	n/a
1955	3500	n/a
1960	5717	93
1965	8901	96
1970	11 328	103
1975	13 517	112
1980	14 772	110
1985	16 454	120
1990	19 742	115
1992	20 116	108
1996	23 439	n/a
2002	28 400	n/a

Source: Department of Transport, Statistics Office.

Table AV.15 Higher Education Institutions offering degree level courses in tourism studies in Great Britain

	1991/92	1993/94	1995/96	1997/98
Institutions*	15	36	43	50
Total courses offered	22	53	75	99
Of which: U-grad	12	27	42	66
Post-grad	10	26	33	33

*Institutions in this table are mainly the former polytechnics that became universities in 1994/95
Source: Association of Tourism in Higher Education, 2003 (*Guidelines 1 to 9*).

Notes on the principal surveys for collecting the published statistics of tourism in the UK

Note: Scotland, Wales, and Northern Ireland also commission their own surveys to provide information to meet their national needs. This note deals only with the UK data.

1 The British National Travel Survey (BNTS; BTS-Y)

Started in 1951 by the British Travel and Holidays Association, this is the longest series of data available on British tourism. From the 1970s, national tourist boards funded and owned the survey until the mid-1990s when it was passed over to the private sector and the data are no longer accessible to the general public. The survey is based on an annual survey and covers longer (four nights or more) holidays in Britain and holidays of one or more nights by the British abroad. The survey is now funded commercially, primarily by businesses interested in holiday travel by the British abroad.

2 The British Home Tourism Survey (BHTS; BTS-M and now UKTS)

Started in 1972 to supplement the data from the BNTS, especially for visits of less than four nights' duration and for purposes other than holidays, this survey is undertaken on a monthly omnibus basis. It measures visits for all purposes away from home including business visits, visits to friends and relatives, and other purposes. Commissioned and owned by UK national tourist boards, the survey became the British Tourism Survey Monthly (BTS-M) and then UKTS in 1989; it measures tourism by UK residents in the UK and abroad. A shift in 2000 to telephone rather than personal interviewing changed the volume of tourism estimates significantly and data back to 1995 was re-estimated to show significant increases in domestic tourism. In 2005, the methodology changed back to the former omnibus methodology and comparability has again been lost.

3 International Passenger Survey (IPS)

Commenced in 1961 (expanded in 1964) to measure inbound and outbound migration and the impact of tourism on the national balance of payments, the IPS is a government owned survey and the only British tourism survey that meets the criteria set for national statistics. Conducted around the year by personal interviews at airports, seaports and on the Channel Tunnel route it measures the volume, value and characteristics of UK residents travelling abroad, and of non-UK residents visiting the UK. Sample sizes have declined over the years to meet government spending requirements, despite the increase in the volume of visits. Sample sizes were around 175 000 interviews in 1987/88 (Pannell Kerr Forster report of 1988) and around 100 000 for 2003 (Allnutt report to DCMS in 2004).

National tourist boards in Britain – What's in a name?

As recorded in Chapters 7 and 8, governments in Britain have always found it easiest to intervene in the tourism sector by altering (some would say 'tinkering') with the organizational structures they fund directly. Although the reach and level of sophistication in process has developed very significantly, and so too has government funding and policy making, the core roles and functions of national and regional tourist organizations – policy, marketing, development, lobbying and co-ordination – have not changed radically in principle over the last half-century.

Within Britain there have been so many organizational changes, however, that it is bewildering and confusing for those not directly involved to keep track of events and who is nominally responsible for what. This short note may be helpful in identifying at least the main changes at national level. Organizational changes at regional and sub-regional level have been even more frequent and defy brief summary.

Pre-war

1920s; The Travel Association of Great Britain and Ireland was formed in 1929. The Scottish Tourism Development Association was created around the same time. Both had very limited government funding.

Post-war to 1969

1946–51; The Travel Association established pre-war continued with the addition of a short-lived British Tourism and Holidays Board; then became British Travel and Holidays Association in 1951 (BTHA), invariably known as the British Travel Association (BTA). The Scottish Association was reformed as the Scottish Tourist Board in 1945 on a non-statutory basis. The first Welsh Tourist and Holidays Board was formed in 1948.

1969 to 1995

The 1969 Act wound up the British Travel Association and equivalents in Scotland and Wales and created four statutory, government-funded boards. The British Tourist Authority (BTA), English Tourist Board (ETB), Scottish Tourist Board (STB) and Wales Tourist Board, each with regional arrangements that changed over time, especially in Scotland and Wales.

After 1995 and Devolution in 1999

In 2000, the ETB structure was changed to become the English Tourism Council (ETC), which in turn was abolished in 2003. Responsibility for tourism in England passed to newly formed Regional Development Associations (RDAs), each with different arrangements for their sub-regions.

In 2003, the former BTA became VisitBritain with responsibility for Marketing England.

In 1999, the new Scottish Parliament took over responsibility for tourism and STB was renamed VisitScotland in 2001 with major shifts in regional/area arrangements. Also in 1999 the National Assembly for Wales took over responsibility for tourism and in 2006, the WTB was wound up to become VisitWales when tourism staff were transferred to the Welsh Assembly Government with new arrangements for regions/areas in Wales.

Selected Bibliography

Adams, G. and Hay, B. (1994). *History and Development of the Scottish Tourist Board*. Conference paper published by Scottish Tourist Board, Edinburgh.

Baker, H. (1982). *The Rise and Fall of Freddie Laker*. Faber & Faber.

Bray, R. and Raitz, V. (2001). *Flight to the Sun*. London: Continuum.

Britain and International Tourism (Central Office of Information Reference Pamphlet 102, 1972). London: HMSO.

British Airways (1996). *Fact Book*. London.

British Tourist Authority (1972). *The British Travel Association 1929–1969*.

British Travel and Holidays Association (1956). *Holidays in 1955*. London: BTHA.

Brunner, E. (1945). *Holiday Making and the Holiday Trades*. Nuffield College and Oxford University Press.

Burkart, A. J. (1974). The Regulation of Non-Scheduled Air Services in the UK. *The Journal of Industrial Economics*, Volume XXIII, September.

Burkart, A. J. and Medlik, S. (1974). *Tourism Past, Present and Future*. London: Heinemann.

Butlin, W. (1982). *The Billy Butlin Story*. London: Robson Books.

Calder, S. (ed.) (2004). *That Summer: What we did on our holidays . . . .* London: Virgin Books.

Carter, J. (1985). *Chandler's Travels – A Tour of the Life of Harry Chandler*. London: Quiller Press.

Cathcart Borer, M. (1972). *British Hotels Through the Ages*. Lutterworth Press.

CIRET (2004). Databases for tourism, leisure, outdoor recreation and sport. Aix en Provence: (CIRET website)

Coleman, T. (1977). *The Liners*. London: Penguin Books.

Department for Culture Media and Sport (2004). Review of Tourism Statistics (National Statistics Quality Review Series; Report No. 33): London: DCMS.

Forte, C. (1986). *The Autobiography of Charles Forte*. London: Sidgwick and Jackson.

Friedman, J. J. (1976). *A New Air Transport Policy for the North Atlantic*. New York, London: Atheneum.

Fyall, A., Garrod, B., and Leask, A. (eds.) (2003). *Managing Visitor Attractions*. Oxford: Butterworth-Heinemann.

Hamel, G. and Prahalad, C. K. (1994). *Competing for the Future*. Harvard Business School Press.

Hartley, L. P. (1953) *The Go-Between*. London: Hamish Hamilton.

Hewison, R. (1987). *The Heritage Industry: Britain in a Climate of Decline*. London: Methuen.

Historic Houses Journal: Silver Jubilee Edition (1998) HMSO (1972). *Britain and International Tourism Central Office of Information Reference Pamp* 102. London: HMSO.

Jeffries, D. J. (2001). *Governments and Tourism*. Oxford: Butterworth-Heinemann.

Jenkins, C. and Sherman, B. (1979). *The Collapse of Work*. London: Methuen.

Jenkins, C. and Sherman, B. (1981). *The Leisure Shock*. London: Methuen.

Johnston, T. (1952). *Memories*. London: Collins.

Lavery, P. (1990). *Insights*. English Tourist Board, London.

Lickorish, L. J. and Kershaw, A. G. (1958). *The Travel Trade*. London: Practical Press.

Lickorish, L. J. and Jenkins, C. (1997). *An Introduction to Tourism*. Oxford: Butterworth-Heinemann.

Lockwood, A. and Medlik, S. (2001). *Tourism and Hospitality in the 21st Century*. Oxford: Butterworth-Heinemann.

Lundberg, D. E. (1985). *The Tourist Business*. New York: Van Nostrand Reinhold Company.

Medlik, S. (1961). *The British Hotel and Catering Industry*. London: Heinemann.

Medlik, S. (1978). *Profile of the Hotel and Catering Industry* (2nd edn). London: Heinemann.

Middleton, V. T. C. (1974). *Tourism Policy in Britain: The Case for a Radical Reappraisal*. Economist Intelligence Unit: Special Report No. 1: London.

Middleton, V. T. C. (1993). *Review of Tourism Studies Degree Courses*. Council for National Academic Awards (CNAA), London.

Middleton, V. T. C. (1998). *New Visions for Museums in the 21st Century*. Chichester: Association of Independent Museums.

Middleton, V.T.C. and Hawkins, R. (1998). *Sustainable Tourism: A Marketing Perspective*. Oxford: Butterworth-Heinemann.

Middleton, V. T. C. (1999). New Resorts for the 21st Century. In *Insights*, Jan 1999. English Tourist Board, London.

Middleton, V. T. C. and Clarke, J. (2001). *Marketing in Travel and Tourism* (3rd edn). Oxford: Butterworth-Heinemann.

Montagu, Lord (1998). *Historic Houses Journal*. Silver Jubilee Edition, p.17.

Moore, K. (ed.) (1994) *Museum Management*. London: Routledge.

Norris, Oakley, Richardson and Glover (1974). *Leisure Industry Survey 1972/3*.

Ogilvie, F. (1933). *The Tourist Movement*. London: Staples Press.

Pannell Kerr Forster Associates (1988). *Review of the Statistical Needs of the British Tourist Sector* (for Department of Employment, BTA and ETB).

Pimlott, J.A.R. (1947). *The Englishman's Holiday: A Social History*. London: Faber and Faber.

Pinney, R. S. (1944). Britain – Destination of Tourists? London: Travel and Industrial Association of Great Britan and Ireland.

Read, S. (1986). *Hello Campers*. London: Bantam Press.

Reed, A. (1990). *Airline: The Story of British Airways*. London: BBC Books.

Review of Tourism Statistics (National Statistics Quality Review Series; Report No. 33, 2004). London: Department for Culture Media and Sport.

Richards, G. (1995). *Politics of National Tourism Policy in Britain*; Leisure Studies 14. London: E&EN Spon.

Richards, P. (2003). *Tourism: Economic Policy and Statistics*. Research Paper 03/73. London: House of Commons Library.

Shaw, S. (1982). *Air Transport: A Marketing Perspective*. London: Pitman Books.

Sherriff, R.C. (1932). *The Fortnight in September*. London: Stokes and Company.

Swinglehurst, E. (1982). *Cooks Tours: The Story of Popular Travel*. Blandford Press.

Taylor, D. (1977). *Fortune Fame and Folly*. Caterer & Hotelkeeper.

The Times (2000). *Travel: A Century in Photographs, 1900–2000*. London: HarperCollins.

The Tourism Society. *21 Years of the Leading Tourism Network*. London: Tourism Society.

Towner, J. (1997). *An Historical Geography of Recreation*. London: Wiley & Son.

Wainwright, A. (1986). *A Pennine Journey*. London: Michael Joseph.

Walton, J. K. (1978). *The Blackpool Landlady*. Manchester: Manchester University Press.

Wood, M. (1982). *Catering Times*. December.

World Travel & Tourism Council (1996). *UK Travel and Tourism: Millennium Vision*. London: WTTC.

Young, G. (1973). *Tourism: Blessing or Blight?* London: Penguin Books.

Reports and strategies

The following are just an indicative selection of the many reports and strategies emerging from government in the last 25 years. The list (which is in chronological order) includes one from the CBI's Tourism Alliance.

1985 ***Pleasure, Leisure and Jobs – The Business of Tourism;***
     Department of Employment.

30 action points to support and encourage enterprise, recognizing above all its role in job creation.

1986 ***Action for Jobs;*** Department of Employment.

First in what was meant to be a series of annual reports intended to evaluate progress against tasks within a framework of *enterprise* as the key word.

Set up an inter-departmental Co-ordination Committee.

1992 ***Tourism in the UK: Realising the Potential;*** Department of Employment.

A prospectus from the Department of Employment before the election highlighting the `remarkable progress that has been made.

1996 ***Tourism: Competing with the Best;*** Department for National Heritage.

This report is based on an extensive analysis by McKinsey Consultants in 1995, commissioned by DNH.

1997 ***Success through Partnership: A Strategy for Tourism;*** Department for National Heritage.

A prospectus from the DNH before the 1997 election.
Foreword by Prime Minister John Major.

1999 ***Tomorrow's Tourism;*** *A growth industry for the new millennium*; Department for Culture Media and Sport.

Foreword by Prime Minister Tony Blair.
Creates the English Tourism Council as a strategic body and formalizes the shift of emphasis to the regions of England.

2001 ***Targeting Tourism: The Agenda for Change;*** Tourism Alliance Confederation of British Industry.

2003 ***The Structure and Strategy for Supporting Tourism:*** Select Committee for Culture, Media and Sport; House of Commons.

2004 ***Tomorrow's Tourism Today:*** A prospectus for tourism development in five key areas: Department for Culture, Media and Sport.

Index